The 1872 Diary of the

Mooresville Macy Farmstead

.....footsteps from the Mayflower to California

By

Donovan L. and Joyce A. Robinson

authorHOUSE®

AuthorHouse™
1663 Liberty Drive
Bloomington, IN 47403
www.authorhouse.com
Phone: 1-800-839-8640

Description of the book cover:
The front cover of this book is a 2009 photo of the Macy Farmstead; the present home of the authors.
The back cover of this book is the original photo of the Macy Farmstead
built in 1859; note Macy family dispersed around the home.

First published by AuthorHouse 2/11/2010

ISBN: 978-1-4490-0629-7 (sc)
ISBN: 978-1-4490-0630-3 (e)

Library of Congress Control Number: 2009913053

Printed in the United States of America
Bloomington, Indiana

This book is printed on acid-free paper.

Acknowledgements

We thank the Macy Family members for sharing information, photos, and enthusiasm.

Morgan County Historic Preservation Society and Morgan County History and Genealogy Association made us aware of the possibilities for researching this story.

Rhonda and Michael Winter provided valuable technical support.

Dedication

This book is dedicated to the Macy family who lived in the Mooresville community in the mid 1800's and to those who appreciate the struggles and contributions of the Macys and their neighbors. The viability of the Mooresville community was surely built on solid foundations of character, industry, and fortitude these early pioneers possessed.

Contents

Illustrations

Foreword

1. Macy Farmstead
2010 Home of Donovan L. & Joyce A. Robinson

Foreword

This story was compiled as part of an effort to protect an Italianate home, built in 1859, from major damage by a government entity. The Indiana Department of Transportation (INDOT) sports a miniscule history compared to this homestead built prior to the Civil War by William Monroe Macy near Mooresville, IN.

The data fragments accumulated by the current owners while pursuing Historical Landmark registration became bulbous. Yet the information is so reflective of the American Evolution to be worthy of consolidation for local family and history buffs.

The Macy Farmstead has been owned by the Macy, Johnson, Richardson and Robinson families over the past 150 years. Among these four families are descendants of Mayflower passengers, Richard the Lion Hearted, and Revolutionary War veterans. One resident became a missionary teacher in South Africa.

William Monroe Macy was born in Tennessee in 1820, migrated to and owned farms in

(Economy) Randolph County, IN	1849-1856
(Mooresville) Morgan County, IN	1856-1882
(Dayton) Yamhill County, OR	1882-1907
(Greenleaf) Canyon County, ID	1907-1911

and passed away in Denair, CA in 1911 at 91 years of age. His family's story is a classic story of the true pioneers who traversed this nation from east to west. They left in their wake cleared land, churches, schools, and homesteads which they constructed with great hope and promise for the future. Apparently, the pioneering spirit was fueled by the diminishing timber, expired soil fertility, and the lure of a profitable sale before attaining near-free land further west.

The Alonzo Johnson family purchased the 342 acre property in 1883. Tough economic times diminished the family's holdings until the death of Alonzo's last unmarried daughter which culminated in the remaining 31 acres being subjected to foreclosure proceedings in 1931.

Willis & Clara Sellars Richardson purchased these 31 acres in 1931 out of foreclosure, and additional acres in 1945 from the only surviving Johnson daughter, Harriet Alden.

Donovan Lee and Joyce Ann Burke Robinson purchased the farm from Clara Sellars Richardson in 1981. Additional adjoining acres were purchased in 1993.

This story traces the genealogy which research has revealed for the Macy family. The record keeping included in the Quaker monthly meeting minutes provided a paper trail which tied the migrations together with reliable authenticity.

There seems to have been a sense of history in these families since autobiographies, love letters, diaries and photographs were created, preserved and available to this 21st century project.

Since the available data would fill a book too heavy to carry, the focus will be on a journal written in 1872 by Alva Perry Macy. Alva was the 14 year old son of William Monroe Macy. As a farm boy, he was required to work as a man and yet he was granted ample time to pursue boyhood curiosities. He had a keen eye for rural farm life and the people who engaged the Macy Farmstead. Tracing the origins of this household hopefully places this family in the timeline of US history and adds perspective to the 1872 activities which Alva so clearly describes in his journal.

We did not take the liberty of correcting spelling where the reader could reasonably understand the thought. Overall, the grammar, and communication skills appear notable for a 14 year old farm boy. Perhaps a few minutes with his journal, summarizing the day's events of his family and local neighborhood, proved more productive for a youngster than an evening with TV abnormalities.

We thank Dr. Thomas Hamm, archivist, at the Lilly Library of Earlham College. He was helpful in gathering and explaining how to utilize Macy family reference materials.

Note:
Mabel Leigh Hunt authored a book, *LUCINDA, A Little Girl of 1860,* in 1934. She later declared that LUCINDA was actually the story of her own mother. The setting of the book is the vicinity around Bethel Friends Meeting house, where her mother, Amanda Harvey, spent her childhood within a Quaker neighborhood during the Civil War. The Macy Farmstead sits within 2 miles of the Bethel Church and school house where William Monroe Macy's son, Aaron, taught during the 1876-77 school year.

After this first book, Mabel Leigh Hunt (11/1/1892//9/3/1971), continued writing and authored a total of 30 volumes of interest to juvenile readers.

She was born in Coatesville, IN, educated at DePauw University, and was a librarian at the Indianapolis Public Library from 1926 to 1938. Many of her stories were highlighted by wholesome Quaker family themes.

Introduction

A Farmstead exists in Brown Township, Morgan County, IN, which has stood as a sentinel on the South West corner of the town of Mooresville since 1859. The home was built immediately before the Civil War. It has been home to 4 families and has undergone two major renovations since it was constructed before modern conveniences which we have grown to expect such as "running water", "electric power", "telephone" and "central heating and cooling".

The home was built by William Monroe Macy (WMM) for his own family in 1859. It stands in 2010 as the residence of Donovan and Joyce Robinson.

It seems WMM was as prosperous as anyone in the local community, however, that did not allow him much leisure. William Monroe Macy was an engaged manager of many diverse businesses. His entire family was hard at work every season of the year.

This book is primarily a presentation of the "personal journal" Alva Perry Macy wrote during 1872 while living on this Farmstead. He turned 14 during that year and the activities he records are through the eyes of a 14 year old who seems fascinated with the industry around him. The farm life of the 1870's would not be considered "the good old days" by most young adults of today.

His focus on local people and their names will hopefully provide today's history buffs a chance to put a bit of life on the stark printed pages of genealogy records. A great effort has been made to correctly identify the people he mentions by researching the 1870 census as well as several other sources for the personal data.

To put the journal in perspective, the family history has been explored to properly identify the Mooresville Macys of 1872. Joyce and I have been fascinated by the Macy family. In our research, we have visited

        —Dayton, OR
          —Denair, CA
            —Vashon Isle, WA
              —Plymouth, MA
                —Nantucket, MA
                  —Greensboro, NC
                    —Dandridge, TN.

We gathered many facts about the Macys in libraries and from surviving descendants. Much of the earliest history has been told numerous times by other authors. Proper credit to each of our sources would dwarf the message. We believe we have compiled an accurate account of these Macys and their Farmstead and offer it to others.

Alva is a 9th generation derivative of the Mayflower passengers of Plymouth. His ancestors also include the early Nantucket settlers who challenged the raw wilderness of the 1600's. They were somehow driven to continue in that vein as they moved inland and westward "from sea to shining sea".

When WMM left Mooresville in 1882, he took Julia Ann, his wife of 33 years, son Alva and daughter Cynthia. He left behind both of his parents, daughter Hannah, and son Aaron who had died during the family's tenure in Morgan County, IN. They are all buried in the White Lick Cemetery.

We Americans owe a lot to the folks who, fortified by true grit and inalterable faith, civilized the wilderness and built our early towns and villages.

We hope this story will entertain and inspire others. It certainly captivated us as we tried to place the 1872 journal in its appropriate light.

The Afterglow is a coincidental addition at the end. It resulted from our chasing the Macy family genealogy until it became apparent that Joyce's ancestors shared the Macy Tree.

Enjoy!

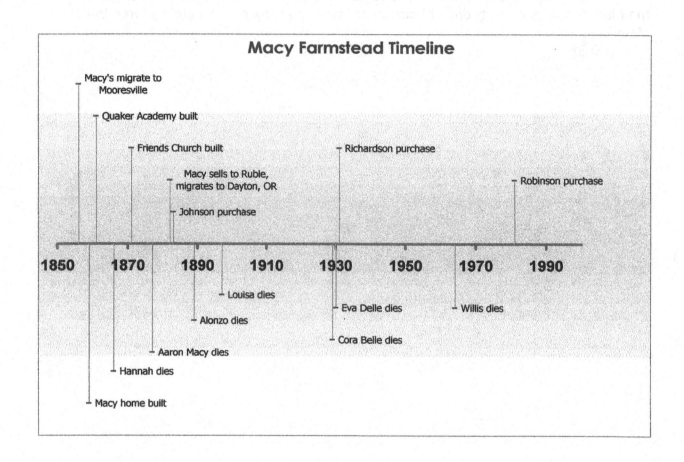

2. Macy Farmstead Timeline

Macy Farmstead

The Macy Farmstead in 2010 is the core of what was a 343 acre farmstead operated by the William Monroe Macy family from 1859 to 1882. William Monroe Macy was a Quaker, a farmer, and a builder. He was extremely industrious. He built the brick Italianate home in 1859 which was the center of much social and commercial activity in Brown Township, Morgan County, Indiana.

His farm included a fruit orchard. He sold peaches and apples and built a "dry house" to preserve the fruit for extended palatability. He raised potatoes, corn, oats, wheat, cows, and hogs which he sold and bartered with other members of his community.

William Monroe Macy was seriously engaged as a timber merchant who bought trees from neighbors, harvested the timber logs and dragged them to Mooresville to be shipped by rail to timber buyers. The tree tops were cut into firewood and sold to Mooresville residents by the wagon load. He operated a huge maple sugar camp which collected the maple tree sap in buckets, and boiled it down to maple syrup. When quantities permitted, his family boiled the syrup further to create 'pralines' of maple sugar which was good trading stock at the local stores.

The MACY FARMSTEAD (1859), along with the Quaker Academy (1861) and White Lick Friends Church (1864), all remain as a testament to his credentials as a builder. The MACY FARMSTEAD has been home to the Macy, Johnson, Richardson and Robinson families from 1859 to 2010. The Friends Church has served the local congregation continuously since 1864. The Quaker Academy was a school until 1972. It was restored in 2000 and serves in 2010 as the Academy of Hoosier Heritage (a local history museum).

The MACY FARMSTEAD is located about 1 mile South West of Mooresville, IN. overlooking Indiana State Road 42 and sits upon 80A bounded by White Lick Creek and Bethel Road. The brick, two story, Italianate home has evolved from its beginning with no electric, no running water, nor central heating & cooling to a residence which includes most features of a 21st century home.

William Monroe Macy was the 1st president of the Mooresville Monrovia Gravel Road Company (a corporation formed in 1865) It was a toll road and a toll booth was located between White Lick Creek and the Macy home. Indiana SR42 evolved from this toll road.

Macy sold the 343A farmstead to Martin Ruble on 4-18-1882 for $18000. Nine months later, Ruble sold the Farm for $24000 to the Alonzo Johnson family. After suffering economic downturns through the early 1900's, the farm had been reduced to 31.68A by the Johnsons. In 1931, Willis and Clara Richardson procured the property from the Johnson estate for $4215. In 1945, they purchased another 46.59A of the original land from Harriet (Johnson) Alden.

Donovan and Joyce Robinson purchased the 78.67A farm in 1981 and annexed 10.41A which had been recently listed as 'owner unknown'. In 1993, another parcel (6.75A) was purchased bringing a total of 95.83A of the original 343A back together. Subsequent grants to INDOT and the Robinson heirs leave 81.26A at this writing.

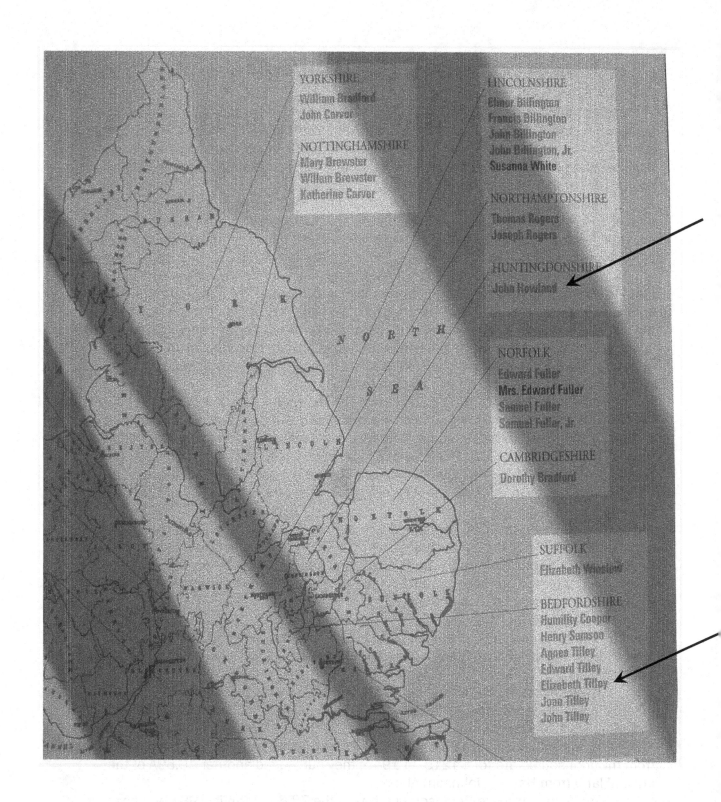

YORKSHIRE
William Bradford
John Carver

NOTTINGHAMSHIRE
Mary Brewster
William Brewster
Katherine Carver

LINCOLNSHIRE
Elinor Billington
Francis Billington
John Billington
John Billington, Jr.
Susanna White

NORTHAMPTONSHIRE
Thomas Rogers
Joseph Rogers

HUNTINGDONSHIRE
John Howland

NORFOLK
Edward Fuller
Mrs. Edward Fuller
Samuel Fuller
Samuel Fuller, Jr.

CAMBRIDGESHIRE
Dorothy Bradford

SUFFOLK
Elizabeth Winslow

BEDFORDSHIRE
Humility Cooper
Henry Samson
Agnes Tilley
Edward Tilley
Elizabeth Tilley
Joan Tilley
John Tilley

3. English Origins of Mayflower Passengers
Note: John Howland & Elizabeth Tilley

Transcontinental Migration of the MACY GENES

John Howland of Huntingdonshire **& Elizabeth Tilley** of Bedfordshire, England travel on the **MAYFLOWER** from **Southampton England to Plymouth, MA**	-------------	**1620**
Barnstable, Ma. And Nantucket Isle,	-----------	1659-1771
Nantucket to Guilford Co., NC (Fitch, Barnard, Macy) Quaker Migration	-----------	1771
Guilford Co., NC to Jefferson Co., TN	-----------	1802
Jefferson Co., TN to Randolph Co., IN	-----------	1820
Economy, Wayne Co, IN to Mooresville, Morgan Co IN	-----------	1856
William Monroe Macy builds Farmstead	-----------	**1859**
Morgan Co., IN to Dayton, Yamhill Co., OR	-----------	1882
Dayton, OR to Greenleaf, ID	-----------	1907
WMM dies in Denair, CA	-----------	1911
Julia Ann dies in Caldwell, ID	-----------	1918
Alva Perry Macy dies in Chico, CA	-----------	1918
Cynthia Ruth dies in Caldwell, ID	-----------	1934

Macy Route to Mooresville, IN

The good ship MAYFLOWER and sister ship Speedwell sailed from Southampton, England August 5, 1620. Problems with Speedwell caused them to stop at Plymouth, England whereupon the Mayflower sailed alone ...... September 17, 1620. The authors of the book (Donovan L. and Joyce A. Robinson) personally set foot and stood on the spot from which the Mayflower sailed from Plymouth, England in 2001.

The Mayflower landed near the present site of Provincetown, MA. After some exploration, the present site of Plymouth, MA was chosen for the settlement where the Robinsons also stood in 2007.

The 102 passengers included John Howland (from Huntingdonshire, England) and Elizabeth Tilley (from Bedfordshire, England) who married sometime after arrival in the "New World". They were also among the 50% of passengers who survived that first winter in Plymouth.

Elizabeth and John Howland had a daughter, Desire Howland, who married John Gorham. Their son, Shubael Gorham (born Barnstable, MA 10-27-1664—d.1730) married Puella Hussey (b.10-10-1677 d.b4 9-23-1748) at Barnstable in May 1693.

Puella and Shubael Gorham's daughter, Deborah (b. 1714 in Barnstable, d. 4-21-1789 on Nantucket Island) married Beriah Fitch (b.8-30-1713 on Nantucket) 12-11-1735.

Thomas Macy (1608-1682) arrived in America by 1639 and was among the original settlers of Salisbury, MA. The Macys have deep roots in American history.

Thomas was a Baptist, but was conflicted by the restrictions placed on religion and persecution of the Quakers. Thomas and his wife migrated to Nantucket Isle in 1659 where they were apparently the first white inhabitants. This line of Macys remained on Nantucket through John Macy (1655-1691), John Macy II (1675-1751), and John Macy III (1721-1795). Barachiah's father, John Macy III, gathered his wife and children and migrated to New Garden, NC in 1771 prior to the Revolutionary War along with the Beriah Fitch and Benjamin Barnard families.

Deborah and Beriah Fitch's daughter, Eunice, married Benjamin Barnard and had a daughter, Lucinda (3-17-1767// 4-5-1810) who married Barachiah Macy (2-24-1760 // 8-28-1832) on 3-20-1783 at New Garden, NC.

Barachiah was the great great grandson of Thomas Macy. This marriage joined the Macy family to the line of Mayflower descendants.

John Macy III died in the home of his son, Barachiah, during George Washington's second term (7-18-1795).

Barachiah's son, William Macy (10-4-1786 // 1-17-1869), was born in Guilford County, NC. In 1801 Barachiah moved his family to Jefferson County, TN.

In 1807, William purchased 200A and signed a note for $500. He married Hannah Hinshaw (2-8-1789// 2-19-1866) on 3-1-1809.

In 1812, William, of strong Quaker persuasion, was drafted into Andrew (Old Hickory) Jackson's Army and refused to serve. Consequently, all his assets were confiscated. By 1815 William worked himself debt free and had built a good house. By 1820 He had 5 sons (including William Monroe Macy (3-8-1820 // 6-4-1911) and a daughter but felt increasingly uncomfortable in the local slavery culture in Tennessee. He explored Indiana (a slave free state) in 1821 and settled in Randolph County, IN.

On 10-16-1849 William Monroe Macy married Julia Ann Mills after a long distance courtship between Mooresville, IN and Randolph County, IN and took her back to Wayne County, IN where a daughter, Hannah Mariah Macy (1-26-1853 // 12-10-1866) was born.

By 1855 The Macy's were on the move again. A son Aaron Mills Macy (5-24-1855 // 9-25-1877) was born in Mooresville and William Monroe Macy completed his move to Morgan County, IN by 8-13-1856. His parents, William and Hannah completed their move to Morgan County on 10-18-1856.

William Monroe and Julia Ann had another son, Alva Perry Macy (1-30-1858 // 8-12-1918) in 1858 and another daughter, Cynthia Ruth Macy (9-17-1861 // 4-18-1934) in 1861.

Meanwhile, William Monroe Macy had become a "mover & shaker" of Mooresville, IN and was engaged in farming, building, and timber marketing. Some milestones of WMM's industry are as follows—

1859 WMM built Macy Farmstead
1860 W M Macy assets = $13200 real estate, $4065 personal property
1860 W M Macy is one of 13 original donors for Quaker Academy School
1860-61 W M Macy built the Quaker Academy (US Historic Landmark)
1864 Macy built the White Lick Meeting House-still in service after 145 years
1865 Macy is 1st President of the Mooresville Monrovia Gravel Road Company
1870 WMM assets = $28000 real estate, $6000 personal property

WMM's mother Hannah Hinshaw Macy (77) died 2-19-1866 and his daughter Hannah Mariah Macy (14) died 12-10-1866. His father William Macy (83) died 1-17-1869 and son Aaron Mills Macy (22) died 9-25-1877. All four are buried in White Lick Cemetery in Mooresville, IN.

In 1882, William Monroe Macy at age 62, sold his farm for $18000 and took his wife, daughter Cynthia Ruth, and son Alva Perry Macy to Dayton, Oregon where he bought a farm and remained until 1907. At age 87, William Monroe Macy and Julia Ann again migrated to Greenleaf, Idaho and bought another farm.

W M Macy died of 'general debility' 6-4-1911 in Denair, CA at age 91.
Julia Ann died 7-22-1918 in Cynthia Ruth's home in Caldwell, ID at age 89 of 'bronchial pneumonia' and was buried next to WMM in Denair, CA.

In 1886, Alva Perry Macy married Ida May Moore (niece of Samuel Moore, founder of Mooresville). They migrated with their children to a farm in Butte County, CA in 1905 where he died 8-12-1918 of Jacksonian Epilepsy at age 63. He is buried in the Chico, CA cemetery (no headstone).

Cynthia Ruth Macy Hatfield was widowed 2-14-1916 and died 4-18-1934 at age 72 of 'strangulated umbilical hernia'. She is buried in Evergreen Memorial Park Cemetery in McMinnville, Oregon.

The Macy's were the truest of American Pioneers who migrated literally from coast to coast and bought land at each juncture. They were hardy stock. They suffered loss of children but survived significant years w/o Medicare, prescription drug benefits, or Social Security checks.

So there it is, a gene pool with roots reaching from a boat ride on the Mayflower in 1620 to serious migrations from the east coast to the solid mid west in the 1800's and finally meeting their destiny in the raw western states of Oregon, Idaho, and California. They were breaking new ground at every settlement.

The diary provides a window on the life of William Monroe Macy's family through the eyes of Alva Perry Macy for the year 1872. Alva was 14 years old as he wrote in the journal and the reader will find he played like a boy and worked like a man.

The activity around the Macy Farmstead reveals a family which had accumulated a greater degree of assets than nearly any one else in Brown Twp, Morgan County, IN. However, the impressive accumulation of assets gave them little or no relief from daily hard work and continued pursuit of cash flow.

The original "Journal" was donated to Earlham College in 1999 by Marilee March Johnson, a great granddaughter of Alva Perry Macy.

This diary was hand written with a 'dip pen' in a bound journal with 4" x 6" pages. During a visit to the Earlham College archives, Joyce Robinson copied every page on a coin operated copier. After careful reading, we determined the content was so awesome that we should translate the journal and type it to permit the mildly interested person a convenient read. Misspells and poor grammar were retained except where communication was jeopardized. Remember, Alva was 14 and it was 1872. He was very aware of the industry around him and focused on personal names of family and business contacts. Each entered name has been compared with the 1870 Census and other sources to determine who that person was and how they fit into the community. Some were never identified; however, those which were found have an asterisk and are foot noted sometimes more than once. A crude code will reveal the assessed value of the person, birth date and place, religion, politics, and vocation when it could be found.

You will notice a great number of Hadleys in the personal contacts. After all, all 6 of William Monroe Macy's sisters each married a Hadley.

Alva Perry Macy's testimony of 1872 in Mooresville, IN includes a major Circus, a visit by Benjamin Harrison, a Ulysses S Grant election rally, and farm produce sales to Samuel Moore, founder of Mooresville. Much of the activity cited by Alva, involved people and events in Brown & Monroe Twps in Morgan County as well as Guilford and Liberty Twps in Hendricks County.

You will note many days when 7-14 workers have been employed in field labor. There is little mention of the home making efforts of Julia Ann, however, it must have been significant as this home had no running water, no electric, and utilized wood for heating and cooking. It is readily apparent that much of the time there were many mouths to feed.

JOHN HOWLAND
13th Signer of the Mayflower Compact

John Howland was born about 1593, the son of Henry Howland of Fen Staten, Huntingdonshire, England. Henry came from London and was identified in the will of Humphrey Howland, a citizen and draper of St. Swithisn's, London. The will was proved 10 July 1646 and mentions his brothers George, Arthur, John and Henry; the last three in New England.

John came on the **Mayflower** as an indentured servant to Governor John Carver at about twenty-seven years old. During the voyage there was a fierce storm out of the west and for many days it was impossible to have any sail. The ship was just drifting under bare masts while the helmsman tried to keep the ship heading into the wind as she wallowed through heavy seas. It was during this storm that John Howland was swept overboard. Luckily, the ship was trailing some topsail halyards and Howland managed to grab one of these and hang on until he was hauled aboard by crew members with a boat hook.

On December 16, Howland was one of the ten men who took the shallop (small open boat) for the third time to search for a suitable location for the Colony. They chose the site which is now Plymouth for their first settlement. When Governor Carver died during that first winter, Howland inherited his estate and immediately bought his own freedom. In 1624 he married Elizabeth Tilley, who had also been a passenger on the **Mayflower** with her parents, John Tilley and his wife. The Howlands had three boys and seven girls.

John Howland's house, along with Samuel Fuller's and Stephen Hopkins'; was built on a slope from the highway to the beach, which is known as Cole's Hill.

From 1627 to 1641, John Howland was in charge of the so-called Undertakers, who were responsible to promote trade in every possible way in order to pay off the Colony's debt to their investors. They established a trading post along the Kenebec River on the present site of Augusta, Maine. With Howland in charge, they did a brisk trade in beaver, otter and other furs with the Abnaki Indians, in exchange for 'coats, shirts, rugs, blankets, etc.".

During his lifetime in Plymouth, Howland was a town officer, partner in the trading company of the Colony, and an assistant or deputy almost continually. He was also prominent in the church, in which he was ordained a pastor.

In Plymouth, records that were kept by Secretary Nathaniel Morton say: *"The 23rd of February 1672 Mr. John Howland, Senior, of the town of Plymouth, deceased. He was a Godly man and an ancient professor in the ways of Christ; he lived until he attained above eighty years in the world. He was one of the first comers into this land, and proved a useful instrument of good in his place, and was the last man that was left of those who came over in the ship called Mayflower, that lived in Plymouth; he was with honor interred at the towne of Plymouth on the 25th of February 1672".*

His wife Elizabeth died fifteen years later, on 21 December 1687, at the age of eighty.

Source: *Signers of the Compact Who Left Descendants* by Esther H Lindsey

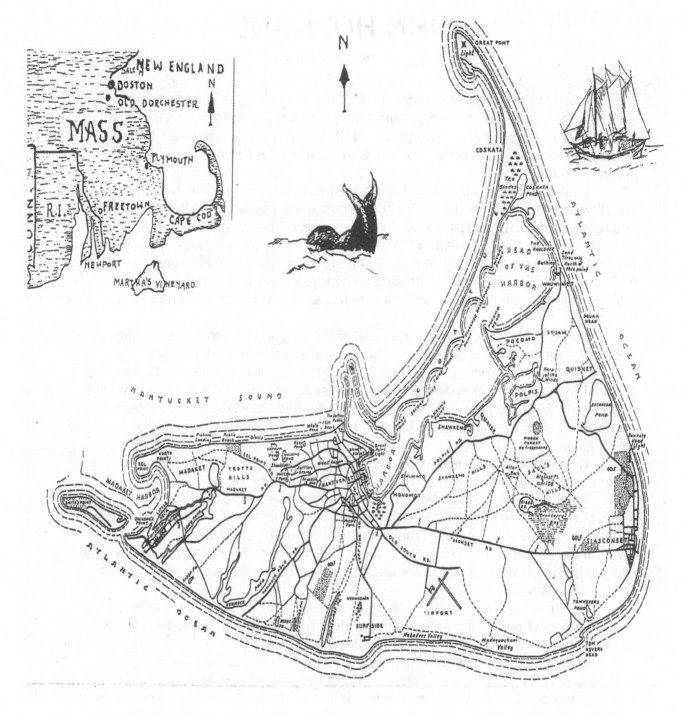

4. Map of Nantucket
Thomas Macy settled on the NW Coast

Thomas Macy's Nantucket

A most definitive work on early settlement has been written by Professor Henry Chandlee Forman who describes the evolution of Sherburne in his <u>Early Nantucket and its Whale Houses</u>. The first dwellings were adjacent to Maddakat Harbor, north of the Ditch and enclosed by Long Pond. The colonials occupied themselves with fishing and farming, and were, to some extent, illiterate. According to Forman they must have built temporary shelters "like dug-outs, puncheon sheds – that is, those having vertical planks for walls stuck in the ground – and wig-wams". The first Proprietors, being fisherman or husbandmen, desperately needed skilled craftsmen. Fourteen more families, or half share men, including seamen, a tailor, a shoemaker, a blacksmith, a fisherman, a cooper, and a carpenter joined the community. The early organization was simple. The earliest Town Records were kept jointly by Robert Pike at Salisbury and at Nantucket by Thomas Macy. On 5-10-1661, these records indicate that Thomas Coffin Sr., Thomas Macy, Edward Starbuck, and Peter Folger were designated to measure and lay out the meadows, woods, and the uplands of the Island, and together with William Mayhew, Richard Swain, John Bishop, all owners, were to determine what should be divided up and what should be retained as common land. They were to designate the town bounds after setting aside a convenient amount of land for public use. Once they had chosen their own lots, (obviously a privilege awarded them for their efforts), the proprietors and their associates were to draw lots for the remainder. On 7-15-1661 each man drew a house lot of 60 square rods (~3/8 Acre). As these were scattered about, they represented a premature form of homesteading. All voters were those residents who were free holders. In 1792, the Proprietors had grown to 500 through purchase, sale, or inheritance, but by 1800 they had decreased to 300. Dr. Guba has described the system thus:

"The peculiar land tenure was conceived and arranged by the original settlers in an attempt to provide for the general welfare by a common ownership of the island and by a common interest in each other".

In 1660 Edward Starbuck moved to the north end of Hummock Pond, while Thomas Macy went to Wannacomet, east of Capaum. Other settlers moved south west via Reed Pond, Wyers and Macy's Pond to the western sections of Hummock Pond; some moved still further to Wesco (or, "the White Stone") which was adjacent to Nantucket Harbor. The various names were derived from two sources; the majority of the names were Indian although modified by usage, e.g., Mattaket, Muskeikat, Tuckernucket, Sasagacha, Nopadea, Aquidnet, Monomoy, Squam, Shimmo, Siasconset, Wescoe and others. Others were English e.g., Northam, Uppertown and Middletown; others like Jeremy Cove, Eel Point, Smith's Point, Reed Pond, Pumpkin Road, Swain's Neck and Tom Nevers Head, either refer to conditions or to owners. At first their properties followed a crescent-shaped scatteration. There was no recognizable town. There were few facilities, no streets, and no order. In 1673 the town of Sherburne extended from Wesco past Capaum Harbor to Hummock.

THOMAS MACY

THOMAS MACY, (1608-1682) the progenitor of the Macy family in America, came to Massachusetts Colony from Chilmark, Wiltshire County, England, about 1635 (possibly the year prior). It should be noted that his arrival occurred simultaneously with the departure of Roger Williams, and that he put into practice the principles taught by Williams.

Thomas was a merchant and dealt in textiles as well as being a planter.
He was absolutely fearless, devout and scholarly for his day. He was first town clerk of Salisbury, now Amesbury. He served as overseer of schools, and was deputy to the general court.

In 1638 he began a relentless opposition to the sale of rum to the Indians. The year later he became a freeman. In the year 1657 the Baptists sought to have the town divided that they might be free to worship as they pleased and to be absolved from supporting the established church. In this they were defeated and were periodically fined for non-attendance. The government of the Puritans in Massachusetts made a strict allegiance to the Protestant church mandatory and a special act passed by the general court denied Joseph Peaslee and Thomas Macy the right of "free speech" upon the charge of "disorderly practices", which consisted of preaching to their fellow Baptists.

The culminating offense of Thomas Macy occurred in 1659. He manifested sympathy for four English Quaker missionaries, whom he sheltered in his home during a rain storm. For this offense he was arrested, convicted and fined 30 shillings.
Two of these missionaries, William Robinson and Marmaduke Stephenson, were hung 10-27-1659 on Boston Common, and buried without religious rites. Their crime was .... being a Quaker!

Upon his departure to Nantucket Isle, he left land, dwelling, cattle, household furnishings – everything except that which he carried in an open boat. Some months prior to his departure, he and nine others purchased Nantucket Island. It was mutually agreed that each would receive twenty-two and one-half acres. They were privileged to sell one-half of each holding, which they did. It was further agreed that the remaining 29,000 acres would be held in trust for the Indians, numbering about 3,000. It was agreed also that any contract with an Indian to purchase his land was null and void. At this time the Indian in Massachusetts could not buy land. Land in Massachusetts Colony was not sold but granted by the King of England. Those who had much money were granted much land; little money, little land; no money, no land. Both Indian and Quaker were subject to the "Vagabond Act". Both were sold as chattels and deported as slaves to the Barbados.

For the first five years, the authority of Thomas Macy upon Nantucket was absolute, there being no other jurisdiction. He established a government upon the principles of peace more than twenty years before the arrival of William Penn. Nantucket was an asylum for Englishmen who were denied their rights upon English soil, and victims of English laws.

In 1664 Nantucket came under the jurisdiction of New York, prior to ceding it to Massachusetts in 1692. In 1664 Thomas Macy returned to Amesbury and disposed of his previous homestead.

In 1676 Thomas Macy confiscated one half barrel of rum, there being a prohibitory law against the sale of rum upon Nantucket and Martha's Vineyard. In a letter to the governor he dwelt at length upon the evil influence of rum upon the Indians. He further says "that for thirty-eight years he had done his utmost in persuading the whites not to sell rum to the Indians." For generations in American history it has been taught "that rum was a Divine instrument sent from God to be used in the extermination of the Indian."

The traits of Thomas Macy have been remarkably reproduced, when times and seasons brought them forth. Descendants of his are numbered in every advanced step in American history and in crucial hours they assumed their measure of responsibility.

Thomas was born at Chilmark, England, 1608, he died on Nantucket 4-19-1682. He married Sarah Hopcott 7-8-1639 (also of Chilmark), who died 1706 at 94 years on Nantucket.

14

JOHN MACY I

JOHN MACY I, b 7-14-1655: d 10-14-1691 .....son of Thomas & Sarah

John was 4 years old when his father migrated to Nantucket. He became a house carpenter. Since he was the only son to reach maturity and marry, he became the slender thread by which present day Macys cling to Nantucket history.

In 1676, he married Deborah Gardner, b. 2-12-1658, d. 4-2-1712. She was the daughter of Richard and Sarah (Shattuck) Gardner.

Richard Gardner was son of Thomas Gardner, b. in Dorsetshire, England, d. in Salem, Mass, 10-29-1674; He was a member of the company of original settlers of Cape Ann and Salem. They came under the Charter of Dorsetshire Company (1624). He was also overseer of a plantation; became one of the earliest settlers of Salem (1626), became a freeman (1636), represented Salem in general court (1637), and held several local offices. He was a large real estate holder.

John, Deborah, and their children were all born and died upon Nantucket.

JOHN MACY II

JOHN MACY II, b 1675, d 11-28-1751.

He married Judith Worth b 12-22-1689; d 11-8-1767. She was the daughter of John & Miriam Gardner Worth.
Their children were all born on Nantucket.
Within the years 1708-11, nine hundred of the thousand white inhabitants of Nantucket espoused the Quaker faith. The history of the inhabitants of the island prior to that date is included in the history of the early Baptists of New England, who numbered about 5,000 in America at the time of the founding of Brown University.
John Macy II, grandson of the first settler of Nantucket, was the first Macy to join the Society of Friends, which he did in 1711. Other members of the family quickly followed.
The will of **John Macy II** indicates he possessed considerable property.

JOHN MACY III

John Macy III b 12-23-1721: d 7-18-1795
John III was born on Nantucket 12-23-1721. He migrated with his family to Guilford Co. NC on 4-28-1771. He died in son **Barachiah**'s home 7-18-1795.
He married Eunice Coleman, b 10-18-1724 on 8-13-1743. She died on Nantucket 12-28-1768 prior to the family migration to North Carolina.

New Garden NC Settlers

The 1754-1770 New Garden settlers from PA, VA, MD, and NC were soon reinforced by other immigrants who also came from old Quaker stock. These were the settlers from Nantucket Island, MA. This movement began in 1771 and Libni Coffin was the first Nantucket man to arrive at New Garden. During the next 5 years from 1771 to 1775, ... 41 of the 50 certificates were from Nantucket.

This migration stopped suddenly with the outbreak of the Revolutionary War. During the war the growth was by local population growth. About the end of the 18th century there began the great migration to the mid west which sapped the strength of all NC Quaker meetings and ended the existence of many. New Garden contributed in large numbers to the movement but had sufficient vitality to withstand the lost membership.

The Quakers have been at the front in settling and civilizing almost every wilderness and plain, in bringing order and law to newly acquired territories which would otherwise have been dominated by pillage and despoliation. They built schools, meeting houses, cultivated farms and founded villages and towns. This migration and development is a blueprint of the Macy genes which landed at Plymouth, MA in 1620 and subsequently made their way to

-Nantucket, MA
- New Garden, NC,
-Jefferson County, TN,
- Economy, IN,
-Mooresville, IN,
-Dayton, OR,
-Greenleaf, ID and settled along the
-Pacific coast states.

This book focuses on William Monroe Macy who carried these genes from Jefferson County, TN to Denair, CA between 1820 and 1911. At every juncture, he and his fellow travelers procured land, contributed to the community settlement and moved on west as if driven by a migratory gene.

History books are largely filled with accounts of wars, land acquisition, political leaders, founding of states, counties and towns and geographical descriptions. Too little is noted of the people who actually settled the various parts of the country. 'Settlers' have been grouped and left there by historians. The Quakers permeated every new land, and with their peaceful ways, their honesty and integrity, were such quiet, though forceful leaders in the building of peaceful civilizations that historians, thinking in terms of wars and strife, have paid them small attention.

It has been said that fully 50% of all American families, now living, and whose ancestors have lived in America since the early days have some ancestral Quaker connections. These are fortunate in that, although they are not likely to be able to establish their lines of descent through other channels, they can nearly always authoritatively establish their genealogical ancestor descent insofar as it connects with Quakers.

BARACHIAH MACY

BY   Aaron Macy
(1948)

Barachiah Macy was born on Nantucket Island, which lies off the shores of the state of Massachusetts, on February 24, 1760. He was the ninth child of John Macy III and Eunice Coleman Macy.

Barachiah's mother died on December 28, 1768, four days after Clement, his youngest brother, was born. This was on Nantucket Island when Barachiah was about nine years old.

In 1771, when Barachiah was about 11 years old, his father, John Macy III and most of his children moved to Guilford County, North Carolina and became members of the New Garden Quaker Monthly Meeting.

Barachiah married Lucinda Barnard (a 6th generation descendant of John Howland) on March 20, 1783 at this monthly meeting. Lucinda was born on Nantucket Island and with her parents, Benjamin Barnard and Eunice Fitch Barnard migrated to Guilford County North Carolina at the same time that Barachiah's father moved his family to the same neighborhood.

Barachiah and Lucinda lived in Guilford County for about 19 years where their 5 older children were born; Mary (1st) who died when about 1 year old; William; Mary (2nd, named for her deceased sister); Jonathan; Anna; Matilda; Eunice, who died when about 3 years old; and Elihu, who died when a little over 7 months old.

In 1800 a brother-in-law was moving to Western Tennessee and Barachiah accompanied him looking for a new location. It was at this time that most all of the Quakers in the Southern states were leaving the South and migrating North and West to "slave free territory".

They bought land on Lost Creek, in Jefferson County and Barachiah returned then to North Carolina to get his affairs in shape to move to the new home.

In 1801 he sent his oldest son, William (about 15 years old) to plant a crop so the family would have provisions when they subsequently moved to their new home.

William made the trip alone for a part of the way and put in a crop which he cared for until fall. He then returned to North Carolina to help the family make the move to the new place. A more detailed story of William's part in this migration can be found in his autobiography.

On New Year's Day of 1802 they started for the new location. As it was winter weather and nearly all mountain roads, they were 30 days making the 300 mile journey with horse and wagons.

Upon arrival, they were able to gather enough corn from the crop William had planted in the year before to keep them going until the new crop was ready to harvest.

On 11-27-1802 Barachiah Macy, Lucinda, sons William and Jonathan and daughters Mary, Ann, and Matilda get certificates to Lost Creek Monthly Friends Meeting in Jefferson County, Tennessee. This is in the Eastern part of Tennessee where they were later received on 2-19-1803.

Barachiah bought more land to add to his holdings and built a new house. He also cleared about 10 acres more for crops and added stock fence. They were now fairly established in their new location.

Barachiah and Lucinda lived here for about 8 years and children Isaac, John, and Lydia were born. Lucinda died here on April 5th, 1810 when Lydia, the youngest child was about 3 years old. She was buried at Lost Creek Meeting House Cemetery in Jefferson County, Tennessee.

Lucinda's life history showed some of the wanderings of our early fore-mothers. Born on Nantucket Island, she was a direct descendant of Mayflower emigrants (John Howland & Elizabeth Tilley). She moved to Guilford County, North Carolina in her early childhood just before the Revolutionary War. This journey was probably made by sea to some port on the Atlantic seaboard of this state and then by wagons to the Western part of the state. Here she was married and several of her children were born. Then life took her to new territory in Jefferson County, TN where the rest of her children were born. And lastly, she died many, many miles from where she first saw the light of day.

In the fall of 1814 Barachiah married Elizabeth Woodard and it was recorded by his son William as a happy union. She was the widow of William Woodard who died at Lost Creek MM (Jefferson Co, TN) on 10-17-1812.

Records show that all his children left Jefferson County, Tennessee and moved to Springfield monthly meeting near Economy, Indiana 9-27-1828.

Barachiah, daughter Emily, wife Elizabeth and step-daughter Lydia were granted certificates of transfer to Springfield Monthly Meeting in Indiana on September 27, 1828 from the Lost Creek Monthly Meeting. Barachiah passed away 8-28-1832. His voyage had taken him from Nantucket to Indiana within a lifetime of 72 years.

This family history reveals how those early families, after the migration from the Southern pro-slavery states to the Northern Free States and territories continued their westward movement. A few would stay in the new location then history would repeat itself again by some staying and others moving on to a further west settlement. Each new migration required abandoning many possessions as well as the graves of their deceased family members.

Guilford County, NC Land Warrants
1778- 1803

952. Stephen Gardner 594A; warrant #1487 issued 4-7-1779 by Ralph Gorrell to Stephen Gardner for 640A on both sides of Russell Creek, joins John Brown on E, John Allen's former land on N, Jemima Gardner on W, & includes the improvement that Patrick Mullen sold; 594A surveyed 3-22-1783 by Alex Caldwell; Henry Ford & **John Macy**, chain carriers; grant #951 issued 11-8-1784.

1500. Nathaniel Macy 320A; warrant #567 issued 11-16-1778 by Ralph Gorrell to Nathaniel Macy for 320A on waters of Bull Run, joined by deeded land of William Gardner on W, land claims of Ruben Bunker, **John Macy**, & James Martin & includes his improvement; 320A surveyed 2-7-1786 by Robert Brattain; Elihu Macy & **Barachiah Macy**, chain carriers; grant #1458 issued 5-16-1787.

1661. John Macy 640A; warrant #1057 issued 2-4-1779 by Ralph Gorrell to **John Macy** for 640A on Deep River and on Bull Run, begins at John Lean's improvement, runs S to THE wagon road, joins Isaac Gardner & includes 2 improvements; 640A surveyed 12-29-1786 by Robert Brattain; Timothy Macy & **Barachiah Macy**, chain carriers; grant #1674 issued 3-21-1789.

1664. John Macy 561A; warrant #1434 issued 4-6-1779 by Ralph Gorrell to **John Macy** for 640A on both sides of Bull Run, a branch of Deep River. joins **John Macy's** entry on S, James Martin & Nathaniel Macy on W, Jethro Macy's lines on N, & includes 2 improvements; 561A surveyed 12-29-1786 by Robert Brattain; Elihu Macy & **Barachiah Macy**, chain carriers; grant #1677 issued 3-21-1789.

2094. Barzillia Gardner 40A; warrant #158 issued 1-18-1802 by John Howell to Barzillia Gardner for 40A joins heirs of **John Macy** deceased, on waters of Rudducks Creek, & entered 10-16-1801; 40A surveyed 4-30-1802 by John Howell, DS for Charles Bruce; Amiel Gardner, chain carriers; 11-29-1802 Barzillia Gardner paid purchase money for 40A in entry #158   (signed) J Craven, comptroller; grant #2098 issued 12-17-1802.

Jefferson County, TN Land Sales

Barachiah Macy	bought	100 A	from	Mary Baker	02-18-1805	@ Lost Creek
Barachiah Macy	bought	100 A	from	Joseph Green	12-25-1809	@Holston French Broad River
William Macy	bought	178 A	from	Benjamin Murrell	10-03-1807	@ Lost Creek
William Macy	bought	1 A	from	Henry Canaday	06-14-1819	
Johnathon Macy	bought	114 A	from	John Vance	06-23-1810	@ Beaver Creek
Barachiah Macy	sold	100 A	to	William Osborn	12-02-1811	@Holston French Broad River
Barachiah Macy	sold	115 A	to	Thomas Nelson	09-08-1828	@ Lost Creek
Wm. & Hannah Macy	sold	190 A	to	Mary Liles	02-12-1820	@ Lost Creek
Johnathon Macy	sold	80 A	to	William Mills, Jr.	03-01-1820	@ Beaver Creek
Johnathon Macy	sold	123 A	to	Henry Derriaux	10-06-1828	@ Beaver Creek

LOST CREEK QUAKER CHURCH

LOST CREEK, TENNESSEE

WILLIAM MACY FAMILY CHURCH
DURING YEARS OF 1802 - 1820

5. Robinson's 2007 Photo of Lost Creek Church

Lost Creek Monthly Meeting
Jefferson County, TN

The theology of George Fox was a very Biblical Christianity with a radical twist. Fox rejected all ceremony and ritual, stressing the essential need for a vital living relationship with Christ. He rejected the concept of a professional clergy, teaching that all believers were ministers of God. He also rejected the idea of a church building as a sacred place or as a "house of God". His followers strongly emphasized the New Testament concept that the church is not a building but a group of believers. Members of the Society of Friends met first in homes and later in buildings that they distinctly referred to as "meetinghouses" to clearly distinguish them from the church buildings and cathedrals of other groups which were mockingly referred to as "steeplehouses".

The Quaker movement, despite ardent persecution from other churches, grew explosively in England, reaching an estimated 50-60,000 in England before Fox's death in 1691. By that time there were also strong Quaker Meetings in Ireland, in the Americas, and elsewhere.

The story of Lost Creek Friends Meeting begins with the movement of settlers from North Carolina into what is now East Tennessee. Large numbers of those settlers were members of the Society of Friends. Some of these early Friends settled near what is now called New Market, Tennessee along Lost Creek. John Mills, a Quaker from Guilford County, North Carolina, brought his family to Lost Creek where they built a log cabin. Mills began meeting with other Quaker families that were settling in the area. By 1787 the local Friends were having what was referred to as a "Voluntary" meeting. They had not yet been formally recognized by the North Carolina Yearly Meeting, but were meeting regularly for worship. In 1793 Lost Creek was recognized as a worshiping group of Quakers, and in 1795 became a Worship and Preparative Meeting.

Lost Creek was a thriving center of Quaker life and worship in East Tennessee. It became an evangelistic center as new monthly meetings were activated throughout the region under the supervision of Lost Creek Quarterly Meeting.

Quakers, however, remained an active part of their local community. A serious social issue of the early 1800's began to challenge the local Friends to take a stand. Friends had begun to reject slave ownership. As early as 1772, it was considered unacceptable for North American Quakers to be slave owners. By 1787 all Quakers are believed to have freed their slaves. Manumission, the freeing of slaves, became an important social concern to Friends and in January 1815 the Tennessee Manumission Society was organized at Lost Creek Church. This was, of course, a controversial position, and many Friends chose to leave Tennessee, migrating North to Ohio and West to Indiana. It is estimated that Lost Creek lost 400-500 members between 1803 and 1832 due to this migration.

During the Civil War, the building was burned by Confederate soldiers. The current wooden building was rebuilt on the original foundation using many of the logs of the original building as part of the structure.

In the late 1800's the two Quarterly Meetings of Friends in Tennessee, Lost Creek and Friendsville, sought permission to establish their own Yearly Meeting.

Of the many Quaker Meetings that once met in East Tennessee, these are the only two of the original meetings that remain. The vibrant spiritual fervor and social activism that characterized these early Friends provides a powerful legacy for modern day Friends.

Our 2007 visit to Lost Creek church had a significant impact on us both.

Macy Family Burials along the Way

NANTUCKET LINEAGE			MAYFLOWER LINEAGE		
Thomas Macy	9-22-1653	Nantucket			
			John Howland	2-23-1671	Plymouth, MA
			Desire Howland Gorham	10-13-1683	Barnstable, MA
John Macy	10-14-1691	Nantucket	Shubeel Gorham	8-7-1750	Hyannis, MA
John Macy II	11-28-1751	Nantucket			
			Deborah Gorham Fitch	4-21-1787	Nantucket
			Eunice Fitch Barnard	11- -1792	Guilford Co, NC
John Macy III	7-18-1795	Guilford Co, NC			
Barachiah Macy	8-28-1832	Wayne Co, IN	Lucinda Barnard Macy	4-5-1810	Jefferson Co, TN

William Macy	1-17-1869	Morgan Co, IN
William Monroe Macy	6-4-1911	Stanislaus Co, CA
Alva Perry Macy	8-12-1918	Butte Co, CA

As the migration progressed, many times the elder members of the family died before the rest of the clan moved on to new settlements. As you can see, the descendants of Thomas Macy (Nantucket Settler) and the descendants of John Howland (Mayflower Passenger) were joined by the marriage of Barachiah Macy and Lucinda Barnard. William, William Monroe and Alva Perry Macy are the first Macys entitled to claim Mayflower heritage

Missouri Historical Map: Missouri
Compromise - 1820 By Maps.com

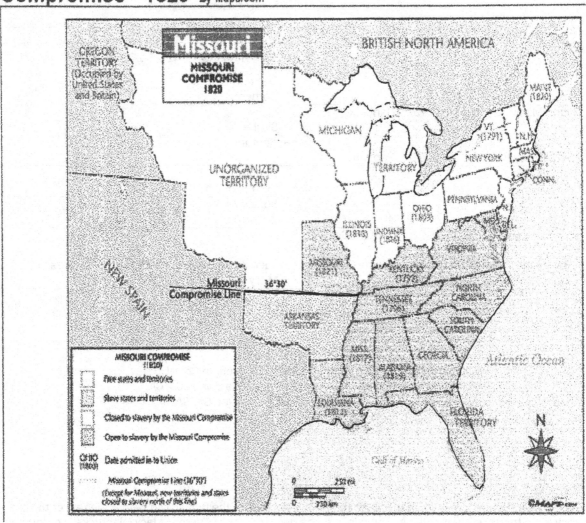

6. Slave States & Free States as of 1820

7. William Macy (1786-1869) Son of Barachiah

Notes on WILLIAM MACY

(1786-1869)

Autobiography, taken from Macy family newsletter Footprints Through Time, 7-1- 1987

Morgan County, Indiana; 9 April 1866

I was born 4 Oct 1786 in Guilford County, North Carolina. My parents' names were Barachiah and Lucinda (Barnard) Macy. Their parents, John Macy III (then a widower) and Benjamin Barnard with his wife, Eunice and their families, emigrated from Nantucket to Guilford when my parents were quite young (prior to the Revolutionary War). They each had a large family of children that eventually married and settled around them although some of them moved to Virginia. My grandfather Macy (John Macy III) lived with my father from my first recollection until his death which occurred in 1796 when I was 10 years old. That circumstance made a deep impression on my mind, which never wholly left me. It was the first time I had ever seen death so near home.

Grandmother Macy died comparatively young (44). She never saw Carolina. Her maiden name was Eunice Coleman and she was the daughter of Elihu Coleman, a public Friend. My grandfather Barnard died when I was very young (1792, during Washington's 1st term as President). I remember seeing him once or twice. His wife's maiden name was Fitch and they were all Friends and descendants of Friends, who fled persecution in England and settled in the Eastern United States.

I was brought up in a compact settlement of Friends until I was 15 years old, and a great many of them were my uncles, aunts and cousins. When I was 14 years old my father went with his brother-in-law to Tennessee to help him move and when they arrived there my father bought a farm on Lost Creek in Jefferson County. It was comparatively new country and the next fall my parents determined on sending me there to raise a crop for them to move to; accordingly I went. I was young and had never been away from home much before that. When I reflect on it, since, it seems a great risk to send an inexperienced lad of 15 years, 300 miles across the Allegheny Mountains, who didn't know a foot of the way nor a single person on the route, to stay twelve months and then come back to assist in moving the family out.

The worse danger in such a situation comes from the surrounding influences in which a youth finds himself, ...out of the reach of his parents and left to his own impulses. I sometimes shudder when I think of the moral dangers I was thus exposed to.

I had the good fortune to have the company of my cousin and his wife for the first 200 miles. They were returning to their home in Tennessee after visiting their family in North Carolina. I did very well with them, but after I left them I had to travel the next 100 miles by myself and I felt very alone indeed. Everything was new and strange and I had a very poor map of the country *in my head*. I took the precaution to get a waybill of the route but nevertheless I got lost two or three times before I got there. Suffice to say I landed safe and found all well. (Jefferson Co, TN)

Having never tasted limestone water until after leaving my cousins, the use of it seriously affected my health and I did not get over it for several months. Now came the trial. I had pious parents and I esteemed and loved them as such but now I was beyond their control and I might take my swing and do as I pleased, Praise be to the merciful God, I was preserved from any gross immoralities. Coming into a strange country, among strange people, I had entirely new associations and it is remarkable to me that I escaped the contamination of evil examples as well as I did, ...which I am bound to reverently attribute to the watchful care of the Shepherd of Israel.

A circumstance occurred in the first summer I lived in Tennessee which made a deep impression on my mind, and I trust never will be effaced while memory lasts. It was the custom of the young men and boys on Seventh Day afternoon, during the hot weather, to go to the river one and a half miles away to bathe. This is a large and heavy running stream. I went with several others one day for that purpose and when we got there we saw a number of others in the water near the other shore. I went in aiming to go to them, unmindful that the river had risen and the water run rapid and waves ran high. I became strangled and sank, which those on the other side, seeing, started towards me, some on horses, some in canoes and some in the water. One young man, more energetic than the rest, succeeded in reaching me as I rose the second time and coming behind me, took me under the arms and held my head above water until others came with a canoe and lifted me into it and thus saved my life. I am certain that in a few seconds more I would have sunk to rise no more. It is remarkable how swiftly thoughts will fly over time and space; while under water, I thought of my parents 300 miles off, and what distress it would bring to them, particularly my mother, when hearing I was sunk in the river, never to be seen again.

After this remarkable deliverance, I got along very well through the summer and raised a good crop and in the fall prepared to go back. In the anticipation of meeting my parents, brothers and sisters, I became homesick and impatient. No one could know my feelings but those who have experienced it.

One of my uncles went back with me and in one place in the mountains, where it was twelve miles from one house to the next, night came on and it grew dark about three miles before we reached our stopping place. As it began to grow dark, we heard a panther about a quarter of a mile ahead of us and about the same distance from the road and immediately another answered it from the opposite side and about a minute later the cry was repeated, it appeared very plain they were coming together so we pushed on trying to escape them. The cry was repeated and answered every time nearer to us but we succeeded in passing between them before they met and the people where we stayed told us it was their custom to call together at dark for the purpose of hunting and woe to the animal that crosses their path when they are thus together, if they had met us at the road we would have been in imminent danger. Our escape I consider as another remarkable deliverance, many of which I have had through a long life.

Nothing further occurred until we reached home and found the family in indifferent health. My youngest brother, some two years old, had been taken from the family circle and now I only had one brother (Johnathan) about five years younger than me and three sisters left. (Mary, Anna, Matilda)

Now we began to prepare for moving. My father being but weakly (@ 42 yrs old), a great deal of the hardship fell upon me and due to circumstances beyond our control, we didn't start until New Years Day 1802. We had a disagreeable time of it through the mountains which were sometimes exceedingly cold and we would seldom get in a house at night. My mother became seriously ill, which added to our distress. We made such slow progress that we were 30 days traveling a distance of 300 miles, but landed safe at last.

When spring came we had plenty of corn to gather to clear the fields for a new crop and during the summer my father and uncle bought another tract of land adjoining the one they lived on and divided their interest. The part that fell to my father had no improvements on it except about ten acres in cultivation. Since my father was no part of a mechanic except that sometimes he made shoes and by this time I had developed into something like manhood I turned my attention to mechanics, partly from necessity, such as building houses, chimneys, etc.

With the aid of a young man that my father hired, we built a double log house and two stone chimneys and cleared the fenced ten acres of ground. (By the way, there was no other kind of buildings seen in those days.)

Having fixed the family in a comfortable way to live, I left them to seek my fortune knowing that my parents had nothing to give me although they continued to furnish me with every day clothes. I went to live with my uncle and remained with him most of the time until I was married – sometimes cropping with him, sometimes hired by the day, sometimes by the job and once by the year. Several times while driving teams for him I narrowly escaped with my life. I had the liberty, while living with him, of going to a profitable job, whenever I found one.

In the fall of 1807 (Thomas Jefferson was President) I bought a tract of land consisting of two hundred acres, paid part down and gave my notes for five hundred dollars on time. It was mostly rich land with about fifteen acres in cultivation but no buildings. After doing this I made every arrangement I could to meet my liabilities. Money became very scarce and since stock was not selling my main resource was mechanical labor.

In the spring of 1809 I married (Hannah Hinshaw) and as I had not yet redeemed my notes I brought additional trouble on my (wife) but she proved a real helpmate.

I was gone from home a great deal of the time, and left her to manage at home which she did effectually. In the spring of 1810 my dear mother died (@ 43 yrs). She was a tender mother of her children and we all loved her.

In 1812 I was drafted into Andrew 'Old Hickory' Jackson's army and of course I refused to go and was fined which placed everything we possessed at risk. It cost us a good deal of money before the fine was paid which was a heavy drawback under our circumstances. (Note: James Madison was President)

In the fall of 1814 I visited my native (Guilford, NC) county for the last time. Great alterations had occurred among the peoples during my absence. While I was in North Carolina my father married his second wife (Elizabeth Woodward) which proved to be a happy union.

In the course of the year 1815 I succeeded in liquidating all my debts, and turned my attention to improving my land, building a good house, etc. Meanwhile my family increased and by the spring of 1820, we had six children. They were all boys but one, (we lost in infancy). I began serious consideration of the propriety of moving my family to a free-state. My friends, except for one, opposed the measure but the idea of my children marrying slave-holders, which I observed frequently happened, overruled every other consideration and in the fourth month I sold out and moved to the State of Indiana where we settled near the head of West River in Randolph County.

In the spring of 1821 I had gone with several others on an expedition westward through the State of Indiana. It was then a primeval wilderness inhabited by Indians and wild beasts of which we saw an abundance. Here again we had to form new acquaintances and new associations and as it nearly always happens, the settlers were mostly of a doubtful character, and so it happened with us.

Here we remained in eastern Indiana until we had raised a large family of children. Our four oldest sons

John H   d 6-1-1849
Jonathan   d 9-15-1850,
Alvah J   d 7-9-1852,
Nathan   d 3-23-1856,

died and left large families. All the rest married and left that part of the country and in 1858 we sold out and moved here (Mooresville, IN). Our youngest daughter (Lydia Ann) married John Franklin Hadley (3-13-1859) shortly after we moved here.

Now to conclude my little story, my dear wife for several years of her life became weakly and gradually grew worse until 19 Feb 1866. She passed away and we doubt not is entered into peace and rest. She gave much good counsel to those around her and frequently expressed, toward the close of her life that all was peace and love and she had nothing left to do but die. (Civil War is concluded, Lincoln has been assassinated, and Andrew Johnson is President)

I have had to pass through many sore trials in the course of my long life but this bereavement overwhelms me with grief. We lived together traveling the chequered path of life in utmost love and harmony for fifty-seven years, wanting nine days, partaking of each others joys and sorrows, tribulations, privations and losses. Again and again has one or the other been prostrated on a bed of sickness, near unto death, and the other was there to administer aid and comfort.

I am bound to believe that a virtuous wife is a gift of God. But now she has gone to reap the reward of a well spent life and enjoy the presence of her Savior forever and left me disconsolate. I take great pleasure in dedicating these lines to her memory. Now, in my old age and infirm state of health, I am left alone but I can truly say I believe I was influenced, in my choice of a mate, by an unseen hand.

Many years ago I was taken down with fever and thought I must die and then I saw that it would not do to make a partial sacrifice. I must give up all. It was an awful time with me. No human being will ever know what I suffered then. I pleaded hard for release, but it would not do. I had a dear wife and a family of children, and the thought of parting with them was bitter. But, after giving up, (without reserve), things were made easy. As a contrast to this, I will state, that several times after this I have been brought to the brink of the grave and had no hope of recovery, yet all was peace within.

And here let me observe, it is much better to become reconciled to God while in health, for diverse reasons:

--one is, sometimes the mind becomes bewildered and unable to concentrate the thoughts on any one subject;

--another is, when the mind is distressed with fears it has an unfavorable effect on the body so that those who have no fear of the result have decidedly the advantage.

I was followed from infancy up with the entreaties of redeeming love, but I was loath to give up, still holding back something I was loath to part with. But now I can truly say that I hope I shall soon follow her (Hannah) and hope to meet her where we shall part no more.

And here I will lay down my pen,

William Macy

Six Macy Brides
for
Six Hadley Grooms

William and Hannah Hinshaw Macy had 6 daughters who each married a man by the name of Hadley.

Lucinda   married   Thomas Marshal Hadley,   son of Isaac & Ruth
                  11-25-1838,   Morgan Co. IN

Margaret Ann married   Levi S Hadley,   son of Simon B & Sarah T
                  5-25-1850,   Morgan co, IN

Sarah   married   Thomas Lindley Hadley   son of Joshua & Sarah
                  11-17-1841, Randolph Co. IN

Ruth   married   Miles S Hadley,   son of Simon B & Sarah
                  3-29-1850,   Morgan Co, IN

Mary Ann   married   Albert Hadley,   son of Joshua B & Mary T
                  4-3-1852,   Morgan Co, IN

Lydia Ann   married   John Franklin Hadley,   son of Aaron & Lydia
                  3-13-1860,   Morgan Co, IN

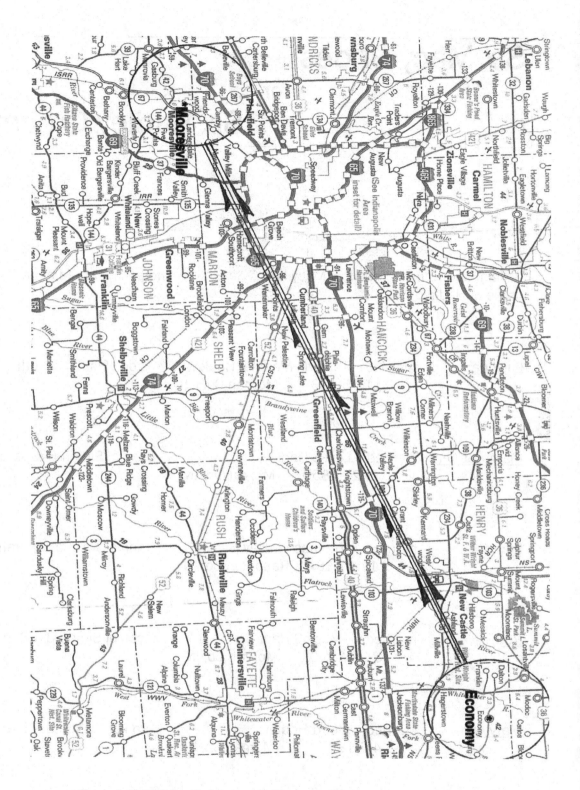

8. 1850's Macy Migration –
Economy to Mooresville, IN map

Notes on WILLIAM MONROE MACY

WMM was born 3/8/1820 in Jefferson Co., TN, the 7th child of William and Hannah Hinshaw Macy. He died 6/4/1911 @ Denair, Stanislaus Co., CA of "general debility or senile decay—he had been confined to his bed several months".

Death Certificate # 90, Buried in Denair Cemetery gravesite 32A 07   6/5/1911

WMM migrated from TN to Wayne Co, IN with his family in 1820.

He married Julia Ann Mills 10/16/1849 in Mooresville, Morgan County, IN after a long distance courtship.

1850 Census indicates WMM is a farmer with assets of $1600 in Wayne Co., IN

WMM & JAM are received @ White Lick MM, Mooresville, 8/13/1856 from Springfield MM

1859 WMM built the Macy farmstead overlooking what is now State Road 42

1860 Census indicates WMM is a farmer with assets of $13200 RE + $4065 PP
   Julia Ann 30, Hannah Mariah 7, Aaron Mills 5, Alva Perry 2 +
   Wm L Macy 21 (live-in student, son of Nathan & Susannah Macy)

9/12/1860 WMM is one of 13 original donors for the Quaker Academy

1861 WMM built the Quaker Academy at the direction of the 6 member Mooresville High School Assoc. Board of Trustees (WMM was one of them)

1864 WMM builds the White Lick Meeting House --Still in service after 145 years

Mooresville Monrovia Gravel Road Co. incorporated with WMM as 1st President in 12/22/1865

2/19/1866 WMM's daughter Hannah Mariah dies of spotted fever @ Macy Farmstead

1870 Census indicates WMM is lumber dealer with assets of $28000 RE + $6000 PP
   Julia Ann 41, Hannah Mariah deceased, Aaron Mills 15, Alva Perry 13, Cynthia Ruth 9, William Andrew 26, Miles Andrew 4, Lyddia Andrew 1, Harvey Aston 20, Julia Heasling 19

1876 Aaron Mills Macy is teacher @ Bethel School

1877 Aaron Mills Macy dies of Typhoid Fever @ Macy Farmstead

1880 Census indicates WMM is a farmer
   Julia Ann 51, Hannah & Aaron deceased, Alva Perry 22, Cynthia Ruth 19 +Lyddia Andrew 11(adopted)

4/18/1882 WMM sells the Macy Farmstead for $18000, migrates to Dayton, Yamhill Co., OR with Julia Ann, Alva Perry, Cynthia Ruth and Lyddia Andrew and acquires a farm

1886 Cynthia Ruth marries Owen Hatfield

9/29/1886 Alva Perry Macy marries Ida May Moore @ New Providence, IA

1905 Alva Perry Macy and family migrates from Oregon to Chico, CA

1907 WMM, JAM, Cynthia, Owen Hatfield, 3 children, daughter-in-law and 1 baby migrate to Greenleaf, ID and acquire farms

6/4/1911 Wm dies in Denair, CA @ age 91

2/14/1916 Cynthia Ruth is widowed

7/22/1918 Julia Ann Macy dies in Caldwell, ID @ age 89 of bronchial pneumonia @ Cynthia's home

8/12/1918 Alva Perry Macy dies @ Chico, CA @ age 60 of Jeffersonian Epilepsy

4/18/1934 Cynthia Ruth dies @ Nampa, ID following a Hernia operation @ age 73

William Monroe Macy was a descendant of John Howland and Elizabeth Tilley who were both passengers on the Mayflower.

John Howland
 Desire Howland Gorham
  Shubael Gorham
   Debora Gorham Fitch
    Eunice Fitch Barnard
     Lucinda Barnard Macy
      William Macy
       William Monroe Macy

— Also —

Thomas Macy born 1608 on Salisbury Plain, England came to America in 1635. His 6th child, John Macy was the first Macy born in America 7/14/1655. He migrated to Nantucket Island in 1659 and the Macys were the first white family on Nantucket.

Thomas Macy (1608)
 John Macy (1655
  John Macy II (1675)
   John Macy III (1721)
    Barachia Macy (1760)
     William Macy (1786)
      William Monroe Macy (1820)

The Thomas Macy and John Howland family trees joined when Barachiah Macy wedded Eunice Fitch Barnard

9. William Monroe Macy at 80 Years Old (1900)

The Coded Love Letters

      While living near Economy, IN William Monroe Macy made the acquaintance of Julia Ann Mills who resided in Mooresville, IN. This relationship was likely facilitated by the 4-12-1848 marriage of their mutual siblings Charity Mills to Perry T Macy. At least, a series of letters between WMM and JAM began about 10-21-1848 and culminated with their marriage 10-16-1849. In both marriages, the bride accompanied her husband to the Economy, IN properties and resided there until the Macy Family migration to Mooresville, IN in 1856.

      In all, there are 12 letters which were exchanged during the "courting" of Julia Ann by William Monroe Macy during 1849.

      Of interest, WMM devised a numerical code to apparently protect the privacy of their letters from curious mail couriers. That code has been deciphered as follows:

1	2	3	4	5	6	7	8	9	0
A	E	I	O	U	L	M	N	R	Y

      All letters of the alphabet unrepresented above would appear in its rightful place in a word.

      The letters included family news, confirmation of personal commitment and declarations of respect for each other. The code certainly was not used to hide elaborate expressions of love or verbalized emotion!

      The following is a poignant letter regarding WMM's brother who died of small pox.

West River, Randolph Co, IN   Sun July 21, 1849

Dear Friend Julia Ann Mills,

      I now take my seat in order to talk to Thee a little by the help of ink and paper. I am in good health at this time and all of our friends and relations are as far as I know, and I hope these few lines will find Thee in good health also. Thy most welcomed letter came to hand the twenty fifth day of last month and I hastily devoured its contents. It was a great satisfaction to read thy letter but much more to talk to thee but as this is all the way that I see we can talk together until fall, let us not omit the chance.

      Thee wanted to know about the small pox. I can tell Thee it was a serious time with us all. I said in my letter that John and Alvah (brothers of WMM) went to see Marshall before they knew what ailed him and there was several others there too; but none of them happened to take the small pox but John. He took sick on six day (Saturday) and died the next fifth day (Friday) in the morning. He left a wife (Elmira Marshall Macy) and four children. The oldest, a boy most ten years and the youngest boy about five years old and two girls.

      When he took sick he went to Marshalls and stayed while he lived. None of us went to see him but our sister, Margaret. She had been vaccinated so she stayed with him a while.

He talked a good deal about dying and said it was hard to be sick so near home yet none of his people could come to see him. But he said if it was the Lord's will he could bear it patiently. He said he was willing to die or he was willing to live "the Lord's will be done, not mine". He said he wanted to see us all if it was so he could, but he requested us not to come for he had nurses a'plenty and we could not help his condition. Only for satisfaction, he said he wanted to see his wife and children but it would not do for them to come and see him. He said he did not want any body else to suffer with the complaint. He wanted Myra and the children to be contented to stay away if they could, and not catch the complaint. It was mighty trying on Myra for her beloved husband to sicken and die within three miles of home and her dare not go and see him. John was asking 'hands' to raise a barn when he 'ketched' the small pox and he took sick before the 'hands' came. But the 'hands' did come on and raised the barn before he died. The workmen wanted to go on and finish the barn. We concluded to have it finished and I had to go and wait on the workmen until the barn was finished, and see to tending the corn until harvest come on Perry's land. He took the ague (illness with fever & chills) again about a week before harvest commenced and did not 'git' to harvest any worth naming, but he is well as common again. Wheat is not much more than worth cutting. It is so spoiled with the rust.

Well, I must tell Thee something more about the small pox. About fourteen days after Peggy (Margaret Ann Macy, sister of WMM) went to see John she took the small pox but she had them so light that she did not know it until she broke out. She only quit work one day. She stayed at home until she broke out, then she went to Marshalls and stayed until she got well. There were four of Marshalls and two hired hands that had the small pox but they have all got well again and gone to work; though one of them was very bad a while. The scare of the small pox is over about here, I believe now. The Cholera is a worse pestilence than the small pox but the people are not so excited about it. There is two family close by Economy that has the Cholera now and Doctor Maulsby, in town, had it but is well again. There was three died out of one family within about a mile of town. There has been twelve or thirteen cases and four deaths and some more not expected to 'git' well in Blountsville (seven miles north west of here).

Julia Ann, Thee wanted me to come down this summer but the way things has turned out I don't think it is possible for me to come till fall the way business is arranged at the present time. Thee wanted to talk to me about something that Thee could not write. I would like to see Thee very much, indeed. Write whatever Thee wants me to know and whatever Thee thinks I would like to hear. Charity Mills was at our house day before yesterday. She said that Seth had the sore eyes so he did not like to come. Perry and Charity went to Monthly Meeting today and I am at home by myself a sawing wood.

so no more—

Farewell,

William M. Macy

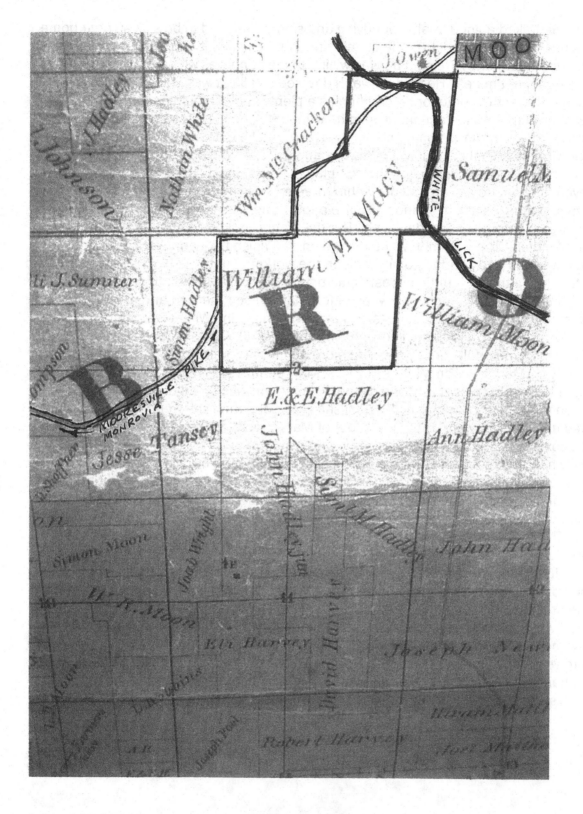

10. W M Macy Farmstead Plat –
SW of Mooresville, IN

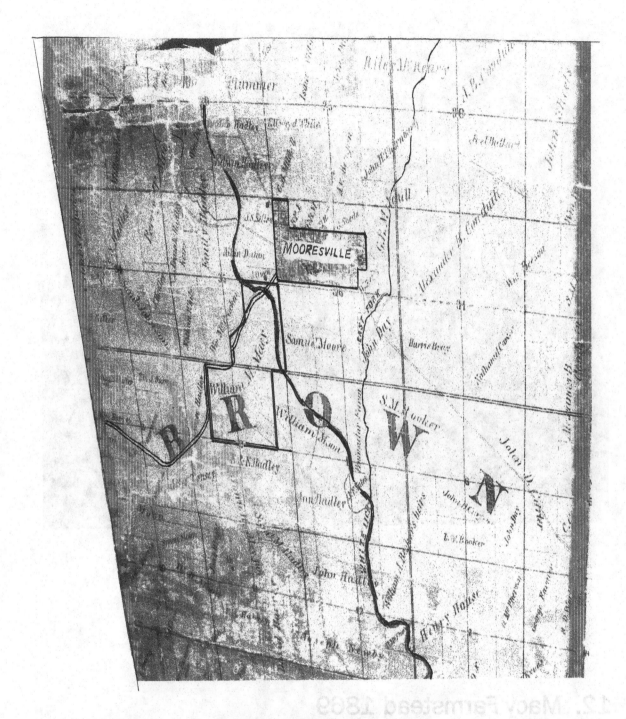

11. 1860 Plat Map–Brown Township, Morgan County, IN

Many of the neighbors are noted in Alva's diary

12. Macy Farmstead 1869
    Note: William, Julia, Aaron, Alva & Cynthia

13. White Lick Friends Church in 2009
Built by William Monroe Macy in 1864

The William Monroe Macy Household

1860 Census

W M Macy	40		valued @$13200/4065
Julia Ann Macy	31	wife	
Hannah Mariah	7	dau	
Aaron Mills Macy	5	son	
Alva Perry Macy	2	son	
William L Macy	21	student boarder	

1870 Census

W M Macy	50		$28000/6000
Julia Ann Macy	41	wife	
Aaron Mills Macy	15	son	
Alva Perry Macy	13	son	
Cynthia Ruth Macy	9	dau	
William Andrew	26	teamster	
Miles O Andrew	4		
Lydda Jane Andrew	1		
Harvey Aston	20	carpenter	
Julia Heusling	19	housekeeper	

1880 Census

W M Macy	60		value not listed
Julia Ann Macy	51	wife	
Alva Perry Macy	22	son	
Cynthia Ruth Macy	19	dau	
Lydda Jane Andrew	11	adopted	

Right of Way for Mooresville Monrovia Gravel Road Co

Recorded July 31, 1871

This indenture made the 22nd day of December, 1865. Witnesseth that whereas the Mooresville and Monrovia Gravel Road Company are constructing a gravel road from Mooresville to Monrovia all in Morgan County in the state of Indiana to accommodate the public in the way of gravel transportation. The said gravel road running over the lands of **William M. Macy**, Simon Hadley, Jonathan Doan, Lot M. Hadley, Jesse B. Johnson, Henny Brewer, Samuel Hadley, Evan Hadley, and Thomas E. Hadley which gravel road the said company agree and hereby obligate to complete and keep in good condition for the purpose above specified. Now therefore in consideration of the above promise **William M. Macy** and Julia Ann Macy, Simon Hadley and Alice Hadley, Jonathan Doan and Elizabeth Doan, Lot M. Hadley and Eunice Hadley, Jesse B. Johnson and Sarah Johnson, Henny Brewer and Sarah Brewer, Samuel Hadley and Eliza W. Hadley, Evan Hadley and Mary Ann Hadley, Thomas E. Hadley and Achsah Hadley do severally and fully relinquish to said Mooresville and Monrovia Gravel Road Company their entire interest in and to such portion of their several tracts of land respectively as is accepted by said gravel road as long as such time as said road shall be kept in good and sufficient repair to comfortably accommodate the public as above specified and it is further agreed that whenever said gravel road shall cease to be used as a public highway or failed to be kept in good and proper repair for the comfortable accommodation of the public then said lands as above conveyed shall revert back severally to the former owners thereof their heirs or assign.

In witness whereof the parties have hereunto interchangeably set their hands and signed

Jonathan Doan	**William M. Macy**	Henny Brewer
Elizabeth Doan	Julia Ann Macy	Sally Brewer
	Simon Hadley	Evan Hadley
	Alice Hadley	Mary Ann Hadley
	Lot M. Hadley	Samuel Hadley
	Eunice Hadley	Eliza W. Hadley
	Jesse B. Johnson	Thomas E. Hadley
	Sarah Johnson	Achsah Hadley

T. E. HADLEY, SECRETARY OF BOARD   **WILLIAM M. MACY**, PRESIDENT OF BOARD

State of Indiana Morgan County

    Before me Jeremiah Hadley, a notary public in the aforesaid county **William M. Macy** and Julia Ann Macy, Simon Hadley and Alice Hadley, Lot M. Hadley and Eunice Hadley, Jesse B. Johnson and Sarah Johnson, Jonathan Doan and Elizabeth Doan, Henny Brewer and Sally Brewer, Evan Hadley and Mary Ann Hadley, Samuel Hadley and Eliza W. Hadley, Thomas E. Hadley and Achsah Hadley.

Thomas E. Hadley, Secretary of Board and **WILLIAM M. MACY**, PRESIDENT OF BOARD acknowledged the execution of the above conveyance and obligation.

Witness my hand and official seal 9th month 3rd day 1866

                              Jeremiah Hadley N P

Wm. M. Macy Farm Census-1880

District #3 Enumeration District #262

1880 Ag. Census for Brown Twp Morgan Co. entered 6-8-1880

by Matt Mathews (enumerator)

-200 acres of tilled or fallow ground of which permanent pastures, meadows, or orchards comprise 85 A.

-58 A. of woodland and forest

- Farm is valued @ $10,000

-Farming implements and machinery valued @ $600

-Livestock valued @ $1700

-Labor cost for 1879 was $500 (plus room & board)

-Produce valued at $3075 for 1879

-His grass lands include 25 mown acres, 15 unmown acres & 15 acres of hay.

-He owns 3 horses and 3 mules as of 6-1-1880

-His livestock includes

1 milk cow, 36 Others, 2 calves dropped, 41 purchased, 5 sold living

7 lambs born + 4 more purchased

as of 6-1-1880 he has

4 fleeces of wool (20#)

66 swine

24 chickens in barnyard +20 in other locations

4 cheeses on hand

PRODUCTION in 1879

-150 lb of butter

-160 dozen eggs

-4000 bu. Indian corn (100 A.)

-1009 bu. wheat (43 A.)

-140 bu. flax seed (20 A.)

-100 gal maple molasses + 20 lb. maple sugar

-100 bu. apples (off 80 trees on 4A.) valued @ $20

-300 cords of firewood (valued @ $400)

14. Mooresville Quaker Academy in 2009
Built by William Monroe Macy in 1861
-on National Register of Historic Places

Donors to the Quaker Academy
Builder – **WMMacy** - 1861

Perry Macy
Jesse Hadley
John F Hadley
A B Conduitt
J L Kelly
William Monroe Macy
Levi L Hadley
Johnathon L Holmes
Aiken Dakin
Samuel Moore
Calvin Moore
John D Carter
John Day

Mooresville High School Board of Trustees

John D Carter
William Beeson
Jesse Hadley
William Monroe Macy
Perry T Macy
Aaron Mills

47

Aaron Mills Macy

5/24/1855------9/25/1877

- Born In Wayne Co, IN
- Son of William Monroe & Julia Ann Macy
- Died at Macy Farm of typhoid fever after 19 days of illness
- Buried in White Lick Cemetery, Mooresville, IN
- He was a superintendent of Mooresville Friend's Sunday School
- He taught at Bethel School for the year 1876-1877*
- He attempted an education at Earlham college but had to return home for health reasons

* Note: This Bethel neighborhood, (1.8 miles west of the Macy Farmstead) was the setting of the book 'LUCINDA, a Little Girl of 1860", authored by Mabel Leigh Hunt. This book records the life of a Quaker girl (actually, Mabel's mother, Amanda Harvey, who grew up in the Bethel Church family) during the Civil War as she matures from 10 to 14 years of age.

Hannah Mariah Macy

1/26/1853------12/10/1866

- Born in Wayne Co, IN
- Daughter of William & Julia Macy
- Died of Spotted Fever at the Macy Farmstead
- Buried next to Aaron in White Lick Cemetery, Mooresville, IN
- Both children share one tombstone

15. Alva Perry Macy as a Young Man

ALVA PERRY MACY
1/30/1858----8/12/1918

- Born 1-30-1858 in Brown Township, Morgan Co, IN

- Son of William Monroe Macy and Julia Ann Mills Macy

- He attended school at the Quaker Academy in Mooresville, IN
  (Note: Quaker Academy, built by WMM is now a National Historic Landmark)

- He married Ida May Moore, (daughter of Alfred Moore)(9-29-1888)

- Alfred was the brother of Samuel Moore (Founder of Mooresville,)

- **Alva wrote the journal (diary) of his life at the Macy Farmstead in 1872**

- He migrated to Dayton, Yamhill Co, OR with his family in 1882

- He and Ida May had 4 children born in Oregon
Norman Kerr	1890-1949
Maude Lavern	1892-1960
Bruce Ward	1893-1986
Ruth W.	b 1894

- In 1905, he settled near Chico, Butte Co, CA where he farmed

- He died 8-12-1918 of Jacksonian Epilepsy @ 60 yrs

- He was buried in the Chico, CA cemetery

Alva Perry Macy's Journal—1872

Joyce and I purchased the Macy Farmstead in 1981. We were alerted in April of 2004 that the Indiana Department of Transportation planned to widen SR42 and that their plan would intrude into the front lawn 54 feet (from the road centerline) and remove 11 trees. Like many homes built during the 19th century horse and buggy era, the home was already too close to 70MPH vehicle traffic of the 21st century.

With considerable help by the Morgan County History & Genealogy Association and Morgan County Historical Preservation Society, we launched an effort to determine whether the Farmstead (built in 1859) would deserve any protection as a National Historic Landmark. This would require evidence of significant architecture, residents and/or events linked to the property. Our attempt at attaining National Historic Landmark recognition is thus far unrealized, however, the history adventure has revealed a remarkable story about the people who have worked and lived on this land.

Within this activity we found heritage lines to Richard the Lion Hearted, Mayflower passengers, Revolutionary War veterans, and one who became a missionary in South Africa.

While pursuing information on the Macy family (Quakers) we visited the Earlham College Library Archives and came upon a life size portrait of Alva Perry Macy and his 1872 journal. Both had been donated by Marilee Frances March, great granddaughter of Alva Perry Macy. She visited the Macy Farmstead in 2006.

Windfall of Windfalls!

The journal, written when Alva was 14, documents daily life at the Macy Farmstead in 1872. The diary was hand written in a 4x7 bound journal. It was written with an ink 'dip' pen and was legible, however, it was a laborious read. In order to share this history, we copied every page and later, I read the 365 daily entries as Joyce typed them into our computer. Since the scores of names he mentioned probably have descendants within our midst, I have notated many names and identified the person via the 1870 census and the Macy family tree which we have compiled.
For instance:

Sylvester Dakin,b. OH1831, M/C1833, farmer, Rep, Quaker, $900/300
> *Born in Ohio in 1831*
> *Arrived Morgan County in 1833*
> *Farmer*
> *Republican*
> *Quaker*
> *$Real estate/Personal property value*

I hope this will add some life to printed names of these **AUTHENTIC PIONEERS**.

Read on>>> > >   >.

Monday, January 1, 1872

Tolerable cold. We all went to Uncle Aaron's**** house. We had a very good time, the children were all gone to school and Aaron* was gone away from home to collect money on the Triddle estate and Aunt Hannah had gone to Pete Seller's*** on a visit and nobody was at home but Molley. Father went to Aunt Mary's** to look for some walnut logs. I got a knife for my new year's gift, it had two blades, a tobacco hook, cork screw, a drill, a horse pleam, a screw driver and a toothpick. It is a very handy knife.

* Aaron Mills Macy, 17, b. IN, 1855-1877, brother of Alva Perry Macy, died @ 22 yrs of typhoid fever

** Aunt Mary Ann Macy, 41, b. IN,1831 d. 1899, widow of Albert Hadley 1831-1866

***Peter Sellers, Sellers & Newman Grocery, b. NC 1834,

****Aaron Mills, 51 b. IN, 1821-1908, brother of Julia Ann Macy

Tuesday, January 2, 1872

I have a very sore thumb. I guess it started from a bruise, it is very painful.

High school commenced today but I cannot go, ground is very muddy. Aunt

Rebecca Macy* came to our house today. She stayed all night. Father***

bought some walnut logs and loaded them on the train. As they were there

already he gained $50 on this. I got a gun wiper at Dorland Grocery Store**

today. It cost 15cts. I went to the depot in the evening and stayed till the

train came.

*Aunt Rebecca Macy, 38, b. IN, 2nd wife of Perry T Macy, widow of Amos Hadley,
    10/24/1833-4/12/1912

**Edwin H. Dorland, 30, b. NY, grocery & hardware merchant, $3200/5700

***William Monroe Macy, b. TN, 1820-1911, son of William & Hannah Macy

Wednesday, January 3, 1872

Still warm in the morning but turned colder in the evening. Mother* went to town on Jacob, (the old black mule) and took some butter. I stayed about home and shot the gun several times at some woodpeckers but did not kill any. I went home with Ida and stopped at Sumner's** and warmed and rested. Cynthia*** went with us to there. I had a very good time in general. I started to school today, I walked to the little creek and rode across the two creeks with Tom Woods**** with whom I fell in company. School went off nicely.

*Julia Ann (Mills) Macy, 43, b. IN, Alva's Mother, 7/3/1829-7/22/1918
**Thomas Sumner, 40, b. IN, farmer, $8230/1400, wife Martha, 40, b. IN
***Cynthia Ruth Macy, 11, b. IN, sister of Alva, 9/17/1861-4/18/1934
****Thomas Woods, 28, b. IN, fellow traveler

Thursday, January 4, 1872

I went to school. I study arithmetic, physical geography, grammar. Father*

went to Thomas Hadley's** to buy walnut logs – he engaged some. It froze

some last night. I set with Clinton*** at school, we killed 5 hogs this year.

They were very nice hogs. Mother went to Thomas Ellmore's**** today.

Liddie***** went with her. Kenneth Elmore has got a very sore breast and

is exceeding painful to him. Louisa Jackson****** is building a new house

by the side of Cal Rushton's*******, it is one story and a half high.

*William Monroe Macy, 52, b. TN, farmer, etc, $28000/6000

**Thomas Marshall Hadley, farmer, b. NC 1810, M/C 1824, 12/14/1810- 10/23/1893,
  husband of Lucinda Macy

***Clinton, schoolmate of Alva Macy

****Thomas Ellmore, farmer 32, b. IL 1839. M/C 1850- 2mi S Mooresville

*****Lyddia Andrew, 3, b. IN, adopted by WMM family, dau of William Andrew

******Louisa Jackson, 47, b. NC

*******Caleb C. Rushton, farmer, 30, b. IN 1844, 1mi NW Mooresville

Friday, January 5, 1872

A nice day. There was a large circle around the moon. I went to school. They have got a new gate to the fence instead of the old style. It is quite an improvement. It was somewhat cloudy today. I got along very well in my studies. Father came home by the way of Aunt Mary's***, Peter Sellers, Uncle William's** and Uncle Miles'* from Thomas Hadley's. I went up in town at noon and swoped diaries with Paul and Jeadey. I went in the evening with Clinton and got 2 lead pencils for our books. They cost 10 cts apiece.

*Miles S. Hadley, b.1828, farmer, $9000/2200, 1 ½ mi NW of Mooresville 6/18/1828-12/29/1911, Husband of Ruth Alma Macy

**William Clarkson Mills, 1816-1899, bro of Julia Ann Macy

***Mary Ann (Macy) Hadley, 1831-1889, widow of Albert Hadley

Saturday, January 6, 1872

Tolerable cold but not windy. Will Carlisle* went to look at some mules at Will McCrary's**. I helped husk shocked corn but it was very cold work. Will came home and hauled the fodder in the barn. Father went to town in the morning and came home in the evening. We killed several mice that were under the shocks. Cloudy all day. Very dark in the night and cloudy. Terrel**** and 3 of his boys husked corn too. It was very cold work to me. Father bought 3 calves of William Harvey*** for 90 dollars.

*William Carlisle, 27, b. IN, employed by WMM

**William F. McCrary, 32, b. NC

***William Harvey, 37, b. OH 1830, farmer, $3150/1000, sold WMM calves 21/2mi SW Mooresville

****Terrill Carlisle, b. NC 8-26-1810, d. IN, 8-20-1885, farm laborer

Sunday, January 7, 1872

A very disagreeable day. Commenced snowing about 9 or 10 oclock in the morning and bout quit at noon. The wind blew nearly all day. Father and mother went to town to meeting. The rest of us stayed at home. In the evening Aaron and I went up in the big woods and about looking for a rabbit or something wild game. Mary Carlisle* come over here in the evening to borrow some books and had a chat about working at Indianapolis. We had a nice time eating snow ice cream which was very good. It commenced snowing again at half past six.

*Mary Jane Carlisle, b. NC 12-6-1851, sister of Will

Monday, January 8, 1872

A cool day. I went to school as usual but I was tardy because I slept too late. Will hauled 5 loads of wood to Thomas Taylor* and 1 load to Craytons**. Wayne Hadley*** come home with us from school. We had a fine time snowballing at noon and recess. I played so long at noon that my fingers got very cold. Father tended the law suit which was brought up by Ira Hadley for work on the planing mill. Cynthia**** stayed at Ira's tonight.

*Thomas J Taylor, wagonmaker, b. OH1815, M/C 1869

**Alexander H Crayton, 41, tailor, firewood customer

***Wayne Coleman Hadley, 18, b. IN, Alva Macy's schoolmate, 12-5-1853/9-5-1913, son of Levi Hadley

****Cynthia Ruth, 11, sister of Alva Perry Macy

Tuesday, January 9, 1872

A tolerable nice cold day. I went to school and took father's watch with me for a rarity. Wayne (Hadley)* went to school with us and took dinner with us. We had a very nice time snowballing each one and then another. Aaron brought Milton Mills' watch home with him to clean out and fix up. It was cloudy most of the day. The clouds were dark and low. Will (Andrew) hauled logs and went to William Harvey's** after the 3 calves which father bought. He turned them in the little clover field.

*Wayne C. Hadley, 8, cousin, son of Levi S. Hadley
**William Harvey, 40, b. OH, farmer, $3150/1000

Wednesday, January 10, 1872

I went to school. Tolerable warm compared with some days. The snow was melted a little so we had a fine time snowballing. I had luck enough not to get badly hurt. Father and Will** hauled logs and old Jim chopped wood. Chauner* gave us a big example in partial payments which is tolerable hard to work. The sun shone most of the day but it turned a great deal colder in the evening. It was very clear in the forepart of the night.

*Chauner, school teacher
**William Andrew, 28, teamster, employee of WMM

Thursday, January 11, 1872

A warm day. I went to school and stayed till noon and then I came home for I was not well enough to pursue my studies at school. I sorted a barrel of apples in the cellar. Huldah* came home with Aaron and Cynthia and stayed till morning. I saw a small turtle in spring branch but it was very stupid. I suppose it had not had luck enough to get into the mud or else it had been washed out of the mud by the late freshets.

*Huldah Hadley, 8, cousin, daughter of Thomas M Hadley

Friday, January 12, 1872

Very warm. I went to school as usual. Huldah went with us to school. Father and Will hauled logs from Deweese's* to the depot. He only bought 2 logs and he has got both of them hauled. The ground is thawed a good deal so it is very muddy everywhere. The sun shone all day pretty steady. We have got nearly through Physical Geography. James Long* chopped wood for father. George has come to Uncle Thomas's house.

*Wm. Deweese, farmer, b. OH1837, M/C1856
**James Long, 52, b. NC, farm laborer, employee of WMM

Saturday, January 13, 1872

Tolerable cold day. We took the steers to a little cornfield by Dakin's*.

Aaron went to town and got his teeth plugged by Dr. Clapp**. I went to

town and helped Aaron grind an ax at Butler & Co. I went to Dorland's and

bargained for a corn popper. Father and Will hauled logs for Newbys****.

I went to town in the evening and got some worm candy for Cynthia at

Milton Hadley's***** grocery and drug store. I paid a quarter for ten small

pieces and were not worth 5 cents.

*Sylvester H. Dakin, 41, b. OH1831, neighbor, Rep, Quaker, (son of Akin Dakin who was previous owner of Macy farm)
**Dr. James R. Clapp, dentist, b. NC1841, Dem, German Reform.
****Newby, sold some timber
*****S.M. Hadley, druggist, b. IN1838, 'Pruitt & Hadley'

Sunday, January 14, 1872

Warm till in the evening. Some cloudy. Father and mother and Aaron went to meeting and the rest of us stayed at home. We all went to the branch to skate. Willie* and I had on skates but Cynthia and Liddie were without any. Cynthia was pulling Liddie Jane** on the ice and they both broke through and got a good wetting. We had some fun skating but we had not run enough. We shot the cross bow and played ball and had a good time generally. I took Willie part of the way home.

*William Seward Hadley, 12, b. IA, 3/19/1860-4/19/1897, Stepson of Perry T. Macy
**Lyddia Jane Andrew, 3, adoptee, bio dau of William Andrew

Monday, January 15, 1872

A tolerable cold day. I went to school. I was not very well in the afternoon.
Cynthia did not go to school because she took medicine for her (healthy
worms). Our mules were brought home today. Father went to summon
some men on the Harvey debts. Will hauled corn out of the sod field. He
got 3 shoes put on Charlie* and fixed our coupling-pole. The new desks
came to school today that they had sent for. They are going to put us little
scholars downstairs.

*Charlie, the horse

Tuesday, January 16, 1872

Not very cold but windy so it is very disagreeable outdoors. I went to school and John went with me and C. Father and Will hauled logs from Amos Marker's* for Newby's. They worked one of the mules. It worked very hard and is a good puller. The Good Templars*** held a convention in their hall. I expect they will have a lively time. James Long worked today in the clearing. Zimri Hadley's** wife has had 2 or 3 sinking chills a day or more ago. She was not expected to live but she is getting some better. We got the word by Zimri himself as he had started up town.

*Amos Marker, 64, b. VA, farmer, $3000/800, sold timber logs
**Zimri Hadley, 41, b. IN,1831-1898 farmer, $7200/1500 (his wife, Luretha lived to 1901)
***Good Templars, an organization advocating temperance

Wednesday, January 17, 1872

Some colder but the wind was settled and it was a pleasant day. I went to school which passed off very nicely. School broke at noon and we come home for they wanted to fix the new desks up and take them downstairs. I come home as I said and fixed fences which had been blown down. Johnny come out with me and went home in the evening. Mother went to meeting and Lydia stayed at Terrel's. Father and Will hauled logs for Newby's. There is a circle around the moon. We shot the gun 3 or four times or five times or six times or 7 times.

Thursday, January 18, 1872

I went to school. We changed rooms today. The upper room looks much nicer with its new desks. They have ink stands on the tops of them. I like ours very well. It is much the warmest room. Some of the largest scholars are not satisfied with the change. Will hauled 2 logs from Sycamore Creek. Jim** chopped wood in the clearing. Father started to go to Martinsville but he got a dispatch not to come till some other day as the trial could not come off. Father bought a calf of William McCracken* for $9. It is a heifer. It is broke to lead by a halter.

*William McCracken, retired merchant, b. NC1800, M/C 1833
**James Long, employee of WMM

Friday, January 19, 1872

Snowed last night and some in the evening beside all morning it was very nice snowballing. Aaron fetched the calf home with a halter. It is a very nice calf. I went to school. Will hauled logs from Sycamore Creek. Father stayed around home most of the day. He went up in the big woods and tree'd a coon up a big poplar. Bill Andrew and Edward Dickenson** come by here in the evening. Will wanted some money for digging the well at Farmer's. He had a rabbit which he caught by Joe Edward's* farm. He gave it to Cynthia.

*Joseph H. Edwards, farmer, b. VA1833, M/C1856, 1mi w Mooresville,
**Edward Dickenson, 37, b. KY, head sawyer @ saw mill, $ /700

Saturday, January 20, 1872

Tolerable cold. Froze some. We all went a coon hunting up in our big woods. We caught 5 coons and one squirrel. We caught one in a very large hollow poplar. It fought very hard for a while. Sylvester Dakin*** and his boys were there (and his hand). We caught 2 in an ash tree. We got a large crowd before we come home. Will got Nance* shod before and Fanny** all around. Father went to town and got a corn popper which cost 25 cts and 50 cts of sugar and a pair of trace chains at Dorland's which cost $1.25. Samuel Hadley**** was here to swap a horse for our mules (but no swap here).

*Nance the horse

**Fanny the horse

***Sylvester H. Dakin, b. OH1831, M/C1833, farmer/meat merchant, Rep, Quaker, $16000/3000

****Samuel M. Hadley, 34, farmer, $4200/2060

Sunday January 21, 1872

Frost and very cold. The thermometer stood about 25F. We did not any of us go to meeting. We stayed at home and popped corn and eat apples and dried beef. Will Carlisle** and father and Aaron* and I went down in the bottom fields and fetched the steers home. Father and Will bled the mules to cure the lampers. The calf we got at town has got its eye hurt but we do not know how. One of our old hens is very sick that I fear she will die. I do not know what ails her. It was very clear all day. The stars shone the brightest in the night they had in a good while.

*Aaron Mills Macy, 17, 5/24/1855-9/25/1877, brother of Alva Perry Macy, Died of Typhoid Fever

**William H. H. Carlisle, 27, domestic, $ /150

Monday, January 22, 1872

Not quite so cold this morning. The snow melted enough to make it good and pleasant outdoors but in the evening the wind rose and made it disagreeable. I got a letter from Hamilton County. It was wrote by Albert Bray**. He said he was going to school and that they and Uncle Isaac's were all well. Will hauled 8 loads of wood and one to Terrel and some sled runners to Taylor's* to get a log sled made. It is very nearly done. The wind blowed very hard in the night. The Rural New Yorkey*** come on today. It had the wrong name on it which delayed it.

*Thomas J. Taylor, wagonmaker, b. OH1815, M/C1869
**Albert H. Bray, 14, cousin, son of Henry Bray, Hamilton County
***Moores Rural New Yorker, a periodic literary and family journal

Tuesday, January 23, 1872

A very disagreeable day. The thermometer was at 22F in the morning and 12F in the evening. I was at school all day. The teamsters hauled logs on the new log sled from Uncle Thomas's* bottom land. There were nine of them. The old hen has deceased on this morning, don't know her desease. I went home with Wayne** in the evening. I guess I broke or cracked Father's watch crystal. The snow did not melt very much anywhere. Our new calf has got one of its eyes hurt very badly. I guess it is put out. I think one of the cows or calves hooked it. It hurts it a great deal of the time.

*Thomas M. Hadley, b. NC1810-1893, M/C1824, farmer, Rep, Quaker, $6000/4000
**Wayne Coleman Hadley, 8, cousin, son of Levi S. Hadley

Wednesday, January 24, 1872

Very cold this morning. The thermometer stood about 4F above zero. The creek was froze over. I had a very good time at Levi's. The old man and Malinda** went to Lodge. I went to school again. I wrote an essay today to read on essay day. Father and Will hauled logs on the sled from Thomas Hadley's* bottom again. When they come they fetched a sugar log to make wood of. It come from the lane by the old potato patch. The horses had icicles all over their legs and tails which would rattle and it was like they would almost freeze but they were used to such.

*Thomas M. Hadley, farmer, b. NC1810, M/C1824
**Malinda Jane Hadley, 4/8/1851-3/14/1925, cousin, dau of Levi S. Hadley

Thursday, January 25, 1872

Still colder. The thermometer stood at 2F above zero. I went to school and was tardy. We took the cattle to the little field in the morning and brought them home in the evening. It was my day to build fires at the school house. We got through the physical geography and are going to review it. The men hauled logs again from Tommy's above the old dam. We had several spectators at school or the board of trustees met and then there were two more, namely Charlie Mills and Joseph Regin (Senior). They had no remarks to make about the school.

Friday, January 26, 1872

School was tolerable dry, we had some visitors at school. They had their

ducks with them. They were Olidah Morgan and Tom Hubbard. They read

their essays some of which were very good. I took the cattle to the little

stalk pasture again. Will and Newboys hauled logs from Thomas Hadley's*

clearing. Newboy stalled in the creek. I found a good place to skate today.

James and Jerry chopped wood. Father tried to settle about the meeting

house but did not entirely succeed. Aaron went to Whitelick to a literary. He

stayed somewhere up there about the school house.

*Thomas M. Hadley, farmer, b. NC 1810-1893, $6000/4000

Editor's Note:
    William Monroe Macy built the Friends Meeting House in 1864

Saturday, January 27, 1872

Tolerable warm again. I staid about home till about 11 o'clock and then I went skating up the little creek. I went by town to get John Hadley* but he had gone hunting so I went by myself. I fell in company with Wayne and we went away up above the little meeting house. I never saw such good slick before I don't believe. I got home about 4 o'clock and sawed wood a while. I went with Cynthia up to Uncle Perry's** in the evening. We got there about a half hour before dark.

*John Hadley, 9, son of Thomas M. Hadley
**Perry T. Macy, 'Macy & Burke', b. IN1825, M/C1856, brother of WMM, Quaker

Sunday, January 28, 1872

Very cold again. The thermometer was at 8F and after awhile it fell to 2

degrees above zero. We had a very nice time talking about different things.

I went to school and meeting and I come home with Levi S. Hadley* and

then Cynthia and Tomas and Will come down after dinner. Father come up

to Levi's and bought a shawl and some overshoes for Cynthia. Rubottom**

and his family were at meeting and went home with Perry T. to get dinner.

There was an association at White Lick in the evening. I did not go to that.

*Levi S. Hadley, farmer, b.1826-1891, Rep, Quaker-3/4mi W of Mooresville
**William L. Rubottom, 44, steam powered saw mill, $2000/2000

Monday, January 29, 1872

Very cold. The thermometer was at 8 below zero. Aaron and I went to school which was somewhat dry. Cynthia did not go for it was too cold. We took some butter (3 pounds) to Aunt Lucinda*. I was tardy. Tolerable clear in the day. The wind blew a good deal of the time. Jim chopped wood. Ben Curtis froze his ears while he was coming to school. There were 2 sundogs and a halo this morning. Terel got some corn and Ragen and Jeff cut down a little sugar tree for firewood which they ought not to have done.

* Lucinda, sister of WMM, b. TN, 1818-1893, wife of Thomas M. Hadley

Tuesday, January 30 1872

Not so cold this morning. I took my skates to school and Willie Jessup took his and we went to the creek skated till time for books. It was very nice skating. School passed off rather dull. **THIS IS MY BIRTHDAY. I AM 14 YEARS OLD.** Elias Andrew come here this evening. Will hauled logs. Tolerable clear all day. Our apples have frozen some in the cellar. Father took the cattle to the cattle pasture. Carlisles took their corn to mill on a hand sled. James and Jerry cut the logs up at Thomas's clearing and then chopped wood in our bottom.

Wednesday, January 31, 1872

Tolerable clear and cold. The morning was 8 degrees below zero. I went to school which was dry and not much life about it anyway. They hauled logs from Thomas's clearing. Jim worked today and little Jim worked. He hauled wood to Crayton*. Elias went home in the morning. Somebody has took some wood out of our bottom. We do not know who it was. Azor Johnson got Dewees's money to give to the girls. Father took the cattle to the little stalk field, all got out but four. They did not want to go very bad because there is not much for them to eat.

*G.W. Craton, brick maker, b. IN1842, M/C1853, Dem, Protestant

Thursday, February 1, 1872

11F below zero in the morning but warmer in the evening. I was tardy at school. Mary went to her home to her sister's wedding. She married Asher Kellum*. Milton took charge of our school. He got along very well only there was a good deal of whispering done. I and Johny went to the creek skating. The ice was very smooth. Old Jim worked. He broke his ax some in the middle. Terel got a bushel of corn. Will hauled logs. We shelled a grist** of corn this evening. The two grammar classes fenced against each other. The class I was in beat.

*Asher Kellum, 47, Guilford Twp., Hendricks Co.,farmer
**grist is grain to be ground at the mill

Friday, February 2, 1872

Warmer again, some cloudy, did not thaw much. I and Johny went skating. The ice was very nice (Will Pool* went too). Some of the scholars chose up and spelled. I and Wayne West went in the choir room and studied our physical geography lesson. There were two visitors. One was Raford Arnold** and somebody I did not know. They hauled logs again. Will Newby*** helped haul in the afternoon. James and Monroe worked. I got out sooner than common. Nate Hadley**** is hauling ice from the big creek. They got very thick ice.

*William H. Pool, 10, son of Joseph Pool, druggist

**Raiford Arnold, 71, b. NC M/C1856, wagon maker, Rep, Quaker, $1500/200

***William Newby, 34, farmer, $3600/700

****Nathan Hadley, 40, farmer, $4000/1000

Saturday, February 3, 1872

Some warmer. I stayed about home all day. I sawed some stove wood and skated a while and made a little sled which I rode downhill on. They hauled logs. Tom and Jerry chopped wood. Aaron went to town and got some sugar (5 1/2 lbs.) and got some coal oil. Snow melted a good deal in the sunshine. I shot the gun 3 or four times. I shot a nail head and hit it. Somewhat cloudy. There was school at Bethel but none of the Carlisle children went. Frank Thompson* come here and got some money which father owed him for logs which he sold for him.

*Frances Thompson, 25, b. VA, farm laborer

Sunday, February 4, 1872

Warmer but a cold wind stirring all the time. Cloudy all day and snowed in the evening. We all went to meeting but Aaron**** and Liddy*****. There were several at meeting. Father and mother and Cynthia and Uncle Thomas** and Aunt Lucinda****** went to John D. Carter's*. I ate dinner at Thomas's and then John*** come home with me. We slid down the hill on our sled and skated a while and shot our cross bows a while and done our work up and played dominos which we had not played in a good long time (still snowing after dark).

*John D. Carter, farmer, b. NC1811, M/C 1822, Rep, Quaker
**Thomas M. Hadley, 61, farmer, b. NC, $6000/1000 , Brother in law of WMM
*****Lydda Jane Andrew, 3, 'adopted' daughter of WMM
****Aaron Mills Macy, 17, brother of Alva Perry Macy
***John Hadley, 11, son of Thomas M. Hadley, cousin of Alva Macy
******Lucinda Macy Hadley, b.1818, TN, wife of Thomas M. Hadley

Monday, February 5, 1872

Not very cold but very disagreeable. Cloudy all day. Johny went to school with us. Aaron give him a cross bow. Cynthia went home with Ella**** in the evening. John Chauner* gave a lecture this evening on the laws of health. They hauled logs most all day from the depot to Comer's*** mill and one from up above the old mill dam. Dave Fogleman** was driving some steers across the bridge in the morning and one of them got crowded off and caught its foot in the side of the bridge and they had to chop it loose. He killed it in the evening for beef.

*John Chauner, School Teacher

**David Fogleman, farmer, stock trader, b NC1828, M/C1833, $13250/5200 Son-in-law of Samuel Moore (Founder of Mooresville)

***Mathew Comer, 46, saw mill operator

****Ellen Zeruah Macy, 17, 10/30/1855-1/19/1955, cousin, dau of Ira C Macy

Tuesday, February 6, 1872

Turning colder all the time. Sleeted and snowed last night. I did not go to school because I had a very bad cold. I took some butter to Aunt Lucinda*** (2 pounds). They hauled logs from Thomas's. Jim and Jerry chopped wood. Mary Carlisle* helped wash. We got snow and melted it instead of carrying water . Lizzie Carlisle** got a peck of potatoes. They took the log to mill which they previously stalled with. It was not hard to pull on the snow. I shot the gun two or three times. Cynthia got a comb at McCracken's**** yesterday. Sold eggs for it, cost 35 cts. Very clear in the night.

*Mary Carlisle, 21, daughter of Terrill Carlisle,
**Rachel Elizabeth Carlisle, 22, wife of William "Will" Carlisle
***Lucinda Macy Hadley, 54, sister of WMM
****William McCracken, 72, b. NC, grocer

Wednesday, February 7, 1872

6F below zero in the morning but turned warmer about noon. I went to school, it was examination day. I was examined in grammar and arithmetic. I don't think I will get a very high percent in arithmetic. Cynthia did not go to school. They helped Newbys haul a big walnut log which their team could not pull. Jim chopped wood. There was a lecture at the town hall on temperance by a man by the name of Baxter. Charly* and Jake* both took their single trees when they hauled the big log. Will brought a little sugar log home for stove wood.

*Charley & Jake the horses 'broke' their single trees

Thursday February 8, 1872

I went to school, was examined in reading and physical geography. There was a she dog came here last evening and stayed about this house and barn. It belongs to John Tincher*. I guess maybe we will keep her and raise a pup. It is only 5 months old. They hauled logs today. Jim and Jerry chopped wood. The thermometer was (below 0 in the morning and about noon it was at 42F degrees). It was very clear all day. The subject of conversation in the evening was about Terel and Co. and their way of doing.

*John D. Tincher, 31, farm laborer b. IN

Friday, February 9, 1872

Two more days rest again. I get tired some a going all through the week. It was a very nice day. Will Carlisle* has a very sore thumb. He got it froze in the first place. We hauled logs. Jim chopped wood and Jerry fussed all day trying to get something to eat. He is three dollars behind so he did not get it. Our dog followed the team all day. Bethel school was out today. Dave Carlisle** wants to go on to school but I guess he will not. I shot the gun this morning. The best caps we can get are 10 cts boxes of whats proof they go every time.

*William H. H. Carlisle, 27, laborer, $ /100
**David E. Carlisle, 13, son of Terrill

Saturday, February 10, 1872

A very beautiful day. It was warm and clear. They hauled logs from Aunt Mary's*. Jim and little Jim built a fence on the inside of the wood rick in the bottom,. Jerry was over here in the morning to get something to eat. He got a bushel. Aaron and I stayed about home and laid a new floor for Bet. And then we tore out the old floor in the upper stable, caught 2 rats. We took the gun and went up in the big woods but we did not kill anything. Tincher come and got his dog. She was very glad to see him. Her name was Brownie.

* Mary Ann Hadley, 10/1/1831-2/25/1899, WMM's sister, Widow of Albert Hadley

Tuesday, February 13, 1872

Not so very cold in the morning. The wind rose in the morning about 10 oclock and kept turning colder. The creek is up a good deal. I went to school. Cynthia went to Uncle Thomas's*** after school was out to stay all night. They hauled one log from Aunt Mary's** and got dinner there. Jim split wood today. He come up here and got a hole bored through a maul. Snider who stole some money from Joseph Edwards* was took to jail at Martinsville today. He did not want to go very bad.

*Joseph H. Edwards, 39, b. VA, farmer, Rep, Quaker, $7850/535
**Mary Ann Hadley, 38, sister of WMM
***Thomas Marshall Hadley, Lucinda Macy's husband

Wednesday, February 14, 1872

The thermometer was 2F above zero and it was windy which made it colder.

This is Valentine day. I went to school as usual. I was sat out on the

rostrum with Clinton for small behavior. I had the headache in the evening.

I guess because I was cold. Will got Charley*, Nance* and Doll* shod at

Ballard and Shrake's** shop. Jim chopped or split wood today. There is a

stray cat here which mews in the night under the house. I intend to kill it if

it does not lose its life before I get a chance at it.

*Charley,Nance, Doll, Horses
**Cornelius Ballard, 34, John Shrake, 34, Blacksmiths

Thursday, February 15, 1872

A very nice day. I went to school. It was my day to build fires. We were nearly out of wood. It was some cloudy all day. Abner Hadley* hauled a load of wood to the school house with 2 yokes of oxen. There were 4 visitors at the school namely Mrs. Davis and Mrs. McNeff and Mrs. Hall and Mr. James Davis. They hauled logs from Mary's They stalled at Richard Hadley's hill. They rolled one log off and come on. There was ice in the road. Jim split and chopped wood. Terel's boys chopped wood in the little sugar orchard.

*Abner Hadley, farmer, b. IN1828, M/C 1863

Friday, February 16, 1872

A nice day, but cloudy. I went to school. We read our essays. There were 13 of them. I took a letter to Maria Mills but she was not at home so I give it to Aunt Achsah Macy** as she boards there. I went to Uncle Thomas's and stayed all night. There was a social meeting there. Joseph Pool was the leader. There were several in attendance. They hauled one load of logs from Elwood Stanley* and they hauled a load of fodder from the sod field after they come home. Jim chopped rail cuts.

*Elwood Stanley, farmer, 34, Monroe Twp, $4450/900
**Achsah Johnson Macy, b. 6/16/1834, wife of Ira C. Macy

Saturday, February 17, 1782

Some warmer. Snowed a little in the night. Very cloudy in the morning. I got home about 9 oclock. Aaron and I went back to town and got a calf which father bought of Alexander Worth* for (9dollars). We led it by a rope halter. Pa and Will hauled logs from Stanley's and James chopped wood. I helped saw some wood and shot the gun several times. I killed a snow bird. The first bird I ever killed with a gun. Carlisle's boys chopped wood in the little sugar orchard.

*Alexander Worth, 66, Secretary of I C &L rail road, b. NY, $16500/1500

Sunday, February 18, 1872

Tolerable warm and cloudy. The snow melted and the ground thawed so it was very muddy. Father and mother and Cynthia went to school and meeting. Aaron had the head ache nearly all day. I slid down the hill a few times. In the evening Aaron and I took a stroll down toward Bethel. We finally got to the water tank down to the railroad and come back by Lewis Robbin's* sugar camp. Father and Mother and Aaron and Cynthia went to meeting to town in the evening.

*Lewis Robbins, 37, farmer, b. OH, $14000/2500

Monday, February 19, 1872

A tolerable pleasant day. I and Cynthia went to school but Aaron stayed at home because he had the headache. He made 170 spiles* for the sugar orchard. School was rather dry. It was cloudy nearly all day but the ground thawed enough to make it slick and muddy. Father went to Martinsville to tend some business. Will Carlisle hauled logs. James chopped wood. Terel got 2 bushels of corn in the evening.

*spiles—hollow spouts to be driven into the drilled hole in a maple tree to collect sap

Tuesday, February 20, 1872

There were some robbers in town last night. They got in McKinzey's and got

some money and in Uncle Ira's*** and got Henry Mills* watch. It is not

known who they were. Aaron's and my watch were stolen at Martinsville

29th of Dec. last with 4 others. They were at Busbee's** to get them

mended. The men who got them dug through a brick wall under a window.

Very pleasant day but quite muddy. Aaron did not go to school. Jim

chopped wood. Father and Will hauled logs.

*Henry C. Mills, 24, blacksmith,

**George Busbee, 48, Watchmaker, in Martinsville, IN

***Ira C. Macy, 42, brother of WMM, shopkeeper

Wednesday, February 21, 1872

Cloudy all day but the sun shone part of the time. Not very cold in the night.

I rode a mule down to the log wagon this morning for Will Carlisle because she was hard to lead. Cynthia and me were tardy. Aaron staid at home and made some new steps to the porch. Will hauled logs and Jim chopped wood. I got my monthly per cent today as follows.

	Deportment	98
	Spelling	100
	Reading	95
	Arithmetic	70
	Geography	99
	Grammar	98
Monthly average		93

Thursday, February 22, 1872

Some colder, the thermometer was at 21F in the morning but it was very pleasant. I went to school. We played shinney at recess and had a great deal of good fun. Will hauled logs from Elwood Stanley's farm. Jim chopped wood. I was looking at a small compass when it slipped out of my hands and broke the glass over it. I intend to pay for it if I can. Aaron took a coffee mill to Ballard and Shrake* to get it mended. Cynthia stayed at Uncle Ira's last night. The Good Templars** held a festival in the town hall tonight.

*John Shrake, 34, blacksmith, b. IN, $600/150
**A lodge devoted to total abstinence of alcohol

Friday, February 23, 1872

A very beautiful day but very muddy. I went to school. We have nice times now playing ball. Will hauled logs and Jim split wood. Father went to Martinsville to court but the trial did not come off. I got 20cts worth of lead and 11cts worth of snare wire to wind around the gun where it was broken. John come home with me in the evening and brought his gun along which is a little shot gun. Aaron Benbo* came after his money (37.25) (he got it).

*Aaron T. Benbow, hotel keeper, b. NC1828, M/C 1832, Rep, Methodist

Saturday, February 24, 1872

I stayed about home all day. Little Jim and Aaron and I hauled fodder from the big field in the forenoon. It was very muddy and it rained most of the time. Will took a log from the toll gate to town and brought our sugar water buckets. There were 198 buckets and 8 iron kettles. We tapped 70 trees in the evening. Mother went to town to meeting. John and I took our guns out and tried to kill some jay birds but did not succeed. Elmira came home with Mother from meeting.

Sunday, February 25, 1872

Quite a disagreeable day. It was damp and cold winds stirring. We hitched the mares to the hack and Aaron and Elmira and Cynthia and I went to Whitelick to meeting. After meeting we went to Uncle Miles'****. Lonzo Hadley* was there and Lottie, Achsah Hadley**, and Wayne and Tommy*** and Willie***. We all had a good time. The roads were very muddy. I went home with Will Hadley***** in the evening and I got my hair trimmed.

*Alonzo Hadley, 13, 2/19/1857-4/30/1925, cousin, son of Mary Ann Hadley

**Achsah Hadley, 17, 1855-1920, cousin, dau of Levi S. Hadley

***Thomas M. Hadley, 9, 1861-1919 William S. Hadley, 10, 1860-1897, sons of Perry Macy
****Miles S. Hadley, 42, farmer, M/C1863, wife Ruth Macy, $9000/2200

*****William S. Hadley, 12, stepson of Perry T. Macy

Monday, February 26, 1872

I went to school. I got Albert's* bullet molds. I don't like to go to school very well. I like to play shinny tolerable well. Father and Will loaded 2 cars. Jim did not work all day. Aaron hauled wood to the sugar camp. Uncle Perry** went to Martinsville to court. Ed Dickenson got a half cord of sugar wood. The sugar water run tolerable free today. Some of the buckets were full but I have luck enough to set on a board all day and not get to enjoy any of the fun.

*Albert Hadley, cousin, b 1853, son of Perry T. Macy
**Perry T. Macy, 45, brother of WMM

Tuesday, February 27, 1872

A tolerable nice day. I went to school. Cynthia** went to town to stay all night somewhere, at Jerry Hadley's I guess. Father and Aaron built a furnace in the camp. Will loaded cars. James helped Will load the cars. Terel's boys worked part of the day. The sugar water run very well all day. I sent a letter to Albert Bray. I come home before school broke. John Greeson* was here in the evening. He wanted to sell some stock to father.

*John Greeson, 40, farmer, $8600/925
**Cynthia Ruth Macy, b. 9/9/1861, sister of Alva Perry Macy

Wednesday, February 28, 1872

Quite a disagreeable day. I went to school with a shinny club in my hand. It was somewhat disagreeable all day. They loaded logs on the cars. Jim helped them. Jim** got his finger between a chain and log and mashed it nearly off. He went to the doctor and got it bound up and then come back. Helped them again. Ezra Olleman* was at school a while in the evening. We went to the sugar camp about dark and brought some sirup home.

*Ezra Olleman, 43, farmer, b. KY, $30000/10000
**James Long, 52, farm laborer

Thursday, February 29, 1872

Tolerable nice day all but in the morning. The wind was stirring. Snowed last night about 2 or 3 inches deep. I went to school but was tardy. Cynthia did not go because of the snow. Father and Aaron finished the furnace. Mother stirred off some sugar. I got a bait once more. Will* hauled logs from Chawner's to the mill and some wood for himself. We had 2 visitors at school. I did not know them. They were both boys.

*William Andrew, 28, Teamster, employee of WMM

Friday, March 1, 1872

A very nice day. I went to school. It was essay day. The subject of the

essays was (What It Takes to Make a Good Scholar). There were some of

them that very near told it. There were 3 visitors but I will not name them.

Father and Jim sawed logs in the big woods. Aaron* boiled sugar water.

Cynthia*** had the tooth ache all day. Will** hauled from Stanley's and

from the sugar camp. I shot the gun twice at a mark and then took it to

pieces and cleaned it out.

*Aaron Mills Macy, 17 Alva's older brother
**William Carlisle, teamster, employee of WMM
***Cynthia Ruth, 1861-1934, Alva's younger sister

Saturday, March 2, 1872

A tolerable cold day. I stayed about home most of the day. Aaron and I cut some stove wood. I shot 2 birds, the most I ever killed before. Aaron Mills* come here this evening. He rode a horse back and his has got scared at some cattle and made it jump and after a while Uncle Aaron and Aunt Hannah*** come in their carriage. Johnny come with them. Johnny Hadley** was here and got 2 pound of butter.

*Aaron Mills, 12, son of William C Mills, Guilford Twp, Hendricks Co.
**John Hadley, 1860-1937, 11, cousin, son of Thomas M Hadley
***Aaron & Hannah Mills, children of Henry Mills

Sunday, March 3, 1872

A damp day, very cloudy in the morning. Comenced snowing about 8 oclock and snowed all day but the ground being so wet it nearly all melted. None of us or our visitors went to meeting. We eat apples, walnuts and popcorn and had a good time, generally. They went home about 3 oclock in the evening. I got a bottle of linament at Ira's for 25cts and a slate pencil for Dave Carlisle yesterday. Aunt Hannah's baby can talk a little.

Monday, March 4, 1872

A very disagreeable day, very cloudy. A damp chilly wind stirring. I went to school. Cynthia* did not go. Aaron and Will hauled wood with 2 horses and the 2 mules. Bet** worked very well for the first time. Father and Jim sawed logs. The sugar water did not run much. Father has sent for 4 dozen more buckets with handles. He wanted a few to carry in.

*Cynthia Ruth Macy, 11, sister of Alva Perry Macy
**Betty, the horse

108

Tuesday, March 5, 1872

A tolerable nice day. I went to school. Cynthia stayed at home. We had a very nice time playing shinny. Father went to Martinsville for Sylvester Dakin's* case but it did not come off. Aaron and Will hauled fodder. I shot a chicken in the evening for breakfast. Emma Hadley*** and Lottie Macy** come down here in the evening. The sun shone nearly all day. Pa and Will went to town to join the lodge.

*Sylvester Dakin, farmer, b.OH1831, M/C1833, Rep, Quaker
**Charlotte L. Macy. 15, daughter of Perry T. Macy, WMM's brother
***Emma Hadley, 24, wife of Benjamin Hadley, 25

Wednesday, March 6, 1872

A tolerable cold day. I went to school and got my leg hit with a stick just below my knee (hurt me awfully for a little bit). Professor Morgan was at school a while. He got some instruments out of the laboratory. I don't know what for. Ella and Nelia*** come here in the evening after school to stay all night. We boiled down some sugar water but did not stir any off. Will hauled logs. Jim* and *little* Jim** sawed logs.

*James Long, 52, farm laborer
**James Long 15, son, helping James Sr.
***Cornelia Hadley, 13, Daughter of Thomas M. Hadley

Thursday, March 7, 1872

A tolerable cold day. Windy all day. I went to school with Ella and Nelia. We were late to school because we stirred off some sugar. Uncle John F. Hadley* was at school a while in the morning. We commenced reviewing arithmetic. We commenced at common fractions. Wayne** come home with me in the evening. Will and Pa hauled logs from Stanley's***. Jim and the other Jim sawed logs.

*John F. Hadley, farmer, b. IN1840, Rep, Quaker, $11600/4345- husband of Lydia Ann Macy
**Wayne C Hadley, 1853-1913, 8, cousin, son of Levi S. Hadley
***Elwood Stanley, 36, farmer, $4450/900

Friday, March 8, 1872

A very damp day. I and Wayne went to school. It was raining in the morning and we were late. It was very sloppy. We did not read our essays this time. Some of our scholars went in the primary room to see the school. I guess they thought they were somewhat noisy. Aaron and Will hauled wood to Ballard** and Shrake***. James* did not work for us. It thundered 2 or 3 times in the evening then rained a while. Father went to Martinsville. He found a knife (3 blades). It is his birthday.

*James Long, 52, farm laborer
**Cornelius W. Ballard, 36, blacksmith, Rep, Protestant
***John Shrake, 36, blacksmith,

Saturday, March 9, 1872

A damp chilly day, very muddy and disagreeable generally. I carried sugar water nearly all fore noon. I dug 4 postholes for the shed over the furnace. The ground was not frozen but about 4 inches. We got it about done. In the afternoon Will* hitched 4 horses to the log sled and drug some logs to the camp. Father went to town and got a new saw (cross cut) for 6.65. Cynthia*** went to Uncle Levi's** in the evening. We fetched one bucket of sirup home about dark.

*William H.H. Carlisle, farm laborer, 27
**Levi S. Hadley, b. 1822, farmer, ¾ mi w of Mooresville, husband of Margaret Ann Macy, $18690/3000
***Cynthia Ruth Macy, 11, Alva's sister

Sunday, March 10, 1872

A tolerable nice day but cloudy. We all went to meeting. There were several there. Will Carlisle went to the Camilite meeting. Father and Aaron went to Joseph Edwards'** in the evening. I stayed about home nearly all day. I played with Carlisle boys part of the time. Cynthia come home in the evening. The sugar water did not run very much. Will went to meeting again in the evening. Mary Carlisle* came home in the evening.

*Mary Carlisle, 24, daughter of William Carlisle
**Joseph H. Edwards, 39, farmer, b. VA, 3 mi SW of Mooresville

Monday March 11, 1872

A very damp chilly day. Cynthia and I went to school. It snowed a little fine frost of a snow all day. Jims (two) sawed logs. Will and Pa hauled one log from Stanley and two from the "big woods". They stirred off a gallon and ¾ of molasses. The rest of them shelled some corn to take to mill. I could not help very well as my hand is sore. Aaron's hand has gotten nearly well.

Tuesday, March 12, 1872

A very nice day. I went to school, had a tolerable good time. Aaron got some more spiles off of Tansey's* place. They hauled one log from Stanleys** and loaded one car then they went to lodge at town. There were several flocks of pigeons flying over all day. I rode part of the way home on the log wagon. I drove some pigs out of the wheat field. Little Jim hauled wood for himself.

*Jesse Tansey, farmer, b. NC1812, M/C1822, $14900/1443
**Elwood Stanley, 34, farmer, $4450/900

Wednesday, March 13, 1872

A very nice day. I went to school. Cloudy all day. Will hauled one log from Stanleys and went to the depot and got the buckets. Father and Aaron tapped some more trees. They run the buckets full by evening. It is very muddy as it did not thaw hardly any last night. Uncle Thomas* come over in the evening to get father to sign a note for which he was security. It was preparative meeting at town. We had a good deal of fun playing if it was muddy.

*Thomas M. Hadley, b. NC1810, M/C1824, husband of Lucinda Macy, $6000/4000

116

Thursday, March 14, 1872

Tolerable nice day. I went to school and got there just before the second bell rang. We had a good fun playing shinny. It was very cloudy all day and rained a very little. Maggie Hadley* come home with us from school and Lonzo Hadley*** come down here in the evening. The rest of them at home tended to the sugar camp. They got 4 barrels of water they hauled with Jake.** We had a little stir off in the evening.

*Maggie Hadley, 17, Alva's cousin, daughter of Thomas M Hadley
**Jake the mule
***Alonzo Hadley, 1857-1925, son of Albert and Mary Ann Hadley

Friday, March 15, 1872

A nice day. The ground was frozen solid but it thawed out again. Maggie went with us to school. Edwin Worth* was at school playing with me when he took a fit. I told his father to come and get him. He did not seem to want to go home. I did not hear from him anymore in the evening. He has these kinds of spell very often. We stirred off a kettle of sugar in the evening and they stirred off one about noon. Aaron and Will threshed out some oats.

*Eddy Worth, 10, son of Alexander Worth, 68, Secretary of I C & L Railroad, $16500/1500

Saturday, March 16, 1872

Very nice bright day. Tolerable cool. I stayed about home till in the evening.

I helped thresh out some oats and then helped stir off about 5 gallons of

molassas. The sugar runs in the evening but not through most of the day. I

got Albert Tansey's* saddle and went to Uncle William Mills****. Father

went to Monrovia to a lawsuit of Levi Hadley** with Will Andrew*** about

digging some wells.

*Albert Tansey, 16, son of Jesse Tansey

**Levi S Hadley, 1826-1891, 50, farmer, ¾ mi W of Mooresville (Alva's uncle)

***William Andrew, 28, teamster, employee of WMM

****William Mills, 36, b. IN, Farm Laborer

118

Sunday, March 17, 1872

A very nice day. We got out of bed about sunrise and fed the horses and cattle and sheep and hogs. I had a very nice time. Aaron or I did not go to meeting. Oliver* and Uncle William** went. We had a good deal of fun. Uncle William has a sore neck so he cannot do much. I come home about 5 oclock. None of our folks went to meeting. Mother went to Uncle Perry's a little while in the evening. We got about 7 barrels of sugar water even if it was Sunday.

*Oliver P. Macy, 2, Alva's cousin, son of Perry T. Macy
**William Mills,

Monday, March 18, 1872

A nice but windy day. The mud is drying up some. I went to school. I did not have any examinations as expected. Will** loaded cars. Aaron*** tended to the sugar camp. Got 7 barrels of sugar water, about a tub full of sirup to fetch to the house. Nola*, the milk cow, had a calf yesterday. It is a bull. There is a lecture on something about spiritualism at the town hall. None of us went to it. They stirred off 3 pounds of sugar and 3 gallons of molasses.

*Nola, the cow
**William Carlisle, WMM's employee, teamster
***Aaron Mills Macy, Alva's brother

Tuesday, March 19, 1872

A very nice day. The sun shone all day but the March wind was still going and made it very chilly. Will hauled wood in the camp. I went to school and was examined in grammar. Cynthia stayed at Uncle Ira's last night. Jeremiah Hadley was at school. Pa and Bill went to lodge. Will got ½ gallon of molasses. Uncle Aaron was here a while in the forenoon. Terels chopped wood near the furnace.

Wednesday, March 20, 1872

A very chilly day. I went to school and was examined in geography. We did not recite any after the last recess. Prof. Chauner made a few experiments with the air pump. There were 3 visitors present. Will hauled wood to town. Aaron tended to the camp. Terel's boys chopped wood. Father was at town tending to the Boon lawsuit. Jake* got his head hurt somehow just below his eye. We stirred off some sugar.

*Jake, the mule

Thursday, March 21, 1872

A nice day but some disagreeable. I went to school. They practiced some on their declarations. I will have an essay on the sugar tree. Mother stirred off about 20 pounds of sugar. Ida Cumuit come down here on horseback. She got here in time to get a good bait of wax. Will hauled one walnut log from Stanleys to the depot. Aaron laid a floor in the lower barn and he also went to Days* Mill. Nola's** calf has got a bad cold.

*Warner L. Day, 34, runs Grist Mill, $6000/600
**Nola the cow

Friday March 22, 1872

Cloudy all day. I went to school. There were a good many visitors present. Professor Johnson of Hendricks County was there. There were several short speeches after school. Mother was there in the afternoon. Teamsters hauled logs from Stanleys. Aaron and the rest of the farm boys caught about 40 rats in the afternoon. I stayed at Uncle Tommys* part of the night. We went to a magic lantern show at the schoolhouse.

*Thomas M. Hadley, husband of Lucinda Macy

Saturday, March 23, 1872

A tolerable windy day. Commenced snowing about 8 oclock in the morning and snowed an hour or two. Cynthia stayed at Ira's* last night. We both come home in the morning. Father*** and Will hauled logs from Stanley. They worked Betty**. Aaron went to mill. We fixed up the little stable in the evening. This was monthly meeting but none of us went. We tried to shoot a turkey but did not succeed. They are getting kind of sly about the gun.

*Ira C. Macy, 43, Hotel keeper, WMM's brother, $1800/460
**Betty the horse
***William Monroe Macy, 52, Farmer, father of Alva, $28000/6000

Sunday, March 24, 1872

A very nice day. Cynthia went to school and meeting. None of the rest of us went. Mrs. Tailer* and her son William** were out here a good part of the day. Johnny*** and Huldah*** and Emma*** come out in the afternoon. It was very clear most of the day. We caught 3 pigs that got in the yard and cut their noses and altered one of them and we run down one of the bull calves and tied him up to alter him. He was hard to catch.

*Margaret Taylor, 55, wife of Thomas Taylor
**William Taylor, 13, son of Thomas Taylor
***John Hadley, 11, Huldah Hadley, 7, Emma Macy, 10—cousins

Monday, March 25, 1872

A rainy day. Commenced raining a while before day and rained till a while in the afternoon. Our little visitors stayed all night and went home about 4 oclock. Jim hauled wood and fodder. Will hauled logs in the afternoon. We got about 10 full barrels of water. Jeff and I took the little wagon and brought a barrel from Scott's* Grocery. It is very muddy. We altered the calf and marked him. We stirred off some sugar (3 pounds).

*Robert R. Scott, 37, grocer, M/C 1857, $1000/2800

Tuesday, March 26, 1872

A very nice day. Some cloudy. The ground was frozen a good deal. I stayed about the sugar orchard all day. We got about 11 or 12 barrel of water. Mother stirred off about 5 gallons of molasses. Pa and Will hauled logs from the bottoms. They worked both of the mules. Terel's boys split wood in the bottom. I took some money to the depot to give to Mr. Fisher of Indianapolis Life Insurance Co.

Wednesday, March 27, 1872

A very warm day. Thermometer was at 56F. A big frost in the morning. The sugar water ran very free. We did not have barrels enough to hold it all. Aaron and I tended to the sugar camp. Father and Will hauled logs from Allen Hadley's* farm. Carlisle split wood in the bottom. Ella** and Nelia** run out here in the evening. School commenced today. They both went, I am not going.

*Allen Hadley, 44, farmer, $12800/4300
** Elizabeth Ellen, 19 & Cornelia, 14, cousins of Alva

Thursday, March 28, 1872

A very warm day. Some cloudy. Ground is drying out very fast. I stayed about home all day. The sugar water did not run much. Too warm. I went in my shirtsleeves all day. We stirred off 14 pounds of sugar today and 36 yesterday. Aunt Achsah* and Lucinda* were out here in the evening. We molded quite a number of sugar cakes in cup shells and other things in the evening. I cut myself while trying to get one of the cakes loose.

*Achsah Johnson Hadley, 38, and Lucinda Macy, 54, aunts of Alva Perry Macy

Friday, March 29, 1872

A kind of a drousy day. We only got 2 barrels of sugar water all day (that in the evening). I got my ax ground at Hill's* shop and chopped a log off at the sawmill and broke a gap out of it. Will hauled logs. Aaron Macy boiled sugar water. Terel's boys split wood. James** and Jim both worked. We stirred off some sugar and made about 30 cakes in saucers and cups. We traded our last cakes for some pans at the tin shop.

*J. M. Hill, blacksmith, b. OH1839, M/C1871
**James and James Long, laborers, father and son

Saturday, March 30, 1872

A very damp chilly day. I stayed about home. Aaron and I shelled about 5 bushels of corn. It rained a while and quit for a while and made it very disagreeable. Will hauled logs. We stirred off some more sugar and caked it. Jim Long took the old cow home with him and her calf. We cleaned the rifle out in the evening. Aaron would have killed a turkey but the powder got wet. Joseph Edwards and his wife and 2 children come here in the evening.

Sunday, March 31, 1872   Egg Sunday/ Easter Sunday

A very cool day. Snowed some but did not cover the ground. Frank Dakin* and Edgar McCracken** come out here in the afternoon. We played in the house a while and then we played knock down the boards and a few other games. Joseph went home about 4 oclock. Very cloudy in the evening. We made some wax and made a few cakes for them to take home with them. Note: Jonas Hastings deceased along in March—do not know the day or the month real certain. He had something like the dropsy.

*Frank Dakin, 14, son of Sylvester H. Dakin, Farmer & meat merchant
**Edgar F. McCracken, 14, son of Willison McCracken

Monday, April 1, 1872

"April fool". A very nice day. Aaron and I sorted apples till noon (10 bushels). Not very many rotten. Will Andrew** was out here a little while in the forenoon to see about some business. I took the rifle out in the sugar orchard and killed 2 birds. We got 5 barrels of sugar water. Will Carlisle*** hauled logs. Terel's boys chopped wood. Mother went to town on Doll*. Father got a collar for Betty*.

*Doll and Betty were Horses
**William Andrew, 28, teamster, employed by WMM
***William H.H. Carlisle, 27, farm laborer for WMM

Tuesday, April 2, 1872

A very nice day. I stayed about home. We only got 4 barrels of sugar water and fetched a tub of sirup home at night. Aaron had the headache part of the day. Ida* and Ora** come here in the evening. I shot a gobbler in the evening. He weighed 16 lbs. I shot him in his head. Will hauled logs from Elwood Stanley's***. Terel's boys worked in the clearing. Will Andrew was out at the sugar camp a while. I made a ramrod for the gun out of hickory.

*Ida Ellen Macy, 10, cousin, dau of Perry T. Macy
**Ora Ruth Hadley, 12, 1860-1921, cousin, dau of Levi S. Hadley
***Elwood Stanley, 36, farmer, Monroe Twp, $4450/900

Wednesday, April 3, 1872

A nice day in the evening but rained a good part of the forenoon. It dried off

very fast when the sun come out from behind the clouds. Ida and Ora

stayed till in the evening. Cynthia went part of the way home with them.

Mother went to see Uncle Abram Woodard* who has had another stroke of

palsy. He is not expected to live much longer. He has had 2 strokes of

palsy. Will and Pa hauled logs from Stanleys. The boys worked in the

bottom.

*Abraham Woodward, 71, b. TN, farmer, $2400/1260, brother of Alva's grandmother,
  Hannah Mills

Thursday, April 4, 1872

A very clear nice day. I husked corn fodder with Terel and his boys. Aaron helped till noon and then he worked in the camp. Got 4 barrels of water, were several mice. The fodder got very dry in the evening. Will hauled logs from Elwood Stanley's. Father freshed some of the sugar trees and loaded some lumber on the cars. Thompson's* cow got in our corn field and borned a calf.

*George B. Thompson, 25, farmer, $5600/1255

Friday, April 5, 1872

Some cloudy but very nice. I cut corn stalks and tended to the camp. Got about 6 or 7 barrels of water. The water had very near quit running by evening. Aaron and mother went to town. They brought a new flag home, cost (7$). Will plowed with the mules. They worked tolerable well. Dave helped cut stalks. Frank Hadley* had a trial about some misbehaving in the Camalite church.

*Frank Hadley, 9, cousin of Alva Macy, son of Thomas Marshall Hadley

Saturday, April 6, 1872

A dark damp day. I stayed about the camp all day. Aaron and Will plowed. They finished the ground they were at. Father stayed about home most of the day. Cynthia went to Uncle Aaron's*** in the evening on Jake*. Come up a big thunderstorm and rained a good deal. I got wet while I was carrying sugar water. Nettie and Lucinda Edwards** come here about dark. They both got wet. Jim hauled fodder.

*Jake the mule
**Lucinda A. Edwards, 15, dau of Joseph Edwards
***Aaron Mills, 51, 1821-1908, brother of Julia Ann Macy

Sunday, April 7, 1872

A very nice day. Some cloudy in the morning. Lucinda and Nettie went home about 10 oclock. Ma and Pa and Lydia went to White Lick Meeting and went to Uncle Miles'* after meeting. Jimmie Long** come and got 2 turkeys (a gobbler and a hen). We run and caught them. Will turned the mules out on the branch lot. We had to boil down the water before it soured. The frogs hollowed some. Very warm.

*Miles S. Hadley, farmer, 1828-1911, Rep, Quaker, 11/2 mi NW Mooresville
** James .L Long, 15, Son of James Long, 52, farm laborer for WMM

Monday, April 8, 1872

A very wet day. It rained just before day and then took it by showers. Father went to Indianapolis. William* went to mill. Aaron and I tended to the camp. Got 5 barrels of sugar water. We did not come till dark. Terel's boys did not work. Jim got his other turkey. It weighed 16 lbs. Some windy in the evening. We got the paper in the evening. Father stayed out at the camp** until in the night

*William Carlisle, teamster for WMM
**maple sugar camp

Tuesday, April 9, 1872

A tolerable nice day. Some colder in the evening. The thermometer was at 46F. We got 5 barrels of sugar water. It is some sappy. Will hauled ash logs from the bottom to the planing mill for flooring. Father* loaded some cars. Terel's boys worked in the clearing. Ed's dog had 5 puppies. Father bought a coconut at the city yesterday. It was very good.

*William Monroe Macy, b. TN1820, M/C1856, Quaker, 1 mi SW of Mooresville,
  farmer/timber dealer, $28000/6000

Wednesday, April 10, 1872

A nice bright day. It is getting warm and everything looks brighter, the grass greener, the elm trees are budding out. I discovered a dove's nest this morning. The hen was on the nest. I stayed about the camp all day. We got 2 barrels of sugar water in the evening. This is about the last day of sugar making with us. We brought nearly all of the buckets home on the sled and wagon. There was a beautiful aurora in the south in the night.

Thursday, April 11, 1872

A very nice day. The south wind blew very steady in the evening. I went to Thomas Elmore's* to get father's road receipt. I got it. I hitched Jake to the sled and fetched the water in that was in them, and one of the kettles and 11 buckets in the afternoon. I harrowed in the oats. Aaron and Will sewed and harrowed in until dinner. Then they hauled fodder. We got the oats done. Doll (the mare) got her breast snagged somehow, about an inch deep. Terel's husked corn.

*Thomas Elmore, farmer, b. IL1839, M/C 1850, Rep, Quaker, 2 mi s of Mooresville

Friday, April 12, 1872

A nice day but some dark in the morning. Rained a very little. Father and I hauled 4 loads of corn from the sod field. Some of the corn was nearly rotten. William Harvey* got one load of corn (22 bushels). Aaron and Will hauled fodder out of the same field. Terel's boys cut stalks. One of our young sows died this evening. She could not born her pigs. One of our turkeys have gone to setting. Father bought 2 calves of William Harvey $4 apiece (not weaned).

*William Harvey, farmer, b. OH1830, Rep, Quaker

Saturday, April 13, 1872

A very nice day. Not much cloudy. I raked stalks part of the forenoon and plowed the rest of the day. Will plowed with the mules. Aaron raked stalks most of the day. Terel's boys cut stalks. Father was out in the field most of the day. He went to town and got 2 sides of leather for some gears. Aaron went to Uncle Levi's* in the evening when he quit work. Will went to town after supper. Pa put a poultice on Doll's** shoulder. We got the paper in the evening.

*Levi S. Hadley, farmer, b. IN1826-1891, Rep, Quaker, Husband of Margaret Ann Macy
**Doll the horse

Sunday, April 14, 1872

A very nice day. All of our folks went to meeting but me. I would have went but all the cows in town got in one of our bottom fields and I and Ed and Jeff and Dave went and drove them out which took till noon. Will got some blood roots and made some tea of it for the mules. We washed Doll's head in the evening. We turned the steers out in the big woods and took the sugar buckets up in the garret (attic) over the kitchen.

Monday, April 15, 1872

A dark damp day. Some colder than common. Drizzled rain a good part of the day. Aaron and Will went to Aunt Mary's after a log. Aunt Mary** has a felon on her thumb. It has been on about a month. Aaron got some strawberry plants of Aunt Patsys'. Father went to Martinsville to pay his tax. Terel's boys split wood. Dave cut stalks but they were hard to cut as they were so wet. I stayed about home all day. Aaron got a book of cousin Albert* (Dr. Livingston).

*Albert W. Macy, b.1853, son of Perry T. Macy
**Mary Ann Hadley, 41, sister of WMM

Tuesday, April 16, 1872

A nice day. The water froze in a tub by the porch. We got the hogs in the mule's stable and cut their noses. One or two did not go in. Will and I plowed. Aaron raked stalks. The ground was some wet. The mules tried pretty hard to have their own way. They would not stop at the corners. Terel's boy cut wood. Mother went to town a while in the morning. Our calves got here this evening. They fetched them in the wagon. Jessie Tansey* got some locust starts here.

*Jesse Tansey, farmer, b. NC1812, M/C 1822, SW of WMM property

Wednesday, April 17, 1872

A dark gloomy day. Very cloudy all day. Will and I plowed. We each one took a mule apiece. They work better that way. Aaron raked stalks and bound them. It rained very steady in the latter part of the evening, so much that we had to quit work. Father and Mother went to meeting at town. Jonas Hastings was buried at Mooresville in the evening at 3 oclock. His disease was something like the pleurisy (Terel's boy cut stalks).

Thursday, April 18, 1872

A damp chilly day. Did not rain any until in the evening. Father and Will and Aaron loaded 2 cars. I stayed about home all day. I shot 8 birds. They hauled a load of stove wood from the sugar camp. Terel's boys cut wood. Joseph Edwards was here a while. He wanted to rent some pasture but did not. They took some molasses to town. Knox* and Hill got it (oh, yes and Snoddy**).

*John L. Knox, 51, b. KY, farmer
**John M. Snoddy, 39, physician, $5200/1000

140

Friday, April 19, 1872

A very nice day. Some cloudy. I did not do much in the forenoon but go to town and get Nance* shod and got some gun caps and 2 nutmegs. Cynthia went to high school on a visit. Bridgeport** born 13 pigs last night. Dave caught a young rabbit. After dinner I went to town and got a flag, one that had been taken to the shop to get mended. And then we all three plowed. Terel's boys cut wood. Dave*** cut stalks.

*Nance the horse
**Bridgeport the sow
***David E. Carlisle, 13, son of Terrill Carlisle

Saturday, April 20, 1872

A tolerable nice day. I plowed all day and so did Will. Aaron plowed till noon and then raked stalks. Terel's boys got done cutting stalks in the big field and then they burned them. Father went to Joseph Edward's to try to buy some calves but did not succeed. Terel got fifty dollars which he drawed at lottery. I went to Uncle Tommy's* about dark on a sort of a visit. Will and 2 of the boys went to town with me.

*Thomas M. Hadley, farmer, b. NC1810, M/C 1824, Rep, Quaker

Sunday, April 21, 1872

Nice, cloudy and rainy and muddy. I had a good time. John and I went to school. All our folks (Pa, Ma, etc.) went to school and meeting. John and I did not stay for meeting but come out here and took some boards over Lady (the sow) and her pigs to keep them from getting wet and cold. After dinner we and "the rest of the boys" tore down the straw stack to keep it from falling on the hogs and killing them. We had a heap of fun.

Monday, April 22, 1872

Very cool day. The horses did not sweat much plowing this time. Aaron got done raking stalks in the big field by noon. Then we all three plowed. I plowed the slow team, namely Jake and Doll and old plow. Father and Terel's boys husked 60 shocks of corn. Jim* commenced plowing in his rented fields. Aaron's little sow has lost 3 of her pigs. Dave cut stalks for Jim as he has been doing.

*Jim Long, farmer, laborer, leased a field from WMM

Tuesday, April 23, 1872

A nice day, some cool in the morning. Froze some in the night. There was a halo around the sun which portends rain. Aaron and Will hauled 2 loads of fodder in the morning. I plowed all day. Father plowed till they got done with the fodder. Then Aaron took his place and Will plowed. Terel and his boys cut stalks in the old sod field. We got a letter from Aunt Hannah Poe*. A good deal of spotted fever up in Hamilton County.

*Hannah Poe, 1833-1914, sister of Julia Ann Macy

Wednesday, April 24, 1872

A nice day, not very cold in the evening. The thermometer stood about 60F. Will and Aaron hauled one load of fodder in the morning. Father plowed in Aaron's place. The horses got very warm and tired. So did I. Terel's boys cut stalks. Terel split some wood. I suppose Lady* has lost one more pig (10 left). John Hussey** come up here to know if father was going to let Jo Edwards have some pasture.

*Lady the sow
**John A. Hussey, 15, b. OH, lives with the Joseph Edwards family

144

Thursday, April 25, 1872

A nice warm day. Some cloudy. Wind was blowing most of the day. Aaron and Will hauled 2 loads of fodder and then they plowed. I plowed all day. Betty* got the thumps. Terel's boys cut stalks. One of Jim's horses got sick. Jim finished raking the stalks. Terel worked in the bottom. Cynthia (10 ½ years old) got one of her teeth pulled and 2 more plugged by Dr. Clapp**.

*Betty the horse
**John C. Clapp, dentist, b. NC1841, M/C1870, Dem, German Reformation.

Friday, April 26, 1872

A warm cloudy day. Thermometer stood about 88F at noon. I plowed Nance* and Dolly*. Will and Aaron hauled fodder forenoon (4 loads). Father plowed till noon. We got the big field done at last. Will worked the mules together. Jim and Terel** worked in the clearing. Terel's boys cut stalks. The cherry trees blossomed April 24. Peaches blossomed 25 April. We burned Jim's stalk in the field he has rented.

*Nance & Dolly, the horses
**Terrill Carlisle

Saturday, April 27, 1872

78F. A nice day. Cloudy most of the day. Come up a thunderstorm but no rain. I raked stalks and burned them before dinner (in the 20 acre sod field). Father plowed all day. Will** and Aaron hauled fodder and corn before dinner. Will and I took a load of corn (30 bu.) to Samuel Moore*. Aaron raked stalks in the six acre field (the boys) cut stalks in the new ground. Jim cut and split wood.

*Samuel Moore, merchant, b. NC1799, founder of Mooresville
**William Carlisle, hired hand of WMM

Sunday, April 28, 1872

A tolerable nice day. Some cloudy. I was unwell all day. I guess I had a slight chill and after that the headache. Mother and Cynthia went to meeting. Father and Will and Aaron went to Waverly to see John Neace* about some business. Mother and Lydia went to Mrs. Sumner's** to see her and her 2 twins (both girls). I made Ed a small windmill. Bridgeport come to the barn with her pigs. Lady's pigs have got the mange.

*John R. Neese, planing mill operator, b.NC1834

**William P. Sumner, 33, wife Martha, twin girls Fannie & Nannie, (both single @home in 1900.)

Monday, April 29, 1872

A nice day. Thermometer was at 86F at noon. Some cloudy. Aaron and I plowed. The ground is getting hard. Will hauled 2 loads of corn to Samuel Moore**and some apples to Hi Johnson* (2 ½ bu.). I got my plow sharpened. Will***, the rest of Terrel's family (9 in number) arrived here in the evening. "The boys" cut wood. Dave cut stalks. Jim split wood. Terel was sick.

*Holman Johnson, merchant, b. KY1817, M/C1847, Dem, Meth. $10000/10000
**Samuel Moore, 73, 1799-1889, merchant, founder of Mooresville
***William Carlisle, b. 2-17-1840, son of Terrill

Tuesday, April 30, 1872

A nice day. Only rained some and thundered some. I had the headache pretty bad when I got up and then chilled between 9 and 10 oclock. Had fever and very bad headache the rest of the live long day. Aunt Mary* and Eli** come here to see father about getting some money but he had gone to Indianapolis. Will and Ed*** and Aaron plowed. Terel's boys split wood, so did Jim. Little Jim plowed. Eliza Hastings and her sister-in-law come to get molasses.

*Aunt Mary Ann Macy Hadley, 41, sister of WMM
**Eli J. Hadley, 12, cousin, son of Mary Hadley
***Edward Carlisle, b. 1858, son of Terrill

Wednesday, May 1, 1872

A damp muddy day. Rained last night like everything. Come up a storm of wind. Rained some. I was not very well. I churned and shelled 2 bushel of corn. We straightened up the room more and put a carpet on the kitchen floor. Ruth* went to town and got 2 boxes of tacks. Aaron** and Ed and Will plowed. Mac and West*** and the rest of Terel's boys split wood. Irvine Moser**** broke up Terel's garden with his mare.

Milton Draper was married to Olive Butler tonight At 8 oclock.

*Cynthia Ruth Macy, Alva's younger sister
**Aaron Mills Macy, Alva's older brother
***John Wesley Carlisle, son of Terrill Carlisle
****Irvine Moser, farm laborer

Thursday, May 2, 1872

A disagreeable day. Rained some in the morning. Tolerable cold. Ed*

harrowed . Will* and Aaron plowed. I commenced chilling about 8 oclock

and had an intense headache the rest of the day. Jim split wood. Mac*

and Wes* and Cage**** and Jeff* split wood. Irvine shingled my hair in

the morning. Lizzie helped mother wash. Father sold 5 logs to John

Birchum.** They come to $88.75. Little James plowed. Lizzie got some

potatoes that were part rotten. Terel*** got 50cts. worth of crout.

*Edward, Mac, John Wesley, Thomas Jefferson, sons of Terrill Carlisle
**John Burcham, 49, Lumber dealer, b. IN
***Terrill Carlisle, b. NC, 1810-1885, Civil War Veteran (Confederate)
****Cager Carlisle, b. 1856, NC, boarder with William Carlisle

Friday, May 3, 1872

Some frost in the morning. I did not chill today. I took 5 doses of quinine.

Aaron, Ed***** and Irvine plowed and harrowed. Little Jim plowed.

Madison** or Mac and Wes*** worked. Cage and Jeff**** worked.

Terel* till noon. Will moved Wm. and Gabe and their families to the Johnas

Hastings house. I shot a pullet and chicken cock, the latter for dinner.

Cynthia and I went fishing. We caught 4 small catfish. They got the plows

sharped.

*Terrill Carlisle, 1810-1885, father of **James Madison b.1850

                        ***John Wesley b. 1846

                        ****Thomas Jefferson b.1856

                        *****Edward b. 1858

Note 10 men working this day
Aaron Macy, Ed, Irvine, little Jim, Madison, Wes, Cage, Jeff, Terel, Will

Saturday, May 4, 1872

A nice day. Some cool in the morning. I helped about the house till noon. Currents are getting considerable size. Aaron and Will plowed. It is very hard, hard plowing in the field where the old road was and around the stumps. Ed harrowed in the "big field". Terel and his boys and Jim worked in the clearing. I worked there a while in the evening. Cage and I went to our house in town and took Aaron a bedstead for Irv. There was an ice cream festival in town tonight.

Note 6 men +Terel's boys worked this day Aaron Macy, Will, Ed, Terel, Jim, Alva Macy

Sunday, May 5, 1872

A nice warm day. They all went to meeting but father and I. Lizzie went with them. Joseph Edwards*** come here pretty soon after they went away. Will Andrew come in the morning and took Lydia**** home with him to play with Ollie*. Aaron and I went to Levi's. All gone from home but the oldest children. We had a very nice visit. Cynthia stayed at town and brought Lydia** home with her. Very warm all day. I had the toothache part of the day.

*Miles Oliver Andrew, 6, Son of William Andrew
**Lydia E. Hadley, 1852-1934, daughter of Levi S. Hadley
***Joseph H. Edwards, farmer, b. VA1833, M/C1856, Rep, Quaker
****Lydia Andrew, 3, daughter of Will but lives with Macy family

Monday, May 6, 1872

88F. A nice day, very warm. They finished the "young bottom". Irv crossed off in the sod field. Ed harrowed. Dave cut stalks. Terel and his boys worked in the bottom. I and Jeff picked and burned brush. I went to Levi's and got a bull tongue plow. Levi*** has some corn planted but are not done breaking up. Jim split and chopped wood. Cynthia went to town and to Sumners to see the babies**. Harvey Chandle* has his ring boned horse in our pasture.

*Harvey Chandle, 45, runs sawmill, $300/100
**Fannie E. & Nancy J., twin babies of William & Martha Sumner
***Levi S. Hadley, 1826-1891, uncle of Alva Macy
Note 7 men worked today Irv, Ed, Dave, Terel, Alva Macy, Jeff, Jim

Tuesday, May 7, 1872

A nice day. Some cloudy. Very warm. Irv crossed off and father planted and Aaron covered with Doll*. Terel and his boys worked in the clearing rolling logs and Jim helped. Cummin's** got done plowing before noon. Mac****is working for Joseph Edwards. I burned brush and cut the sprouts off stumps. I killed a large blacksnake. Will Tailor*** snared 5 or 6 mockacines at the bridge amongst the rocks. They are very plenty there. We need some more ink don't we?

*Doll the horse
**Joseph Cummins, 50, farmer, B. NC, $12000/1000
***William Taylor, 13, son of Thomas Taylor, wagon maker,
****Mac, one of Terel's sons

Wednesday, May 8, 1872

56F 90F 85F. A nice warm day. Wind blew most of the day. David and I dropped corn. Aaron crossed off and Irv covered. Father and Wes and Jim and Terel and Cage and Jeff and Will worked in the bottom. Will plowed part of the time. Edward harrowed. Little Jim harrowed. Silvester Dakin* got done planting corn in the evening (16A). Gabriel worked for us. Will fetched a load of wood home with him for us. 2 of our turkeys run off or walked off to Will Sumner**.

*Sylvester H. Dakin, farmer, b. OH1831, M/C1833, Rep, Quaker

**William Sumner, 33, teamster, $ /500

Note 14 men working this day: David, Alva Macy, Aaron Macy, Irv, WMM, Wes, Jim Long, Terel, Cage, Jeff, Will, Edward, little Jim Long, and Gabriel

Thursday, May 9, 1872

A rainy forenoon. Rain by little spells so that we got wet. David and I dropped corn and Irv covered and Aaron crossed off. We got the "big sod field" done by 8 oclock at night. Will plowed. Jim split wood most all day. Gabe and Wes, Jeff, Cage all worked in the bottom. The sky was covered with thick and heavy clouds all evening. Good deal of thunder and more lightning. Cynthia went to town to get Lydia a new hat. She took 2 lbs of sugar to Mrs. Taylor*.

*Margaret Taylor, 55, b. PA, wife of Thomas Taylor

Note 10 men working this day: David, Alva Macy, Irv, Aaron Macy, Will, Jim, Gabe, Wes, Jeff, Cage

Friday, May 10, 1872

A nice day, some cloudy, very warm. Ed finished the "big field" and the "young bottom" and harrowed some on the sandy bottom sycamore field. Father and Gabe and Jeff and Cage reset the fence between Jones' field and sandy bottom. Irv and Wes laid off corn ground in the big field. Aaron took sick in the field in the forenoon and was sick the rest of the day. Wes only worked half a day with the plow. I went to town and got a box of Frost's pills* for Aaron. I helped Bill haul the oats to the barn forenoon and helped reset fence in the evening.

*Frost's Pills, a patent medicine of the day

Note 10 men working this day
Ed, WMM, Gabe, Jeff, Cage, Irv, Wes, Aaron Macy, Alva Macy, Bill

Saturday, May 11, 1872

A disagreeable day. Rained every little while in the forenoon. Tolerable cold. Did not rain any in the evening. This was quarterly meeting at Mooresville. None of us went but Ruth**. Will*** laid off in the sandy bottom with Fanny*. Irv and Wesley laid off in the "big field". Terel and I took a load of wood to Gabe and 2 sacks of corn to mill and waited till we got them ground and stopped the team too long and liked to had a fuss. I feel very bad over it. I got a scoldin – a scolding. It is a great pity.

*Fanny the horse
***William Carlisle, farm hand of WMM
**Cynthia Ruth Macy, sister of Alva

Note 5 men working this date: Will, Irv, Wesley, Terel, Alva Macy,

Sunday, May 12, 1872

A nice day. Looked somewhat like rain. Sprinkled a very little. We all went to meeting (quarterly). Had a good meeting. A drove of calves got in the mule lot, just when we departed. They were hard to drive out. They all went to the evening meeting but me. I went to Lewis Robbins* residence on a sort of a visit. Had a very good time. They had all gone to meeting but Charles** and Oscar**. I fetched some pieplant*** and greens home with me. Our old turkey has hatched her eggs.

*Lewis Robbins, farmer, b. OH1833, $14000/2500, 1 ½ mi s of Mooresville

**Charles, 14, & Oscar, 12, sons of Lewis Robbins

***pieplant is rhubarb

Monday, May 13, 1872

A nice day, some cooler than usual. Will crossed off the young bottom the other way and Ed planted till noon and Jeff and Cage and Terel and Aaron covered with hoes. They got it done. They planted a large potato patch. Irvine and Wesley crossed off in the "big field". Gabe and I plowed in the sandy bottom. So many trees that it is hard work. Father helped about planting the potatoes and cleared off our lands in the bottom. Irvine got ½ gallon of apple butter. The Mooresville band is in order again. They played tonight.

Note: 11 men working today Will, Ed, Jeff, Cage, Terel, Aaron Macy, Irvine, Wesley, Gabe, Alva Macy, WMM

Tuesday, May 14, 1872

Some frost in the morning. Sprinkled some in the evening. Jim got done planting corn and then he got the roller and rolled the field. Irv** and Will covered and Aaron and Wesley crossed off. Ed and Jeff dropped corn. Gabe plowed and hauled posts and rails. Father and Cage and I split some stove wood, blocks and chunks and piled up the heaps. Irv's dog caught a ground hog by the road. I took the hide to Gray's* Tanyard and swapped it for another and I got a dimes worth of powder. Cynthia Ruth went to Uncle Perry's a while in the evening. --------- not I.

*Frank Gray, tanner, 32, b. Ireland, M/C1868, Dem, Catholic, $1100/1200

**Irvine Moser, laborer of WMM

Note 11 men working today: Jim, Irv, Will, Aaron Macy, Wesley, Ed, Jeff, Gabe, WMM, Cage, Alva Macy

Wednesday, May 15, 1872

The prodigal turkeys come home. I think they enjoyed their visit. Rained some through the day. Gabe plowed. Will and Aaron crossed off and Irv and Wesley covered. Ed and Cage dropped corn. Father and Jeff and I dug off the steep bank in the sandy bottom. Will Andrew is digging a well for Tom Elmore*. Jim split logs in the clearing. Little Jim rolled. He got done. Cage got a midling (2.10). We fetched a load of wood home with us. Irv's dog (Guard) has been poisened. He is very weakly.

*Thomas Elmore, farmer, b. IL1839, M/C1850, Rep, Quaker

Note 12 men working today: Gabe, Will, Aaron Macy, Irv, Wesley, Ed, Cage, WMM, Jeff, Alva Macy, Jim, little Jim

Thursday, May 16, 1872

Damp and cloudy in the forenoon and rained a good deal after 5 oclock in the evening. There was a halo around the sun most of the forenoon. Gabe plowed in the sandy bottom. Irv and Wes covered corn and Ed and Cage dropped and Aaron and Will crossed off. Jim and Jim hauled wood in the clearing. Father and Jeff (or Tom) worked about in sandy bottom. They built fence after dinner. I went to the dentist office (Clapp*) and got 2 jaw teeth extracted – hurt pretty bad for a while. I helped father the rest of the day.

*J. C. Clapp, dentist, b. NC1841, M/C1870, Dem, German Reform.
Note: 11 men working today
Gabe, Irv, Wesley, Ed, Cage, Aaron Macy, Will, Jim, little Jim, WMM, Jeff

Friday, May 17, 1872

A wet day. Rained most of the night but very slow and kept on till nearly noon when it quit. Rained again about dark. Rain was much needed. The locusts around the house are in full bloom. There is a continual hum of bees which are gathering honey. We shelled about twelve bushels of corn for meal and for the horses. Joseph* and his hand (Mac) come here in the morning and staid most of the day. They took the corn to mill. I split some wood and Aaron and I sorted all the apples and "taters" in the cellar.

*Joseph H. Edwards, farmer, b. VA1833, M/C1856, Rep, Quaker

Saturday, May 18, 1872

A very wet day. Drizzled till noon and then came a regular shower. Wes and Ed, Jeff and Cage cleaned out the stables. Father and Aaron hung a gate opening to the gravel road. Irvine and Gabe hauled the posts for the gate and rails till noon. In the evening Gabe and I went to mill. Will and I plowed till noon. Would have finished if it had not rained. One of the sows killed a pig. The colored brethren worked part of the day. They did not get the gate hung just right. One of the hinge needs turning. It is made of rock. (no more at present).

Note: 10 men working
Wes, Ed, Jeff, Cage, WMM, Aaron Macy, Irvine, Gabe, Alva Macy, Will

Sunday, May 19, 1872

A very nice day, clear in the morning but clouded some during the day. We hitched up the mules and all got in the expressor hack and took a ride to Aunt Mary's. Lonzo*** and one of the girls had gone to meeting. All the rest at home. All well within. A very nice visit and we got a puppy (a brown puppy), part bull. They had four. Gancy Marley and his family come over to Mary's in the evening. Aaron and Lonzo went to Aunt Patsy's a while. We came home by the way of Uncle Bennie Woodards** and Perry's****and Will Deweese*. The mule worked very well to the express.

*William Dewees, 35, farmer, b. OH, Dem, Quaker, $4500/1400
**Benjamin Woodward, 66, farmer, b. TN, $20580/5200
***Alonzo Hadley, 1857-1925, Alva's cousin, son of Albert Hadley
****Perry T. Macy, 1825-1889, brother of WMM

Monday, May 20, 1872

A nice day. A little cool. Aunt Betsy Bray* and Aunt Hannah Poe*** come

down from Hamilton Co., Ind. to stay a while, mainly to go to the conference.

I got a letter from Henry Poe**. Father and Gabe and Wesley and Will

loaded cars. Irv finished crossing the big field and Aaron and I took the

mules and finished covering and lastly, we have got the big field done.

Cage covered with the hoe and helping Jim he caught a young weasel. Jim's

2 hauled wood. Irv and Aaron and I crossed off in sandy bottom. Ed and Jeff

harrowed. I helped harrow till 11 oclock.

*Betsy Bray, 53, b. TN , living in Hamilton Co. IN

**Henry Poe, 14, son of Hannah & Isaac S. Poe, Hamilton Co., IN

***Hannah Poe, 1833-1914, sister of Julia Ann Macy

Note 12 men worked today
WMM, Gabe, Irvine Moser, Aaron Macy, Alva Macy; also Jim Long, little Jim,; And
    William, Cager, John Wesley, Edward & Thomas Jefferson Carlisle

Tuesday, May 21, 1872

A very nice day. Tolerable warm. Aaron and I hitched the mules to the express and took Mother and Aunts to the conference. Lydia went to her father's* for the day. They had a very good time. We took dinner at our new house in town. Aunts went to Uncle Aaron's after the conference was over for the day. Aaron and Cynthia planted some melon seeds in the garden. Ed got done harrowing. Irv crossed off. Father and Will and Wes and Gabe loaded cars. Jim and Jon hauled rails and wood.

*Lydia's father was William Andrew. She resided with the WMM family

Note 8 men worked this day Ed, Irv, WMM, Will, Wes, Gabe, Jim, Jon

Wednesday, May 22, 1872

Rained in the morning and after dinner. They all went to the conference but Lydia and I. Will and Wes hauled wood and rails in the clearing. Ed and Jeff and Cager worked in the clearing. I tore down part of the garden fence and dug new holes and dug up some burdocks which are very plenty. I took Lydia to Terel's and Gabe and Irv and I went a sort of squirrel hunting but did not get any. Mac is sick at Gabe's house. They went to the night meeting and Joshua Trueblood* come home with them. He is a noted minister.

*Joshua Trueblood, b. 9/17/1804 in Pasquotank Co., NC

Thursday, May 23, 1872

A nice cloudy day. This was the last day of the conference. All went but Ruth, Lydia and I. I dug some more docks and got some hogs out of the "big field" and put up a fence where it had got knocked down. Will took the 4 sows and their pigs out to the big woods because the pigs got in Long's* corn. We had to catch 4 of them. We took one of the sows pigs and have got it in a box. It has learned to drink milk. Its mother does not give any milk. Just about dark there was a great deal of thundering in the west. I guess it will rain.

*Jim Long, rented crop land from WMM

Friday, May 24, 1872

A little cooler than common. Cloudy all day. Aaron and Will crossed off and Ed and I dropped and Irv and Jeff and Cage covered. Finished at one oclock pm. Gabe and Wesley and Jims hauled wood and rails. Aaron hauled in the evening. "The 3 small boys" picked chips and piled brush. I went to Joseph Edwards to take a note for mother and a summons for father. I rode Irv's mare. Irv got four dollars of father last night. Madison* is very sick – ague. Miram got 17 lbs of dried apples in the morning. Father and Will loaded one car of logs. Ureka (some butter).

*James Madison Carlisle, 20, son of Terrill

**Miriam Catherine Carlisle, 2nd wife of Terrill

Note 11 workers this day
 Aaron Macy, Will, Ed, Alva Macy, Irv, Jeff, Cage, Gabe, Wesley, 2 Jims

Saturday, May 25, 1872

A nice day. Warmer than common. Aaron and I hitched the mules to the express*** and mother** and Aaron and I went to Perry's*. When we left, Ruth and Lydia and Aunt Betsy****** and Hannah got in and we went to Aunt Polly Woodard's sale. There were a great many there. They sold 3 horses and several cattle and thirty six hogs, one walking plow, harness, six shares of the Plainfield and Mooresville Gravel Road, 80lbs of yarn. Aunt Betsy stayed at Uncle William's. Aunt Hannah at Uncle Aaron's. Lottie**** and I stayed at William's*****.

*Perry T. Macy, b. IN1825, M/C1856, $16000/3000, Bro. of WMM

**Julia Ann Macy, b. IN 1829, Alva Macy's mother

***express= the buggy

****Charlotte L. Macy, 15, cousin, daughter of Perry Macy,

*****William Clarkson Mills, 1816-1899, brother of Julia Ann Macy

******Betsy Jane, 1819-877, and Hannah, 1833-1914, sisters of Julia Ann

Sunday, May 26, 1872

A beautiful day. We had a very nice visit. I and Amos rode to meeting in a buggy and Aaron rode a horse and Oliver* and his mother and Lottie** and Aunt Betsy*** rode in a carriage drawn by 2 mules. Uncle Aaron's***** folks and himself and Aunt Rebecca**** come home with us as father and mother went to White Lick. Had a very good meeting. There was a black cloud appeared in the west and kept coming over. A great deal of thunder and lightning. Rained some but I can tell better by tomorrow.

*Oliver P. Macy, 2, son of Perry Macy
**Charlotte L. Macy, 15, daughter of Perry Macy
*** Betsy Mills Bray from Hamilton Co, sister of Julia Ann Macy
****Rebecca Macy, 36, 2nd wife of Perry Macy
*****Aaron Mills, 1821-1908, bro of Julia Ann Macy

Monday, May 27, 1872

Hauling chips. The main go, piling chips – Ed, Jeff, Cage, Jim and Jim

hauled wood. Will and Wes worked on the Bethel road. I hitched Nance**

and Doll** to the express and took my Aunts to the depot. They stopped at

W.H.P. Woodard's* house a little while. Mother and Cynthia and Lydia went

to town with us. Father went to Indianapolis to get some money but failed.

The largest (Jeff Davison) sow had 7 pigs last Saturday. They are very large

and stout. A great deal of thunder in the night accompanied by a

considerable rain rain rain.

*William H.P. Woodard, b. VA1816, M/C1835, dry goods merchant
**Nance & Doll the horses
Note 7 workers this day Ed, Jeff, Cage, Jim, little Jim, Will, Wes

Tuesday, May 28, 1872

Rolling logs and burning brush is the rage. Aaron hauled two loads of chips to Will and one to Gabriel. Gabe is working for Sil Dakin* ($25 per month). I hauled one load of wood to Terel and Aaron and I hauled chips to the wood house which is about full of the things. Will and father and Wesley and Jim rolled logs. Little Jim hauled wood and chips. Cage helped me and Ed helped Aaron and Jeff helped Jim. We about finished the chip business. Joe Hutton**has fixed a porch in front of the toll house and sells candy and peanuts.

*Sylvester H. Dakin, farmer, b. OH1831, M/C1833, Rep, Quaker

**Joseph P. Hutton, b. NC1839, M/C1869, Toll Keeper for The Mooresville Monrovia Gravel Road Company. The booth was located between Alva's home and White Lick Creek.

Note 10 workers this day
Aaron Macy, Alva Macy, Will, WMM, Wesley, Jim, little Jim, Cage, Ed, Jeff

Wednesday, May 29, 1872

Got done rolling logs and commenced plowing. Will and Jim (the second) plowed. Irv and Wes and old Jim helped roll logs and then picked and burned brush. Aaron and Cage hauled 2 loads of tan bark to Frank Gray*and took the beard plow to Hill** to get it sharpened and the cutter fixed up. Ed carried water and picked brush. Jeff and I hauled gravel to the hill on the Bethel Road north of the sulpher spring. It finished the road tax. We got too big a load on and broke Charlie's***single tree -- and his trace.

*Frank Gray, tanner, b. Ireland1840, M/C1868

**J. M. Hill, blacksmith, b. OH 1839, M/C1871, Rep, Christian

***Charlie the horse, pulled through his harness

Note 10 workers this day
Will, little Jim, Irv, Wes, Jim, Aaron Macy, Cage, Ed, Jeff, Alva Macy

Thursday, May 30, 1872

Cleared ground, broke up, hauled wood and rails and harrowed and crossed off and planted. Irv plowed corn in the sod field. Not hardly any missing. Will and Jim plowed. I took the harrey to Hill's* shop and got it sharpened and the cutter fixed on and a large hook welded. We took a small double shovel to the blacksmith shop to get new shovels. I got started to plowing by nine oclock. It is very rough work. Terel got four dollars of Pa today. Jim helped about riding up the fires and clearing off the lands. Jeff and Ed and Cage planted and covered corn.

*J. M. Hill, b. OH1839, blacksmith, M/C1871
Note 7 workers this day Irv, Will, Jim, Alva Macy, Jeff, Ed, Cage

Friday, May 31, 1872

A nice day. Very warm in the evening. Will hauled logs in the forenoon from the new ground and Aaron harrowed and crossed off till noon and plowed the rest of the day. Will plowed in the evening. Wes plowed in my place. Jim plowed all day. I took the big harrow to Hilll's shop and got it sharpened. Then I helped Wes and Cage and Jeff dig down the steepest banks. Wes only plowed ½ day. We got done the banks and replanted corn in the "big field". Moles have took a great deal.

Note 6 workers today Will, Wes, Jim, Alva Macy, Cage, Jeff

Saturday, June 1, 1872

A wet day. Did not rain much till after dinner. I and Jim and Will broke up. We got done about noon. Aaron harrowed and crossed off. Jim and his wife planted. Got done planting about four o'clock. Cage and Jeff and Ed replanted corn. Wes did too (I forgot). Father went to town and got 4 plows - $5 a piece ($20). Aaron went to Uncle Levi's*. Irv plowed in the sod field. Little Jim and me went a fishing after we got done planting. Did not catch many. Mac shot a squirrel with our rifle.

Note 11 workers this day
Alva Macy, Jim, Will, Aaron Macy, Jim & wife, Cage, Jeff, Ed, Wes, Irv

*Levi S. Hadley, farmer, 1826-1891, $18690/3000, Brother in law of WMM

Sunday, June 2, 1872

A wet day. Rained extremely hard for a while in the night. Did not any of us go to meeting because it rained considerably in the forenoon. Johny come over in the afternoon. We had a great deal of fun. He went home in the evening. Commenced raining about dark and is still raining. Aaron come home about 7 oclock. The lesser "Jeff Davis" sow has got 8 pigs. Very nice ones. Thundered and lightninged a good deal about dark. We got the paper last evening (I must go to bed).

Monday, June 3, 1872

Another wet muddy day. Rained more in the night and off and on till about 3 oclock in the afternoon. Irv and Wes hauled rails from the road by the new ground. Irv and Will went to Aunt Mary's and got a log. Cage helped Wes after dinner. Aaron and Jeff and Ed and I reset the west fence of the north little orchard and part of the north fence of the old sod field. It was very dirty work. We put Bridgeport* and her family in the branch lot.

Father** went to Martinsville. Aunt Ruth and Uncle Miles*** come a while.

Note 8 workers this day   Irv, Wes, Will, Cage, Aaron Macy, Jeff, Ed, Alva Macy

Editor's Note: Irvine Moser was mentioned earlier in the year. Cage Carlisle, 14, was a farm laborer boarding with Wm. Carlisle in 1880. Wes, Will, Jeff & Ed were Terrill's sons.

*Bridgeport the sow

**William Monroe Macy, farmer/timber dealer, b.TN1820, $28000/6000

***Miles S Hadley, farmer, 1828-1911, Rep, Quaker, $9000/2200, Brother
        in law of WMM

Tuesday, June 4, 1872

A nice day. Did not rain any in the night. The sun shined and a cold wind

stirring. Aaron*** went to Waverly to get some figures of John Neese*

about the Harvey trial. Irv and Will hauled logs. They broke one of the tires.

Father and Jeff and Cage and Ed and me finished resetting the north fence

of the sod field and laid up the loose rails along the pike**. Wes hauled

rails. Cage and me went to town and got one of the plows…. been fixed.

*John R. Neese, 34, planing mill operator, $1000/350
**The 'pike' was the gravel road now known as SR42
***Aaron Mills Macy, 1855-1877, brother of Alva Perry Macy
Note 7 workers this day Irv, Will, WMM, Jeff, Cage, Ed, Wes

Wednesday, June 5, 1872

Corn plowing the go. Aaron and Fanny* and Will and Bet* and Irv and Mol* and Cager and Charlie* and Ed and Doll* and Jeff and Jake* and Alvah and Nance* (best of all) (7 in all). We got the six acre field and the sod field done. Will*** quit at noon "cause he had a boil under his arm and one on his rist". The little stag got out again. He had better stay in or he will get eat up. Jim and Jim** plowed in their field. Part of our field was very wet. Father went to Martinsville.

*Fanny, Bet, Mol, Charlie, Doll, Jake, Nance (horses and mules)
Note: 7 workers-- Aaron Macy, Will, Irv, Cager, Ed, Jeff, Alva Macy
**James Long 52, & son, James L Long, 15, were working the land he rented from WMM
***William Carlisle, hired hand of WMM

Thursday, June 6, 1872

A cloudy day. Commenced clouding up early in the morning. Did not rain until about noon. Rained very slow till about 3 oclock. Then it came a little faster. We all plowed till noon in the Big field. Irv got 2 bushels of corn and took it to mill. Aaron and I went to lodge which met again at Clark Hadley's house. Changed the Young Templars to Cold Water Temple. 24 members present. The rest of the hirelings plowed some after 5 oclock (got to the banks)

Friday, June 7, 1872

Wet weather. Rained a good deal in the night. Rained off and on all forenoon. Pa and Will hauled 1 log from Zimri Allen's*. Jim and son plowed a while in the evening but it rained very hard between 3 and 4 oclock. Aaron and Ed and I finished replanting the Big Field. Father went to town after he come home and got the mattock sharpened. Aaron made some trussel benches in the evening of June 7th.

*Zimri Allen, 71, b. NC, farmer, $7000/4000

Saturday, June 8, 1872

A nice day. Cloudy most of the time. Father and Terel's boy built a fence from the corner of the garden to the corner of the barn and from that to the big field (part plank). So we have the barns fenced in all but a gate. Irv helped them. Aaron hauled a load of rails from the new ground to the south side of the Big field and put them up. I was not well enough to do anything till noon. Then Aaron and Ed, Jeff, Cage, Dave and I replanted the sandy bottom . Not much missing. I fixed a pretty good hatchet afore dinner. Rained very hard before night.

Note 8 workers this day WMM, Irv, Aaron Macy, Ed, Jeff, Cage, Dave, Alva Macy

Sunday, June 9, 1872

Some cloudy. Sprinkled some. We all went to meeting and school. After meeting we went to Uncle Tommy's* and Lydia** went to Will Andrew's. Cousin Wayne*** come here just after dinner. Seems like we always go away when somebody comes. Topengburg the temperance lecturer delivered a lecture at the Friends meeting house at Mooresville in the evening. Jim's new-ground corn is coming very nicely and some of our oats is falling down. Looked some like rain at sunset.

*Thomas Marshall Hadley, farmer, 1810-1893, $6000/4000, Brother in law of WMM

**Lydda Andrew, daughter of William Andrew, "adopted" by WMM

***Wayne C. Hadley, 18, cousin, son of Levi S. Hadley

Monday, June 10, 1872

A nice day. Some windy. Father went to court. The trial was put off two days more because the lawyers wanted to go to the political conventions at Indianapolis. Will hauled four logs from Aunt Mary's. Eli* got some lye in his eyes. He was playing with Lonzo**and one of Harper's boys and they run in their wood house and he was after them. There was a kettle of lye and one of rainwater so they throwed some on Eli and hit him very badly. Jeff and I plowed in the six acre field. Aaron, Cage, Ed grubbed sprouts.

*Eli J. Hadley, 12, cousin, son of Mary and Thomas Hadley
**Alonzo Hadley, 15, 1858-1925, son of Mary and Thomas Hadley
Note: 6 workers today – Will, Jeff, Alva Macy, Aaron Macy, Cage, Ed

Tuesday, June 11, 1872

Nice day. South wind blowing most of the day. We all plowed corn in the "big field". I layed in bed too late and got a little behind. Ed and I swapped plow horses. Doll** got so she would not mind him. Aaron*** took sick just a little while before night. Not very bad. Father watched us plow a while in the morning to see if we done good work. He went to Monrovia in the evening to see John Greeson*. I have got my feet poisoned with dew.

*John Greeson, b. NC1830, farmer, $8600/925
**Doll the horse
***Aaron Mills Macy, 17, brother of Alva Perry Macy

Wednesday, June 12, 1872

No dew in the morning. Scarcely very cloudy and I thought it would rain

before night but it did not. Very hot in the morning. Wind rose in the

evening and cleared off. Aaron was not well enough to work. We all

plowed. Got the great field done one way and about 18 acres the other

way. I plowed Doll most of the day. Aaron fetched Fanny* out and took

Doll* for mother to ride to meeting about 1 oclock. Father plowed Fanny in

the evening.

P.S. One of Miriam's kinfolk got here in the evening.

*Fanny & Doll the horses

Thursday, June 13, 1872

Nice forenoon. South wind blowing almost all the time. We all plowed till noon. Before we started to work , it commenced raining very hard. Rained by jerks all evening. Irvine's wife got one pound of butter (20cts). Will got one midling (24 ½ lbs.) ($2.45). Ed and I caught 2 of the biggest Jeff Davis sow's pigs cause she did not give milk enough for them. One got away but I guess we can catch it again. We built a pen of plank for them and put Cynthia's pig with the remaining one. Still raining now and it is nearly bedtime. Much thunder and lightning. ------ and Pa went to Martinsville. He has not come home.

Friday, June 14, 1872

A nice muddy day. Too wet to plow. Aaron and Cage hauled rails from new ground to the east side of the meadow. Jeff and Dave cut weeds. Will and I hauled logs from Aunt Mary's. Eli* is very bad off with his eye. He cannot see any at all. It pains him very bad. I stayed there for dinner. Mac went with Will in the evening. Ed was not well. Father has not come home yet. The suit is still in progress. There was a turkey nest in the big burdock leaves on the hillside. I fetched 3 duck eggs home with me from Auntie's.

*Eli J. Hadley, 12, cousin, son of Mary Ann Macy and Albert Hadley

Saturday, June 15, 1872

Nice day. Some cloudy. Dave and Johnathan, Ed and Jeff and I cut thissles and burrs. Will and Irving hauled logs from Aunt Mary's. Aaron and Cage hauled rails in the morning and afternoon. Jeff and Aaron and Cage plowed corn in the big field. Jeff and Cage plowed their garden this morning. Fido* got out where Bridgeport** and Co. were and they like to have eat him up but we got them off. They bit him under his hind leg very badly and bruised him up. He is getting some better. The trial come to an end. Harvey gained most of it. Father got about ----

*Fido the dog
**Bridgeport the sow
Note 9 workers this day
Dave, Johnathan, Alva Macy, Ed, Will, Irvine, Aaron Macy, Cage, Jeff

Sunday June 16, 1872

Very pleasant day. All went to meeting and school but me. I stayed with our patient Fido. He has one of his forelegs broke. We did not know it. Joseph Edwards* come down and stayed a while. Aaron and I and Cage and Ed and Dave got about 40 town cows out of Moon's meadow and then we all went in swimming. We killed a ground squirrel. Had a heap of fun. Father and mother and Ruth and Lydia went to Levi's***. Ruth went to Uncle Perry's** to stay all night. No more on this day.

*Joseph H. Edwards, b. VA1833, M/C1856, Rep, Quaker, 3mi SW Mooresville
**Perry T. Macy, 1825-1889, brother of WMM
***Levi S. Hadley, 1826-1891, uncle of Alva Perry Macy

Monday, June 17, 1872

Nice day. Very warm. We all went to the big field and finished plowing it the second time and then went to the old sod field and begun and finished it and then went to the sandy bottom and plowed a round or two. Father went out to Gasburg to see Bill Allen* but he had started to his home in Kansas. Fido has a hard time. Cannot move about much. John Fogleman** bought the Marley stag. He weighted 348. Got $27.82. It's very clear night so far. Terel is working for Billy Sumner***.

*William Allen, 45, farmer, b. NC, $1000/725
**John Fogleman, farmer-butcher, b. NC1827, /C1848, Dem, Methodist $1000/500
***William P. Sumner, farmer-teamster, b. IN1840, $ /500, ½ mi W of Mooresville

196

Tuesday, June 18, 1872

Nice day but very warm and sultry. I thought it would rain but no. We all went to sandy bottom and finished it. Pitched into the big field. Here we got a touch of knowledge. Seems like father wants it plowed deep and close. We took a new start and done some good plowing. Better than we had been doing. Father and Will went to the IOGT lodge*. Puppy, I think, is improving. He can sit up a good deal, does not use his leg much. Badly chawed up. (nice day).

*International Order of Good Templars—Promoters of Temperance, Peace and Brotherhood

Wednesday, June, 19, 1872

Very hot day. Full swing at plowing. Got to the gate. Will did not plow in the evening. He was not well. Wesley plowed for him. Terel got a bushel of corn and 2 ½ gallons of molasses (75cts). S. B. Maulsby* come here and engaged 25,000 feet of walnut timber. Fido walked some. No wind stirring at all. Father stayed about home and hoed in the garden and fed the hogs and done up the chores generally. Some of the raspberries are getting ripe. The old fashioned cherries are getting ripe. The peaches and apples are falling off trees. Rot to do so.

*Silas B. Maulsby, 35, Marion Co. IN

Thursday, June 20, 1872

Very warm again. The thermometer was up to ninety at noon. We finished

the big field and plowed 2 or 3 acres in the old sod or west field. Father

went to Joseph Edwards' to see if he might not hire his reaper. Terel plowed

for Sumner**. Aaron and I took our shovels to Hill* and got them

sharpened. It was after dark I mean and Irv fetched them home the next

morning. Aaron took Pa's watch to the silversmith to see about getting it

"fixed up". Left it with him.

*J. M. Hill, blacksmith, b. OH1839, MC1871, Rep, Christian
**William P. Sumner

Friday, June 21, 1872

Nice day. Some wind moving. Got done the west field and the young bottom also and some in the sandy bottom. Jim and sons plowed in their new ground. Father was not well. Had a bad headache. Uncle John* come to see about some money business. Turned much cooler in the evening. Cynthia went to the last day of high school. She says they had a good time. She took some books back for Aaron. Cage broke his plow, nearly 2 rounds and one again – 3 in all. (Grass sod)

*John Franklin Hadley, farmer, 1840-1898, 1 ½ mi W of Mooresville, Rep, Quaker
   $11600/4345

Saturday, June 22, 1872

Nice cool day. We finished the sandy bottom field about 3 oclock then we all took Saturday evening. Went to the creek and washed off. Fixed up the meadow fence some. Will got ½ gallon of apple butter (37 ½ cts). Terel got ½ gallon of molasses (87 ½ cts). Father cut weeds where we were at work. Went to the town of Mooresville in evening. Irv and Will fetched our calf home from Richardson's**. A nice bull. Ida* and Ora*** come here in the evening. Irv killed a woodpecker with our rifle. I could not hit at all.

*Ida Ellen Macy, 10, daughter of Perry Macy
**Thomas A. Richardson, 35, tinner
***Ora R. Hadley, 11, cousin, daughter of Levi S. Hadley

Sunday, June 23, 1872

Cloudy all day. We all went to school and meeting. Johny come home with us. Tommy and Ira come in the afternoon. We went to the creek and washed. Then we went to a mulberry tree and got all we wanted. Ed and I went part of the way home with them. Will and Irv took some leather to Dave Farmer's*** to get some harness made for the mules. Terel's Aunt Fanny Crayton* is very sick. Cynthia rode Jake** to meeting. She intended to go to Aaron Benbow**** after meeting but did not. The cherries are now good ripe.

*Francis M. Crayton, 62, b. NC, wife of George Crayton

**Jake the mule

***David D. Farmer, b. IN1834 farmer-harness maker, Rep, Protestant 3 ½ mi E of
    Mooresville

****Aaron B. Benbow, 43, b. NC, farmer, $13000/2500

Monday, June 24, 1872

Nice day. Not quite so warm as usual. We all plowed in the big field.

Father went to Indianapolis to see a man about some business. Jim and

son plowed up their field here. Dave went to Joseph Edward's and got some

cherries. I shot a red head. Thought I done big business and I quit a while

before night and took my plow to Hill**and got the beams crooked again. It

straightened it some while I was at work among the roots of sandy bottom.

Fogleman* killed one of his calves.

*John Fogleman, butcher, b. NC1827, keeps calves on WMM's land
**J. M. Hill, 33, b. OH, blacksmith, Rep, Christian

Tuesday, June 25, 1872

Nice day, very cloudy in the evening and thundered some. Joseph* cut our 3 acre field of meadow. Aaron went after the reaper with the mules but Joe fetched it with his horses. Will thinned the corn till Aaron come back. We got the big field done about 5 oclock. Then we all thinned corn but Aaron took the mules and went to Jo's and got his rake. I shot 5 more birds in the cherry tree and missed one. One of our pigs or sows is dead. Do not know when it died. Ed and I swapped back plow mares. My plow runs too deep for Doll.**

*Joseph H. Edwards, b. VA1833, M/C1856, 3 mi SW of Mooresville
**Doll the Horse

Wednesday, June 26, 1872

Nice day. Very warm. Aaron raked the little meadow with Fanny. Will and

father and the colored folks put it up. Got done about 10 oclock. Aaron

took the rake . "WARREN'S GREAT SHOW" All went.

Circus, Menagerie and Museums.

An Elephant weighing 12,880lbs besides 3 Lions,

    a Bengal Tiger, Hyenas, Rhinoceros, African Buffalo,

    Llama of South America, Reindeer of Siberia, Camels,

    Rocky Mountain Badger, Coons, Monkeys and the Zebra, Ostrich, and

several trained horses. A man without arms,

a woman 20 inches high weighs 17lbs.

Many other things.

2005 Note: The "KELLY MILLER CIRCUS" visited Mooresville in May of

2005. The Robinsons attended for comparison to the show of 137 years

ago.

It included 12 Ponies, 3 Elephants, 3 Camels, 2 Horses,

2 Miniature Donkeys, 2 Llama, 6 Dogs, a Juggler, Dog Act,

4 Trapeze Performers, Clowns, Vertical Balance Bar, and

a Balance & Chair Climb Act.

Thursday, June 27, 1872

Warm again. Had a shower big enough to lay the dust. Irv and Will helped Joe take care of his hay. They took the mares and a wagon. Thundered good deal in the evening. We thinned and hoed corn, father is included. Jim got over his corn the fourth time. The raspberries are getting very near their highest glory. I killed 2 rats while we were resting at noon. I caught them in my hands. One of them bit me. They all come out to get a drink. Nearly all young. I guess they all come out just cause they had a big crowd.

Friday, June 28, 1872

Doubtful weather. Looked like all forenoon and past after we went to the field. Joe cut part of the big meadow after dinner. Cage and Jeff and Ed hoed corn. Aaron helped Jim stack his hay – 3 stacks. Will and me layed by the 6 acre field. Aaron hoed corn till dinner. Irv's wife is sick therefore he did not work. Looks like nice weather from the way the sun set. Father walked about and bossed the hands. The frogs and our (big woods) whipperwill are holding a concert.

Note 9 working this day
Joe Edwards, Cage, Jeff, Ed, Aaron Macy, Jim, Will, Alva Macy, WMM

Saturday, June 29, 1872

Nice day. The thermometer was at 92F at noon. Looked some like it would rain the evening but passed north of us. Will raked hay till he got done what was cut. Aaron hauled 5 loads to the barn and Will too. Jim and son helped us get it all stacked up. Father was not well. Cage and Jeff and Ed and I plowed in sandy bottom till noon then we packed away hay in the barn. Father went to town and bought a pitch fork and got a bolt fixed that belongs to my plow. Irv was sick and his wife was not well.

Note 8 workers today Will, Aaron Macy, Jim, little Jim, Cage, Jeff, Ed, Alva Macy

Sunday, June 30, 1872

Pleasant day. Some cloudy. All went to meeting but me and Lydia. I was

not very well, but not sick. Uncle Thomas* and Aunt Lucinda**** come

home with them. After dinner Aaron and Dave and Ed and I went up in the

big woods and got some soapstone and whittled it. Then we went to

Tansey's**sulfer spring. I forgot that Emma*** come home with them.

She is going to stay all night and Uncle and Aunt went home. We watched

for rats a while but could not kill any. Caught one in the trap.

*Thomas M. Hadley, farmer, b. NC1810, M/C 1824, Rep, Quaker

**Jesse Tansey, farmer, b. NC1812, M/C1822, $14900/1443

***Emma Macy, 10, cousin, dau of Ira C Macy

****Lucinda Macy Hadley, 1818-1893, Sister of WMM

Monday, July 1, 1872

Nice day. Very warm but a nice wind blowing nearly all the time. Some of our calves have got out sometime last week. Have not found or heard of them. Father cut wheat. Irv and Will and I hauled hay till noon then they took Joe's rake home and intended to haul for Joe* but he had not cut any more so they come home and hauled 2 loads in the evening. I helped Aaron bind in the afternoon. Father got a sack of flour at the mill. Ed and Jeff and Cage laid by sandy bottom.

*Joe Edwards

Note 8 men working this day
WMM, Irv, Will, Alva Macy, Aaron Macy, Ed, Cage, Jeff

Tuesday, July 2, 1872

Warm day. Father and Aaron got done what wheat was ripe. Will and Irv finished hauling what hay there was cut. Cage and I mowed away (2 loads). Then they went to Joe's*. Cage and Jeff, Ed and I plowed in the west field. The corn is about up to our arms. Jeff broke Irv's plow last evening. A black cloud rose in the west accompanied by very much lightning. Did not rain any but cooled the air some. Cynthia** went to Sumner's*** a while in the evening.

*Joseph H. Edwards, farmer, b. VA1833, M/C1856, Rep, Quaker, 3mi SW of Mooresville
     $17850/535
**Cynthia Ruth Macy, 11, sister of Alva Macy

***William P. Sumner, farmer, b. IN1840, ½ mi W of Mooresville

Note 8 men working   WMM, Aaron Macy, Will, Irv, Cage, Alva Macy, Jeff, Ed

Wednesday, July 3, 1872

Mother's* birthday. Forty three years old. Very nice before noon but warm. Will and Irv hauled hay for Joseph. Aaron helped Joe too. What was left of us plowed in the west and would have done it if it had not rained two good showers in the afternoon. We had just went 3 rounds when the first shower come up. It rained very hard for a few minutes then we went and plowed till very near time to quit when it come up a big shower and wet us all again.

*Julia Ann (Mills) Macy, wife of WMM, 43, dau of Henry and Hannah Woodward Mills

Thursday, July 4, 1872

Ninety six years ago the declaration of independence was declared. It was a very nice day. Joe got here with his reaper about 10 oclock and finished cutting the wheat. Father shocked and Aaron and Irv and Will and Mac bound. Cage* and I were going to bind but he was so long in coming. We caught our horses (which we had turned out) and went to plowing. We finished the west field and got 12 acres of the big field done. Of course Ed and Jeff plowed. Irv broke two fingers out of the cradle.

*Cager Carlisle, 16, farm laborer
Note 9 men working WMM, Aaron Macy, Irv, Will, Mac, Cage, Alva Macy, Ed, Jeff

Friday, July 5, 1872

Nice day. Plenty of dew in the night. They hitched the mules to the wagon and Irv and Will and Mac (for he stayed with Terel) and Pa and Ma and Ruth and Lydia and Terel went to Joe's to harvest. We four boys plowed, got past the oak trees, even to the walnut beyond. They got two gallons of cherries. Dave got 2 ½ gallons of cherries at Tansey's* farm. We caught four rats and one mole. The back band has made a sore but I have moved it. One of her shoes come off. **

*Jesse Tansey, farmer, b. NC1812, M/C1822
**Horse's harness back band rubbed a sore on the horse's back. Also the horse lost a shoe.
Note Irv, Will, Mac, WMM, JAM, Cythia Ruth, Lydda Terel joined the threshing ring

Saturday, July 6, 1872

Nice cool day. We got up early and took a good start. Father and Aaron and Irv and Will went to Joe's. What was left of us plowed. Got to the lower corner of the orchard, yes, even beyond. There was a big hawk come and lit on a limb of a tree close to where we were plowing. We tried to run him off for he was after a little bird but he would not go. I went and got the gun and got ready to shoot and away he went. Rebecca* got 2 lbs of butter. They got Joe's wheat all cut.

*Rebecca H. Bowles Hadley Macy, 1833-1912, 2nd wife of Perry T. Macy

212

Sunday, July 7, 1872

Nice day. All went to meeting and school. Cynthia rode Jake* and after meeting went to Uncle Aaron's**** and stopped at Levi's**. Said Aunt Marguret*** was sick and Uncle John was sick. Aaron***** and I and Ed and Jeff went to the creek and went swimming while father went about the bottom and found our calf which got out. The thermometer was at seventy four about dark. Ah yes getting warmer. Ed and I went through the wheat field and got us some straws to plat. We went to Sumner's and got a few cherries and apples.

*Jake the mule

**Levi S. Hadley, farmer, b. 1822, husband of Margaret Ann Macy, 50

***Margaret Ann Macy, Hadley, 50, sister of WMM

****Aaron Mills, 1821-1908, brother of Julia Ann Macy

*****Aaron Mills Macy, 1855-1877, brother of Alva Perry Macy

Monday, July 8, 1872

A nice warm day. Joseph cut grass. Us lucky boys finished laying-bye the big field -- done laying and plowing corn. Will took Nance* and the mules and got them shod. Aaron bound wheat for Sumner till noon. Irv and Cage and Jeff cleared and arranged the lower barn for the hay after they got done the plowing. I plowed the garden. Got 9 loads hauled. Ed and Cage and I went to the creek and washed off. Father went to look for the stray calf but did not get it. Will raked hay in the afternoon.

*Nance the horse

Tuesday, July 9, 1872

Nice day. Working in the hay all the go. Joseph* stayed all night. Got done cutting about 10 oclock. I raked it. Jeff and Ed moved away. Irv pitched up in the mow. Will and Aaron and Cage loaded. I mowed away till Joe got done. Father helped and bossed the job. When I got done raking I hitched Nance** and Charlie** to the express and took the rake home. Got 2 or 3 gallons of cherries. Nettie and Mattie come home with me. Ruth*** went with me. Borrowed 2 bushels of wheat.

*Joseph H. Edwards

**Nance and Charlie the horses

***Cynthia Ruth Macy, 1861-1934, sister of Alva Perry Macy

Note 9 workers putting up hay
Alva Macy, Jeff, Ed, Irv, Will, Aaron Macy, Cage, Joseph, WMM

Wednesday, July 10, 1872

Warm and cloudy. Got the hay all in the barn by three oclock. The barns are about as full as we could crowd them. Jeff and Irv were not able to work. Ed and Cage and Will unloaded. Aaron and father loaded. I helped load and unload. Rained about 5 oclock then quit and rained again about 7 or 8. Father and Aaron and Will hitched the mules to the wagon and hauled some rails to stack the wheat on. Ed and Dave went to the creek and washed and then went to the wheat field and got some straw to plat.

Note 7 men working Ed, Cage, Will, Aaron Macy, WMM, Alva Macy, Dave

Thursday, July 11, 1872

Wet day but not till afternoon. Will and Pa hauled a log from Aunt Mary's*.
Rained so much in the evening Will did not go back. Father stayed at
Mary's for dinner and consequently had to stay over all night. Aaron and I
hauled four loads of rails from the new ground to where father intends to
stack the wheat in the mule lot. I have got enough of straw plated to make
a hat I guess. Aaron and I shelled a bushel of corn while it was raining.

*Mary Ann Macy Hadley, b. 1831, sister of WMM, widow of Albert Hadley

Friday, July 12, 1872

Pretty slick. The big rain beat down the oats considerably. Aaron and I hauled Ensminger ½ a cord of wood and one load of rails to the orchard fence. I took my platting to Emaline Moser*** to get a hat made of it and Aaron took two bushels of wheat and three of corn to Day's* Mill to get flour and meal. Will hauled logs from Aunt Mary's. Father stayed all night there and come home at dinner. We hitched Jake and Doll to the express and my parents and Aaron went to town. Father got some money from the city. Cynthia and I took Tom Sumner's** pitch forks home.

A daughter was born to Miram and Terrel—name, Hannah Carlisle

*Warner L. Day, 36, Grist mill operator

**Thomas C. Sumner, farmer, 1 ½ mi SW of Mooresville

***Emeline Moser, 28, wife of William Moser

Saturday, July 13 1872

A real nice day. Heavy dew. Sun rose and set unclouded. Will hauled one log from Aunt Mary's. Father went to Martinsville to see about some pressing business. Days could not grind the corn and wheat so Aaron went and got it and took it to the Monrovia and got it ground. Mother went with him and got some yarn. Cynthia and Lydia and I stayed at home. Bill Moon's* horse jumped the fence and got in our pasture. I turned him back and layed it up and he knocked it down and come on. Pa has gone to see Moon about it.

*William Moon, 42, farmer, $36000/4000, 3 mi SW of Mooresville

Sunday, July 14, 1872

The day of rest again. We all went to meeting. Will went to Farmer's* to see if the harness were done. He had not commenced them. Father and Will took a stroll about the bottoms to see if they could find the runaway calf and have not got back yet while I am writing. Aaron and I went to Levi's. Willie Hadley** and John*** and Ira**** come home with me but went back in the evening. Joseph Edwards and John Hussey *****come over in the evening. Terel bought Joe's old cow. Give forty (40.00) for her and calf.

*David D. Farmer, b. 1834, farmer-harness maker, 3 ½ mi E of Mooresville

**William Hadley, 12, son of John F. Hadley

***John Hadley, 11, son of Thomas M. Hadley

****Ira W. Hadley, 9, son of Levi S. Hadley

*****John A Hussey, 15, lives with Joseph Edwards' family

Monday, July 15, 1872

Rain! Rain! Rain! Will and Irv and Aaron and Ed and me commenced stacking wheat. Got 4 loads hauled and begun raining. Had to quit. Went to the camp and got the planks and covered it. Aaron went to town and got 2 barrels of salt after dinner. Emaline** commenced sewing my hat together. Terel got 33 pounds of salt (50cts). Will and Gabe and I went in the big woods and looked some for squirrels. Did not get to kill any. Father took Bet's* harness to get a hook mended then went to look at Levi's two mules which he will sell.

*Betty the horse
**Emaline Moser

Tuesday, July 16, 1872

A nice day for a wet one. Rained long spells all night and a good part of the day. But Pa and Will hauled one log from Allen's. Will and Irv went to Uncle Levi's* and fetched 2 mules home which father had bought. One horse mule and a mare. Jim** and Kit (bob)**. They worked the new mules to the tongue and true leaders before. They are 3 years old. Aaron and I worked all day cleaning the upper barn. Irv worked one third of the day. He had the toothache. Ed and Jeff and Cage a half day. Irv got $5, Caught 28 rats.

*Levi S. Hadley, 1826-1891, WMM's brother in law
** Jim & Kit, the new mules

Wednesday, July 17, 1872

Terrible wet day once in a while although Will and Irv went to town and got 2 backbands, three pairs of traces, two pairs of hames, 2 bellybands, 1 hitch strap, 1 collar, four hame strings. Total amount $14.25. 83 town cows got in Jim's upper field of corn. Joe Cummins* saw them get in and drove them out immediately. Aaron and father repaired the fence. I worked at the manure and dirt in the barn all day and got it all out. Will and Irv hauled a log apiece from Milton Cook's***. Pa borrowed or hired Comer's** wagon. Will worked all the mules. Irv had the old team and his mare.

*Joseph Cummins, b. NC1820, M/C1856, farmer, $12000/1000, Dem., Methodist
**Stephen Comer, 47, was a teamster
***Milton Cook, 43, farmer, $9487/1484

Thursday, July 18, 1872

A nice day only it was raining when I got up but that did not last long and such a time we had laying up water gaps. Only 7 to put up and the culvert across the Bethel Road caved in. The supervisor and his hands made a new one. Washed the big elm log lengthwise with the branch. We layed up all the gaps, had what wheat there was stacked to take down and shock up to dry. The freshet washed away 3 or four of the shocks in the field. I went to Farmer's* and got those gears, what there was of them.

*David D. Farmer, harness maker

Friday, July 19, 1872

Beautiful day. Father and Aaron cut oats all day. Will and Irv cut a while in the morning. They got Dakin's* cradles. They went to Mary's** and got a log apiece. They were large. Will stalled in the Greencastle ford but doubled teams and come out all right. I went to Uncle Tommy's*** to get our sickles but Mr. Feasel had borrowed them and was using them at Uncle Miles'**** farm. I went and got two. We have another one somewhere. Don't know where it is. Our oats are down very bad.

Ben. Harrison*****lectures at town tonight.

*Sylvester H. Dakin, 41, farmer-meat merchant, b. OH, $16000/3000

**Aunt Mary Ann Macy Hadley, 1822-1899, sister of WMM

***Thomas M. Hadley, 1810-1893, brother-in-law of WMM

****Miles S. Hadley, farmer, 1828-1911, 1 ½ mi NW of Mooresville

***** **Benjamin Harrison, 1833-1901, Civil War General, 23rd President of the USA-1889-1893**

Saturday July 20, 1872

Very nice day. Will and Irv hauled a log apiece from Milton Cook's*** (poplar). Aaron helped Sumner's**** thrash wheat till noon. Father and I cradled oats till noon. This was the first of my experience with a cradle. I like the work. After dinner we bound and shocked. Gabe and Wes bound in the evening. Will helped after he got home. Don't know what he done. Cynthia went to Uncle Levi's (just so). And Ella* and Nelia** come out here to stay all night. Oh, I forgot, Ed helped Aaron thrash. Aaron and I and Jeff and Ed went in swimming after we were dismissed.

*Ellen Zernah Macy, 17, daughter of Ira C. Macy
**Cornelia Hadley, 13, daughter of Thomas M. Hadley
***Milton Cook, farmer, Center Valley, Hendricks county
****Thomas C. Sumner, farmer, 1 1/2 miles SW of Mooresville
Note 9 men working   Will, Irv, Aaron Macy, WMM, Alva Macy, Gabe, Wes, Ed, Jeff

Sunday, July 21, 1872

Very nice day. None of us went to meeting. Ella and Nelia and Aaron and I went up in the big woods to the soapstone branch. We whittled the soapstone a while then we come home and eat dinner about 2 oclock. Wayne come down about dinner time. Johnny Hadley* and Ed Naugle** and Ed McCracken***come over and we went to the creek and took a good souse and a swim. Ella and Nelia***** went home after dinner. Mother and Lydia went to the tollgate with them. Wayne**** is going to stay all night (Cynthia got home safe).

*John Hadley, 11, son of Thomas M. Hadley
**Edward E. Naugle, 11, son of John Naugle, a blacksmith
***Edgar McCracken, 14, son of Wilkinson McCracken
****Wayne C. Hadley, 18, son of Levi S. Hadley
*****Elizabeth 19, & Cornelia Hadley 14, daus of Thomas Miles Hadley

Monday July 22, 1872

Very nice and warm. Father went to Martinsville on the Dakin* trial. Will

and Irv hauled logs from Cook's. Aaron and I cradled and reaped oats. Got

50 dozen cut, bound and shocked. Wayne went home about ten oclock. He

went with us to the oats field and cut a little oats. One of our spring pigs

died. I guess it had the cholory – for several farmer's hogs have been dying.

I noticed a "Katy Did" singing - - 6 weeks till frost. Irv's colt has a sore leg.

* Sylvester Dakin, a farmer, neighbor

Tuesday, July 23, 1872

Very warm and sultry. Rained early in the morning and about 5 oclock in the evening. Father was at the county seat all day. His cause come off but not decided. Will and Irv hauled a log from Cook's. Aaron and I cradled all the oats that was standing. And reaped 5 shocks of down. Irv has bought a rifle of Will Crayton*. $5. And he has got a new whip sometime along. He uses Will Sumner's** saddle. Cynthia is not well. I will write more some other time and we fetched the calf home.

*William C. Crayton, 39, tailor
**William P. Sumner, 33, teamster

Wednesday, July 24, 1872

Nice day. Looked some like rain. Will and Irv hauled logs from Allens. Father went with them. Aaron and I fixed the road on the west hill where it washed out a hole. We made a ditch by the side of the road. This took till noon. After dinner we reaped oats. I sowed some turnips in the garden. Aaron went to town and got some nails and hinges. Irv and Will hauled a load of oats to the barn after they got home. The Katy Dids and frogs are holding a concert.

Thursday, July 25, 1872

Nice day. But most intolerably hot. Will and Irv hauled a load from Cook's. Father went to Uncle Aaron's* and bought some oak logs. Aaron and I reaped and bound oats. We could not work steady. Just before dark a cloud appeared in the west. It kept coming up slowly. About dark the wind blew very strong. Almost incessant lightning. Did not rain very much. They were thrashing at Thompson's. We had green corn for dinner.

*Aaron Mills, Julia Ann Macy's brother

230

Friday, July 26, 1872

Nice day. Very warm. Will and Irv hauled four logs from Uncle Aaron's for lumber to make seats for the "old settler's picnic". Father and Aaron hung 2 doors on the stable and fixed up elsewhere about the barn. I stood around and looked on. Aaron took the big clock down and to pieces to clean it out. He has just got the little clock cleaned. Pa and Ruth and I went on a sorty of a berry hunting and took Dakin's cradle home. We got ½ gallon of berries, not plenty.

Saturday, July 27, 1872

Nice day. Mother and father and Aaron went to meeting. Irv and Will hauled one load from Uncle Aaron's. Ruth and Lydia and I stayed at home. Johnny** and Willie* come home with Aaron. John went home and Willie is going to stay all night. Aaron went to Uncle Miles' after he come home. Willie and Ed and Jeff and Dave and I had an old fashioned game of fox in the barnyard and orchard. Will got eight and ½ lbs of meat, Irv got two dollars and Will one dollar. They hauled the rest of the logs from Uncle Aaron's (3 logs).

*William Seward Hadley, 1860-1897, adoptive son of Perry T. Macy
**John J. Hadley, 1860-1937, son of Thomas Marshall Hadley

Sunday, July 28, 1872

Little cooler. All went to meeting to White Lick. After it was over they went to Uncle Aaron's. They had a big party at Uncle Miles'**. Willie and I stayed about home and played and tended to feeding and watering the mules. We went to the creek and took a souse and a swim. Jeff hired to Johnathon Doan* for a month if it suited. He broke the spring of his steel trap and I got the chain of him. Aaron got his watch last evening. Cost one dollar and fifty cents to get it mended.

*Johnathan Doan, 71, b. TN, farmer, $9600/2500
**Miles S. Hadley, 1828-1911, Husband of Ruth Alma Macy

Monday July 29, 1872

Very sultry and cloudy most of the day. Sprinkled some in the afternoon. Will nor Irv neither one worked. I guess their folks are sick at home. Father and Aaron and I stacked wheat. Got about one hundred and forty dozen stacked. The wheat was very muddy and sandy next to the branch. The trash and dirt had filled up amongst them so that we could hardly pull them out. Most all the heads are good, nearly all. Isaac Jones* finished hauling his wheat out today. Pa killed a big garter snake.

*Isaac Jones, b. OH1824, M/C1870, teacher, Rep, Quaker

Tuesday, July 30, 1872

Mostly nice but very warm. 90F. Pa and Aaron and I stacked wheat. I and father pitched up and Aaron loaded after dinner. I cut off the butt end of the muddy bundles that come from the bank of the branch. Mother and Cynthia went visiting. Mother went to Aunt Polly Woodard's* who is very sick, scarcely able to talk. Ruth**stayed at Aunt Ruth's***. Irv had a son born unto him yesterday. ------ Neither of them worked for us. Commenced blowing and raining at five oclock and rained very hard. Blew down an elm tree in the mule lot.

*Polly Woodward, Julia Ann Macy's mother was a Woodward
**Cynthia Ruth Macy, Alva' sister
***Ruth Alma Macy Hadley, 1830-1909, WMM's sister

Wednesday, July 31, 1872

Cloudy and sultry and very warm. Irv and Will hauled logs from the depot to Matt Comer's* sawmill. Aaron and I hitched Jim** and Kit** to the wagon and hauled rails to the lower side of the wheat field where the fence had washed away. Then we built it up. We put nearly all of the scrub hogs in the stubble field. Alvah Hadley*** come down here to see if he could not rent some wheat ground. Had a very hard shower about 5 and 6 oclock.

*Mathew Comer, 46, saw mill operator, $ /500, Rep, Methodist

**Jim & Kit, the new mules

***Alvah Macy Hadley, b. 1851, son of Miles S. Hadley

Thursday, August 1, 1872

Very nice day for a new one. Will and Irv loaded a car with logs before dinner. Did not work after grub. Father was about town till noon then he took the cross cut saw to John Sanderson to get it filed and set. Aaron and I pulled weeds and deadened locust trees till noon. Then we turned over the wheat which was not stacked and straightened up the oats shocks. And then we went to Jim's cornfield below the barn and drove 44 "town devils"* out of it. Destroyed about an acre of corn.

*town devils are cows owned by town residents which are grazed on the "commons".

Friday, August 2, 1872

Some cooler. The thermometer was at 66F this morning. Will worked all day and Irv ½ day. Irv's wife was worse in the evening. Father went to Uncle William's looking at some timber. He did not engage any certain. Aaron and I hauled rails to the lower side of the field where the cows got in. We made it 10 rails high. That took till noon, then we hauled along the meadow fence and part of a load to the exposed part of Cummin's corn. Terel got five dollars this morning. John Anderson* worked ½ day for Father.

*John Anderson, 24, farm laborer

Saturday, August 3, 1872

66F in the morning. We, (Pa and Aaron and Will and I) stacked oats. Aaron and Will hauled and Father stacked and I picked up from the wagon. Made 2 stacks and took one load and half another to the barn. Done oats harvest. Guess there was about 260 dozen of wheat was cut. Left about 40 dozen for the hogs that was down and that Aaron and I cut and did not bind. I was not very well. Felt some like chilling but took some quinine. Willie Hadley* come down in the evening. Cynthia went to Sumner's** a while in the evening.

*William A. Hadley, 12, 1860-1946, cousin, son of John F Hadley
**Thomas C. Sumner, b. 1837, M/C1854, farmer, 1 ½ mi SW of Mooresville

Sunday, August 4, 1872

Pretty nice day. We all went to meeting and school. Willie went to Uncle Levi's*** after meeting. We all went home. After dinner, they all went to Aunt Polly's. She is very low. I stayed at home and Charlie Robbins* come up here and we had a good time. We found 3 pigs dead – the demon "cholera" has got to them. Several others mopey. Johnathon Moffit** has lost 70 pigs – hard on farmers. Cynthia was not quite as well as common. Jim Long and his family come to see if there were any beens.

*Charles Robbins, 14, son of Lewis Robbins
**Johnathan Moffit, 39, farmer, Guilford Twp, Hendricks Co., $10200/3614
***Levi S. Hadley, 45, farmer, brother in law of WMM

Monday, August 5, 1872

Cooler yet. 58F in the morning. Father and Aaron and Will and me hauled a load of lumber "walnut" from Chanderor's Mill to the depot. One of poplar to a vacant lot there in town to be out of the way. Will was not able to work after dinner. Father got Aaron and me an ax apiece. Aaron's cost 1.80 with handle and mine 1.65. Aaron helped Sumner thrash wheat in the evening. Pa and I went to Wilk. McCracken's* and sawed 3 cuts of a big oak. Rode home with Albert Hadley** who was breaking ground for wheat for Billy McCracken***.

*Wilkinson McCracken, 40, b. NC, Farmer, $3000/2000
**Albert M. Hadley, 40, farmer, $1000/150
***William McCracken, retired, 72, $8000/1000, b. N.C.

Tuesday, August 6, 1872

Warm day. Irv and Will hauled logs. Aaron helped Sumner and Dakin***

thrash wheat. Got done at noon. Father helped Will and Irv. I chopped

wood most of the time. Aaron chopped a while in the evening. Then we

hitched Jake and Doll to the wagon and hauled a load of wood to Jim

Crayton* and took the 2 log wagon wheels to Hill's shop to get the tire put

on. Cynthia is very hoarse. Mother got a letter from Aunt Hannah**. Aunt

has been sick a while back. Our axes chop very well. Aaron's is a little the

best to his notion. Ah.

*James M. Crayton, 36, shoemaker, Dem, Protestant
**Hannah Poe, Julia Ann Macy' sister
***Sylvester Dakin, farmer

Wednesday, August 7, 1872

A nice day. Will hauled logs from Cook's. Father and Aaron made a new barn door. I caught Jake* and Doll* and Kit* and father rode Doll to Uncle William Mills'*** to see about some walnut timber. I rode Kit to town to tell Aunt Lucinda** she need not come to help mother till tomorrow as the thrasher did not come. I also went to Sumners and got 20 sacks. After dinner Aaron and I cleaned off the barn floor and the grain boxes. Then we cut some wood. Ruth is still hoarse.

*Jake, Doll, Kit,--mules & horses
**Lucinda Macy Hadley, 54, sister of WMM, wife of Thomas M Hadley
***William C. Mills, 56, 1816-1899, farmer, $28950/5490, Julia Ann's bro

Thursday, August 8, 1872

Nice day, very warm. Cale Burris* and Co. thrashed our wheat and 110 dozen of oats, 162 bushels of wheat, and 87 ½ of oats. They were bothered by part of the machine getting out of order so it took all day. Two of the men put up for the night and 6 horses. Macy Hadley*** and Albert Macy**** and James Hunt** helped. Maggie Hadley***** come to help mother. Will Sumner****** and Tom******* helped. Irv's baby died and his wife is not expected to live. Will did not work. Terel and Mac and Cage helped on the straw. Maggie is going to stay all night.

*Caleb Burris, 49, farmer, b. OH, $1000/300
**James Hunt, 29, farmer
***Alvah Macy Hadley, 21, farmer, 1851-1924, son of Miles S Hadley
****Albert W. Macy, 19. son of Perry T Macy
*****Margaret Ann Hadley, 17, dau of Thomas M Hadley
******William P. Sumner, 33, teamster
*******Thomas C. Sumner, 40, farmer

Friday, August 9, 1872

Nice day, very warm. Some lightning in the north in the evening. Irv's baby was buried at Bethel. Aaron took a load of the folks down. Mother went to town and stayed at Rebecca's till they got back. Maggie went home. Ruth went to Uncle Ira's. Before they went home they went to Uncle Perry's, Aunt Rebecca* is sick. Father and I topped off the straw stack and fenced the oats stack. After dinner father went to town to see about the log wagon wheel. They are ready for use. The trees we cut are between the big woods and the big field.

*Rebecca, 39, 2nd wife of Perry Macy

Saturday, August 10, 1872

Very warm. Rained in the night and blowed some. Father and Aaron and me chopped and sawed wood. Cut down 3 trees and cut one all up and about half another and sawed off 5 cuts of another. Very hot work. We got a watermelen and a musk melen from the garden. A black cloud in the west. It's lightening considerable. Ruth got a kitten of Maggie yesterday. Is very pirt. Name "Katy". There was quarterly meeting at West Union but none of our folks went.

Sunday August 11, 1872

Cloudy and warm. We all went to meeting to town. There was no school. Had a good meeting. Uncle William* and part of his family come home with us. We had a nice time. They went home about six oclock. Rained about dark. Buried another pig in the morning. One dead in the branch lot. More sick. There is a peach tree whose fruit is ripening in the little orchard. There was quarterly meeting at West Union. About quit raining now 8 oclock.

*William Clarkson Mills, 1816-1899, Bro of Julia Ann Macy

Monday, August 12, 1872

Very warm. Rained 2 or 3 times. Will hauled a log from Cook's. Father went to Uncle Perry's* to see if he could engage any walnut trees but he did not. Uncle is very sick with the bilious stomach**. Father went back about dusk to sit up with him. Aaron and I cut and split what wood we could in the evening. Will got the wagon wheel and put them on. The tires are ½ inch thick. We buried a pig and fixed the road.

*Perry T. Macy, 47, one of the original 13 donors to the Quaker Academy and member of the Mooresville High School board of trustees, brother of WMM

**bilious stomach.... upset stomach usually includes vomiting

Tuesday, August 13, 1872

Tolerable nice day but very warm. Will and Irv hauled 2 logs from Cook's. Old Settler's Picnic. Aaron and I and Ruth went to it. Father was there a while. There was a great many present. I guess we had a good time, several old speakers. Maggie* come over and got 2 chickens and over a bushel of apples. We got the paper when we come home. The Martinsville band was at the picnic. Played very well.

*Margaret Ann Hadley, 17, cousin, dau of Thomas M. Hadley

Wednesday, August 14, 1872

Very cloudy, rained a little. Will and Irv hauled logs from Cook's. Aaron and I helped Uncle Thomas* and Fuson** thrash all day. Long's steamer did not get started till late. Some of us eat dinner at Tommy's and some at Fuson's. Aunt Lucinda*** and John*** and Huldah*** are not at home. They are at Charlottsville. Looked for them home but they did not come. Mother and Ruth and Lydia went to Uncle's to help the girls get dinner****. One of our boars is getting sick.

*Thomas M. Hadley, 62, farmer, alva's uncle

**John Fuson, 52, farmer, Independent, Protestant

***Lucinda Macy Hadley, 54, John, 11, Huldah, 8, wife, son, & daughter of Thomas M. Hadley

****This would be for the threshing ring workers

Thursday, August 15, 1872

Nice day, some cooler, heavy dew, did not get done thrashing. Aaron* went home last night and I stayed at Uncle Levi's**. Got done thrashing about 10 oclock. Aunt Lucinda got home. They went to Uncle Miles'*** from there. Mother and the 2 girls went to Levi's. Mother and Aunt Marguret**** went to see Aunt Polly, she is not expected to live overnight. Will Crayton***** died last night and buried today. Aaron and father sawed up a sugar maple and I trimmed part of it. Made 2 saw logs.

*Aaron Macy, 17, son of WMM
**Levi S. Hadley, 1826-1891, brother in law of WMM
***Miles S.Hadley, 1828-1911, brother in law of WMM
****Margaret Ann Macy, 1822-1899, sister of WMM, Wife of Levi S Hadley
*****William Crayton, 39, tailor

Friday, August 16, 1872

Nice day. Pretty cool. Irv and Will hauled logs from John Scotten. Father went with them. They brought a load apiece of ash lumber. Aaron and I chopped wood and split most of the day. Aaron went to Dave Farmer's and got some breeching which he made for us. As I hunted Doc up and cut his tail off to bleed him. He can hardly walk. Maggie Williard is very sick. Guess she has the fever. Father bought a figured tree of Scotten. Got a ripe watermelon and a muskmelon from the garden yesterday and a watermelon today.

Saturday, August 17, 1872

A nice day, very clear most of the day. Will and Irv hauled logs from Scotten's*. Father went to the depot to see a man by the name of Harden about some walnut logs. Aaron and I cut a small sugar down and cut it and split it up. It had a bumble bee's nest in the butt. We had to whip them out. I cut my finger with my ax just after dinner so I could not chop any more. I gathered a few peaches and apples. Father fetched a side of sole leather home. Cost $5.50. Huldah** and Emma*** come out in the evening.

*John Scotten, 59, farmer, b. NC, $2000/600

**Huldah P. Hadley, 8, daughter of Thomas M Hadley

***Emma M. Macy, 10, daughter of Ira C Macy

Sunday, August 18, 1872

A nice day. Sun rose and set beautifully. Emma and Huldah and Ruth and Lydia stayed at home. Us four went to school and meeting. Aunt Polly was buried today at Sugar Grove and Catharine Beeson* was buried this evening at the town graveyard. She had been weakly a long time. Ed Williard had a chill today. Maggie is better. We buried 2 pigs. Emma and Huldah went home in the evening. We had a watermelon in the morning. A man named Vestile wanted to hire but was refused. His mind is deranged.

*Catherine Beeson, 46, b. VA, wife of (William F. Beeson,47, b. OH, farmer, $12000/1200, Mooresville High School trustee)

Monday, August 19, 1872

A nice day, tolerable nice day. The horses got in the corn again. Will and Irv took our log wagon and the four mules and Nance and Doll and went to Scotten**** and put on a big log and broke the fore bolster and come home empty. Father took Comer's wagon home and took 15 ½ bushels of wheat to mill. Aaron and I hauled 5 loads of rails along that cornfield fence. Will Sumner* has bought Dakin's place ($6,000) "Thanks to Billy" Father and Sparks*** settled up and he settled with John Sanderson. Father sold 322 feet of poplar lumber to Eli Sumner.**

*William P. Sumner, 33, teamster
**Eli J. Sumner, 60, b. OH, Pattern maker, $ /6000
***William J. Sparks, 51, farmer, $6000/2500
****John Scotten, 59, farmer, b. NC, $2000/600

Tuesday, August 20, 1872

Nice day, very warm. Will and Irv hauled the log they left yesterday. Aaron and I hauled rails. I helped till noon then Father and I went to Uncle Perry's and helped thrash. Did not get done. I stayed overnight and Father went home. Long's machine*. Aaron hauled on in the evening. Terel worked for Bill Sumner. Aaron hauled 2 cords of wood to Joseph Butler and 50 cts worth to Mrs. Polly of Mooresville. Father bargained with Joe Butler - the planing mill for 20 acres of land --- -------.

*Long's machine is the steam powered threshing machine moving from farm to farm

Wednesday, August 21, 1872

A nice hot day. The thermometer stood at 94F at noon. Irv and Will hauled another big walnut log with 6 horses. Aaron went to the institute at town til noon. Then he went to Sumner's and got a hack bed and took it to Hill's shop and the running gears of the hearse. I went to Uncle Levi's with the machine and helped the rest of the day. They got done and went to Robert Harvey's*. Cynthia went to Sumner's in the evening.

*Robert Harvey, 60, b. OH, farmer, $12620/2453, Rep, Quaker

Thursday, August 22, 1872

Extremely hot till it rained about 4 oclock. We had a very nice shower.

Father went to Anderson's to see about some trees. Will got a coupling pole

and Jim* shod fore dinner. Aaron and I hauled a load of old lumber from

the new meeting house from town on the wagon we got of Moon. It is a very

good wagon. Father finished the trade with Butler****. Ruth rode Jake**

to town to put a letter in the office. I rode Kit*** to Uncle Levi's to borrow

some log chains. I had to go to Uncle John's for he had borrowed them.

Levi paid me 30cts for a days work.

*Jim the horse
**Jake the mule
***Kit the mule
****A planing mill for 20 Acres of land

254

Friday, August 23, 1872

A nice day, not quite so hot. Aaron and Will hauled logs from Scotten's. Aaron drove the horses. Father sold $60.00 worth of poplar lumber to Eli Sumner. I sold my old iron –come to 1.76. Ruth sold 25cts worth. They got the money safe in the bank this evening. Weight 4500 lbs. After dinner Father and I sawed off a log at the mill. Before dinner I nailed on some picket on the garden fence and mowed some weed along the young bottom fence. We had a musk mellon or two. Very good ones.

Saturday, August 24, 1872

A very nice day. Pretty warm. Aaron and Will hauled logs from Scotten's. Mother and I went to monthly meeting. Had a very good meeting. Rebecca Clawson was granted a request to visit the poor house of this county and appoint meetings in some of the adjoining counties. John Hadley*come home with me. I finished the garden fence. Aaron got 6 snaps at town. Cost 50cts. We had a mellon in the morning. Ruth went to Uncle Perry's after we come home on Jake.

*John J. Hadley, 11, cousin, son of Thomas M. Hadley

Sunday, August 25, 1872

A very nice warm pleasant day, some signs of rain. Mother and father and Lydia went to school and meeting. Ruth stayed all day at Uncle Perry's and come home late in the evening. Mother and father went to the association and night meeting. Aaron was not well in the morning. John and I stayed at home. Lydia stayed with us in the evening. We had 5 or 6 mellons. Father got his new shoes last evening which Terel* made. He got 12 lbs. of nails at town.

*Terrill Carlisle, 62, b. NC, farm laborer

Monday, August 26, 1872

Very hot. Rained about 5 oclock very hard and hailed some. Will and Aaron hauled 4 walnut logs from Zimri Allen's*. Father went as far as William Long's. He bought a walnut tree of Long**. I went with them to Allen's. Rained a little before we got home but we did not get much wet. John Fogleman*** turned 2 yearling calves in the mule lot and killed one this evening. I got its tongue and part of its liver. Cage and Ed helped Mitchel thrash wheat – but that is none of my business and the thermometer was at 98F in the SHADE.

*Zimri Allen, 71, farmer, b. NC $7000/4000
**William K. Long, 50, b. KY, farmer, $6000/1300
***John Fogleman, b. NC1827, M/C1848, farmer-butcher, Dem, Methodist, $1000/500

Tuesday, August 27, 1872

A little cooler but not pleasant yet. Father and Aaron and I builded a dry house all but shingling and making the riddles. It is 6 x 8 ft square. Going to have a stove in it. Will did not work. There was a temperance mass meeting at the Friends church. Ruth went I guess and there was a public speaking in town about politics of course!! Fogleman come to butcher his other fatling but it had escaped from the lot. And he knew not wither it went. Reverend Butler got 10 bushels of oats 25cts.

Wednesday, August 28, 1872

Commenced raining at 6 oclock in the morning and rained pretty steady about 3 hours and then it quit and cleared off. Father and mother and Aaron and Ruth went to town in the afternoon. Mother went to trade. She bought a pair of shoes for herself. (3.10). Goods and groceries of Sheets* amounting to 5.37. Ruth went to finish the load. They fetched the 2 stoves home and a few other things. Aaron went back and took a load of wood to Will Carlisle** and Isaac Shelly***. A peck of pairs and a peck of peaches got 25cts for pears , 10cts peaches. Fogleman put 3 steers in pasture.

*Fredrick Sheets, 49, b. VA, dry goods Merchant, $9750/10900
**William Carlisle, b. NC1805, M/C 1833, Rep, Methodist
***Isaac Shelly, b. 1844, confectioner

Thursday, August 29, 1872

A nice day to take it all over. Very cloudy and rained a little in the morning. Mother and Cynthia went to Uncle Levi's to help them quilt. Father finished covering the dry house. Johnson come here and cleaned 61 bushels of wheat and did not get done either. He has a patent fanmill. He follows this as his business now. Turned much cooler since the rain. Will come over and got a chicken for Fanny. Aaron and I got on Kit and Bet and looked at the water gaps. None of them were down. Some of them had holes under them. That's all.

Friday, August 30, 1872

Not such a cool day as it was. A person needed a coat and shoes (58F). Will and Aaron hauled logs from Scotten's. Johnson cleaned 32 bushels of wheat in the morning. 93 bushels in all. 7cts x 93bu = $6.51. He stayed here all night. Father laid the floor in the dry house and put the stove in it and fixed the place for some riddles. I went to town and got some stove piping. Cabe Burris*, Caleb's son, was turning some of the cogwheels and caught his right thumb between them and tore it to pieces, had to cut it off at the doctor's office in town. Took Shelly 1 3/4 peck of pears—Got one shoe put on Bet and one on Kit.

*Caleb A. Burris, 13, son of Caleb Burris 49, b. OH, farmer

Saturday, August 31, 1872

Cool day. Will and Aaron hauled 4 logs from Scottens*. Jake** fell down and broke a hame so they had to borrow one which was hard to do on this occasion. They were late getting home. Father sold the big field of corn to Dave Fogleman*** for five hundred and fifty dollars. 11 dollars an acre. He fixed the shelves in the dry house and got 4 bushels of peaches in and a fire in the stove. Did not get the door hung. Joe Edwards was here about noon. He said that Huffie run off on the sly. No loss.

*John Scotten, 59, b. NC, farmer, $2000/600

**Jake the mule

***Dave Fogleman, b. NC1828, M/C 1833, farmer-stock trader, $3250/5200,son in law of
    Samuel Moore, founder of Mooresville, IN

Sunday, September 1, 1872

A nice day, tolerable cool. All went to meeting but Aaron and me. Aaron's throat is very sore. I kept fire in the dry house and Ed watered the mules and whipped out a bumble bee's nest in the barn. I got stung just under my eye. Aunt Lucinda* and Aunt Aachiah** and Hulda* and Emma**, we had a big bait of water and musk mellon. Wayne*** come down in the afternoon. Ruth's pig died this morning. Took sick last night. Will**** come in the evening. We filled 3 scaffolds with peaches and finished picking all the trees.

*Lucinda Macy Hadley 54, & Huldah 9, family of Thomas M. Hadley
**Achsah Johnson Macy 38, & Emma 10, family of Ira C. Macy
***Wayne C. Hadley, 18, son of Levi S Hadley
****William Carlisle, laborer

Monday, September 2, 1872

Cool and pleasant. Will hauled one log from Scottens's*. He got home about 4 oclock. Father and Aaron took 6 double shovel plows to Billy Carlisle** to get sharpened and 2 to Taylor*** to get the legs put on new or new legs. Got 3 single trees fixed up. Took 2 bushels of pears to Shelly****. They fetched some stripping to put on the dry house and 3 plows. Wayne went home about 9 oclock. Fogleman***** killed 2 beeves today. He wants them for the fair. Will Sumner****** come over to see about our hogs getting in his corn. Will took Nance and Jim******* and went to town to be ready for the trip.

*John Scotten, 59, b. NC, farmer, $2000/600
**William Carlisle, 67, b. NC, blacksmith, $2800/300
***Thomas Taylor, 56, wagon maker, b. OH, M/C 1869
****Isaac Shelley, 28, confectioner
*****John Fogleman, 35, butcher
******William P. Sumner, 32, farmer1/2 mile W of Mooresville
*******Nance and Jim are horse & mule

Tuesday, September 3, 1872

Nice day, some cloudy. Father ceiled the dry house and raised the stove pipe some. Now it gets much hotter and we can dry in the loft. Will did not go to Indianapolis because Billy did not get the money to pay for his coal. He sowed wheat in the big field and Aaron and Ed and I plowed in. Cage* plowed after dinner. It's very bad plowing. The foxtail is very tangled (scary in some places). Will got 8 bushels of wheat on four acres (for that was all we plowed) where he should have got five. Pa says that will not do. The fair commenced ---- ----- ------- -------

William Elliot was married to Elderadofranciseodoriaprasisnodder today.

*Cager Carlisle, 16, farm laborer, lives with William Carlisle

Wednesday, September 4, 1872

A cloudy and sultry day. Aaron and I plowed in wheat all day and Jeff and Cage half day. Will sowed half day. Becca took much worse and sent for them. Father sowed in Will's place. Ed is sick, got the chills. Mother went over to Irv's. There is a good deal of sickness in the surrounding country. We got some over a bushel of dried peaches out of the house. Gravel Road* got $2.40 worth of lumber to make a culvert. Terel got 24 cts worth of quinine. We got 10 or 12 mellons out of the garden. Gathered about a little wagon load of peaches after we quit work.

Elias Andrew was married to a Mendenhall today----wish them much joy.

*Mooresville Monrovia Gravel Road Company, maintained the toll road which is now IN 42

Thursday, September 5, 1872

A nice day. Rebecca died this morning about daylight. We all went to the fair but father and Lydia. The fair was hardly as good as last year. I went to a show and seen an alligator and a few other curiosities. Mother went to Irv's in the evening. We got a brass kettle at Rusie's** tin shop ($1.25). They had some very nice horses but very few cattle and hogs. Father cut peaches and tended to things about the house. Aaron bought some pencils. They had a good many stands there (140 – 190). Uncle Levi*** got father a suckling mule.

Monroe Staley* married a Britton. (Josaphen Britton, 22)

William Johnson married Hannah Keller,16.

*Monroe Staley, 33, son of Hiram Staley, 67, both farm laborers

**John H. Russie, b. VA1834, tinner, Russie & Richardson

***Levi S. Hadley, 1826-1891, Farmer, ¾ mi W of Mooresville, Brother in law of WMM

Note:

After much study of "Irv Moser" who appears continuously as a farm laborer, the following revelations are tantalizing..

>>>Rebeca, daughter of Terrill Carlisle married Joseph E Moser 3-31-1861 in North Carolina. Terrill's family was still in NC in 1870.

>>>On 7-29-1872, "Irv had a son born unto him"

>>>On 8-8-1872,"Irv's baby died and his wife is not expected to live"

>>>on 9-4-1872, "Becca is much worse and sent for them"... "Mother went over to Irv's"

>>>on 9-5-1872, "Rebecca died this morning about daylight"

>>>On 9-6-1872, "Irv is going to live with Gabe"

>>>Joseph E Moser must have been Joseph Ervine Moser and Alva Macy spelled the nickname as he imagined it, Irvine

>>> since so many of these people had the same first name, a preponderance responded to their middle name.

Genealogy is more like detective work than science!

.

Friday, September 6, 1872

Very warm. Looks a little like rain which surely will come pretty soon.

Rebecca was buried at Bethel at ten oclock. Aaron took the hack to town

and took some of their folks. I took the wagon and took all that were over

here but Ed and Mag. She chilled. Irv is going to live with Gabe. Aaron got

half dozen glass cans ($1.40) and fetched the plows home. We cut 2

bushels of peeches and put them in the dry house and took out about a half

bushel of dried. Father went to town and measured some lumber at

Comer's* Mill which he had sold. Come to $318.00.

*Mathew Comer, b. 1826, sawmill owner, Rep, Methodist

Saturday, September 7, 1872

A nice day. Father went to Indianapolis to pay off an insurance debt. He

bought a brass kettle up there that holds 5 gallons for three dollars and 90

cents. Would have cost five dollars here. Aaron and I cut peaches and

filled up the dry house about a half bushel. We cut some apples. A man

come here and wanted to buy peaches for 30cts. We don't sell that low. He

went his way. Macy Hadley *come down this very evening. We hauled up a

load of peaches within the morning. Ed and Terel went to the Sanderson's.

*Alvah Macy Hadley, 1851-1924, son of Miles S. Hadley

Sunday, September 8, 1872

A very warm day, clear nearly all day. We all stayed at home. We got about a bushel of dried peaches out of the dry house then we filled it up with green ones or new ones. Will Andrew come over in the morning to see how we were getting along. Will** and Irv*** were over here the same time Andrew was. Uncle John* and Aunt Lydia* and two of their children come a while after dinner. Uncle hurt his foot on a nail pretty badly. They have got their house nearly done. Macy and them went home about six oclock. I made a whip.

*John F. Hadley, 32, & wife Lydia Ann Macy, 38, sister of WMM. JFH was one of the original 13 donors to the Quaker Academy

**William Carlisle, laborer

***Irvine Moser, laborer—perhaps Ervine Moser?

Monday, September 9, 1872

A very nice day, only sultry. We sowed wheat till noon. Irv and Aaron, Cage and I plowed. Will** sowed, father tended to the dry house, Lonzo* went down and tried to buy Irv's colt. He wanted 50 dollars and Lonzo would not give but 45 so they did not trade. Come up a little shower just after dinner then we watered our horses and concluded to wait a while. In about a half an hour commenced again and rained and blowed very hard. Father paid Will five dollars and Terel ten. A man by the name of Harden was here. He bought 17 pigs of father.

*Alonzo Hadley, 1857-1925, cousin, son of Mary Ann Macy Hadley

**William Carlisle, farm hand of WMM

Note 6 men working today Irv, Aaron Macy, Cage, Alva Macy, Will, WMM

Tuesday, September 10, 1872

A nice day. Only not much wind stirring. Aaron and Irv, Cage, Jeff and I plowed. Will sowed. It was very nasty work till nearly noon. It was so wet we could not go only a round at a time without resting. Charlie got the thumps* very badly. Fogleman** killed a beef this evening. Father cut peaches and helped about the house. Will took Jim and Nance and the wagon to town. He intends on going to the city in the morrow. Irv and Wes are going with him. We got to the oaks and fetched our plows up.

*"Thumps" is a symptom similar to hiccups probably due to dehydration.
**John Fogleman, 45, butcher, Dem, Methodist
Note 7 men working today Aaron Macy, Irv, Cage, Jeff, Alva Macy, Will, WMM
Note: Charlie, Jim & Nance are work horses

Wednesday, September 11, 1872

A cloudy day. Rained about 3 oclock then stopped and commenced about 5 and rained till dark. Will and Irv went to the city. We all stayed about the house and gathered peaches and cut them. Aaron and Ruth and I went to town to the wedding of William Hadley and Hattie Fuson* at the residence of the latter. They took the car at the depot and went to Charlottesville for their honeymoon. Several present. Molly Hadley and Lewis Hoskins were the waiters. Fogleman killed another beef. Cage borrowed 2 corn knives. He was going to cut corn for Samuel***. William Macy Hadley** married Hattie Fuson* at 3 oclock.

*Hattie Fuson, 20, school teacher, dau of John Fuson
**William Macy Hadley, 1845-1882, cousin, son of Lucinda Macy Hadley
***Samuel Moore, founder of Mooresville

Thursday, September 12, 1872

More rain about noon and sprinkled some occasionally. We got about a bushel of peaches dried and about a peck of dried pears. After we got the house filled we hauled rails and made a fence across the 7 acre field and turned the fatling hogs in there – on the north side. I dug a bushel of potatoes after dinner. Will and Irv hauled rails to the orchard fence. Fogleman killed another beef. Father bought the steer of John Greeson*. Give $26 for him. Mother made some peach pickles. Terel mended my boot and put eyelets in Ruth's** shoes.

*John Greeson, 40, farmer, b. NC, $8600/9215
**Cynthia Ruth Macy, 11, Alva's sister

Friday, September 13, 1872

Clear and cool. Wes and Irv hauled a load of wood to Mrs. Polly** (paid 1.60) and another to Rebecca Greeson* fore dinner. We got about a peck of pears and about a bushel and 3 pecks of peaches (dried). After dinner Irv hauled rails from the bottom to the orchard fence. While father and Aaron and Will and I reset it. John Hadley got 2 chickens for dinner tomorrow. Mr. & Mrs. Hadley have returned. Jim Levy is on a big drunk spree again. Irv hauled Will a load of wood. Lydia has the headache pretty badly in the evening.

*Rebeca Greeson, 45, b. NC, head of household
**Anna Polly, 32, wife of Stephen Polly, printer

Saturday, September 14, 1872

A nice day. Some cooler. Will and Irv loaded a car with walnut lumber. They hauled the lumber from Comer's mill. Will sprained his foot in the bargain but he worked. Irv got a bushel of dried peaches. Father and mother went to Uncle Tommy's***. They had a big dinner there, 47 were there for dinner. Pa got a barrel of H. Johnson* (.25) and a comb (.45) and a pick parer of Gregory** (1.50). Aaron and I cut peaches and apples and moved some lumber and fixed a better place to put the boards on that hold the peaches.

*Holman Johnson, b. KY1817, M/C1862, dry goods merchant, Rep, Methodist,
    $10000/10000
**Abner B. Gregory, 29, druggist, $7700/3500

***Thomas Marshall Hadley, 1810-1893, husband of Lucinda Macy Hadley

Sunday, September 15, 1872

Got a very nice day again and a bushel of dried peaches too. We all went to meeting. Hugh Woody was there and another minister or two. Jes Young and Howard. We went to Uncle John's*** after meeting. They have remodeled their house - put an addition to it with 2 rooms down and 2 room upstairs and a kitchen. Aaron and mother and Aunt Lydia*** went over to see Hannah Bray* who is very sick. Aaron stopped at Levi's. Stayed with them. Lydia** was sick a little while in the evening. Joe Edwards come and took dinner while with Levi (what of it).

*Hannah Bray, 81, wife of John H Bray
**Lydia Andrew, 3, "adopted" daughter of WMM
***Lydia Ann Macy Hadley wife of John Franklin Hadley, 1840-1898

Monday, September 16, 1872

Cool dewy, very heavy dews now. Will and Irv cut corn in the west field. I took one of our old mowing scythes to town to Billy* and had 2 corn knives made. Father cut corn till I got back then he went to the house and fixed handles on them. Aaron come home in the morning and filled up the dry house and cut peaches and apples. After dinner us there that cut corn went to the speaking at the train ground. Thomas Brown was the speaker (Republican of course). Aaron went to town in the evening on business told hereafter.

*William Carlisle, b.NC1805, M/C1833, Rep, Methodist

Tuesday, September 17, 1872

A nice cool day. Irv and Will cut corn in the west field. We each one cut across at the north end (22 shocks). Aaron and father tended to the dry house and went to mill. Joseph come and got Jim and Kit to plow a while. This is Ruth's birthday. She had a party of little girls and boys, namely Ida H., Emma M*., Ira H.**, Huldah H.***, Malinda H.****, Mattie E.*****, Ira H., Willie H.******, and Tommy H*******. I guess they had a very good time. Ruth was 11 years old. It was Jane Edward's birthday too. Mr. McNutt******** spoke at town tonight and he's a democrat is what he is. Will and Irving cut two bushels.

*Emma Macy, 11, dau of Ira C. Macy
** Ira Hadley, 9, son of Levi S. Hadley
 ***Huldah Hadley, 8, dau of Thomas M .Hadley
 ****Malinda Hadley, 21, dau of Levi S .Hadley
 *****Mattie Edwards, 4, dau of John Edwards
******William Hadley, 12, stepson of Perry T. Macy
*******Thomas Hadley, 11, stepson of Perry T. Macy
********Cyrus F McNutt, 34, lawyer, $7000/6500

Wednesday, September 18, 1872

Cool and cloudy. Drizzled some through the day. Aaron and I cut forty shocks. Will* has got sorty dissatisfied about working here. Irv nor him neither worked. Mother went to meeting. Got some over a bushel of dried apples and about half bushel of peaches. Aaron went to mill in the evening after we quit work. Two pigs died today. Belonged in the mule lot. Spoon and Mac put up 32 shocks in a day. Ed is poisoned with the corn or something else. His face is swelled up and red, they tie with broom corn.

*Will Carlisle, farm laborer

Thursday, September 19, 1872

Cool and pleasant. Mother and father and Ruth and Lydia went to White Lick to Hannah Bray's funeral. Uncle Henry Bray was there. Aaron and I cut corn from ten oclock till noon and from 3 till 5. Got 28 shocks. Hiram Cope* cut 16 shocks. He only worked today. He has took his horses off our pasture. Ruth gathered some of our popcorn in the evening. Terrels cut corn for Fogleman. Terel's baby is sick too. Will said he had another chill last night. Father cut peaches and tended to the dry house.

*Hiram Cope, b.OH1821, M/C1864, farmer, Methodist, $ /300

Friday, September 20, 1872

A nice day. Pretty cool. Heavy dew. Will sowed wheat till noon, then he plowed and father sowed. Jeff and Aaron and I plowed. We plow the other way from what we were plowing. It plows much better where the corn is cut up. Got about 2 thirds bushel of dried peaches and the same of apples. We turned the steers into the mule lot in the evening. One of Jeff Davidson's* sons died very suddenly after dinner. Jeff and I buried her. Aaron took Linzy Poe** a load of wood. Got a barrel of Jonathons*** (.25).

*Jeff Davidson the sow
**Linzie H Poe, 39, b. NC, butcher, $400/100
***Johnathon apples

Saturday, September 21, 1872

A tolerable warm and cloudy day. Sprinkled some in the morning. Aaron, Cage, Jeff and I plowed wheat all day. Will sowed till noon then father sowed. Made some sign. A cat got in the house last night and on the bed it went. And Pa got hold of it and went to throw it out at the door when it scratched him on the hand. Got about a bushel of dried apples and a peck of peaches. Ed was sick again. Fogleman was over here. He took out shocked corn and paid Terel.

Note: 6 men working- Aaron, Cage, Jeff, Alva, WMM, Will

Sunday, September 22, 1872

A nice day and a warm day and a pleasant day and a cool morning and warm noon and a sickly time generally. None of us went to school but Ruth. She had a chill while she was there and come home before meeting. Molly Mills and Melinda and Ida Curnut and Johnny and Belle come here this morning and stayed all day. We had a very nice time. We hunted rocks and shells along the branch and eat peaches and cut peaches for the dry house. Lydia and Belle had an uncommon good time. Lydia* had a light chill after they went home.

*Lydia Jane Andrew, 3, lived at WMM's house, daughter of William Andrew

Monday, September 23, 1872

A nice warm day. The same old wheat sowers around and Ed and Irv besides. We got to the corner of the orchard. Wes and Terel cut corn in the west field. Father cut peaches and tended to the dry house. Peaches are nearly all gone. After we quit work, Cage and I went to Mike Wilson's* to borrow his wagon for Will Carlisle's future use. We come back through the woods and got some papaws and then come through several bur patches. Did get plenty of burs and Spanish neddles.

*Michael M. Wilson, 33, b. NC, M/C1865, farmer, $3900/2450, 1 ½ mi SW of Mooresville

Tuesday, September 24, 1872

And another cloudy day. And the plow boys had full sway. We finished the big field about 10 oclock and went into the west field. It is much better plowing in the latter. Father tended to the dry house. Ruth** chilled in the night and had high fever most of the night. Will Sumner* come down to tell us about our climbing pig which was out in the road. We put it in with the fatlings.*** We had got 3 of 4 rounds when the black cloud gave good signs of rain and we got to the barn in a hurry. Rained a good big shower.

*William P.Sumner, 33, teamster

**Cynthia Ruth Macy, 11, sister of Alva Macy

*** a fatling is an animal being fed for slaughter

Wednesday, September 25, 1872

School again. All three of us went. Chawner and Isaac Jones**and Mary R. Hadley are the teachers. We stayed till noon then come home and Aaron and I and Jeff plowed what wheat in that there was left on the field. About 3 acres. I plowed Bet* and Aaron – Fanny* and Jeff – Doll*. Will and Irv took a big notion and took three of our horses and Moll* and took a wagon load of people to Monrovia to the big Greely speaker. G. W. Julian was the speaker. Got about a bushel of peaches and nearly a basket of apples.

Mary Carlisle*** married James Crayton**** today.

*Bet, Fanny, Doll, Molly, the horses
**Isaac Jones, 50, b. OH, teacher, $7000/700
***Mary Carlisle, 24, dau of William Carlisle, blacksmith
****James M. Crayton, 36, shoemaker

Thursday, September 26, 1872

A nice cool day. Will and Cage and Jeff and Ed and Aaron and I plowed in wheat. Pa sowed nearly all day. Will sowed a while after dinner and I plowed Bet and let my nag stand. We got nearly to the walnut. I went to town in the morning and got a box of pills for Ruth (.25). She has nearly got the fever. Father went to town and got a (Febrofug?????) for Ruth. Cost (30cts). Mary Carlisle married James Crayton last night. Frank Herman* was killed by a team of horses running away which he was driving.

*Frank Herman, 17, part of Elwood White household
Note 6 workers today   Will, Cage, Jeff, Aaron Macy, Alva Macy, WMM,

Friday, September 27, 1872

Considerable frost. Got done sowing wheat a little before dinner. Will did not have to work but about 2 hours fore dinner. After dinner him and Irv hauled wood to town. They hauled to Crayton** and one load to Sparks* and one load to McVay***. Ruth is getting better. Aaron and I went to school in the evening. Terel and his boys cut corn in the new ground. Aaron went to town after school and got ½ gallon of coal oil and 5cts worth of cheese. It's better for Ruth. My studies are Algebra, Latin, Physiology and Grammar.

*William J. Sparks, 51, farmer, $6000/2500
**Alexander H. Crayton, 41, tailor
***John McVey, 58, b. NC, carpenter, $800/150

Saturday, September 28, 1872

Very cloudy. Almost steady south wind blowing. Will and Irv hauled 2 cords sugar wood to Thompson Woodard and Co. and a half cord to McVay and half cord to Will, one cord to Billy Carlisle and one load or half cord to Joe Hutton and 2 other loads to town and one load home. Aaron and I cut corn in the new ground. We both cut ten shocks apiece. The corn is tall and tangled. Terrell and his boys cut corn in the same piece and Wes. Father went to Joseph's. I went to Uncle Tommy's after we quit.

Julia Elma Thompson, daughter of Oswell Thompson died today.

Sunday, September 29, 1872

Rained in the night. Very cloudy most of the day. I did not go to school or meeting. I got a physiology book of Maggie*, borrowed it. John and Aaron Mills** come home with me. Aaron was in town and we met him and just come over. We had a great deal of fun. Charlotte Jenkins given in marriage yesterday at meeting. I do not know her intended. Mother and father went to meeting. Aunt Lucinda and Aunt Acksah went to Bethel to meeting. Aaron and Johny went home in the evening. It is sprinkling rain now and 8 oclock in the night.

*Margaret Ann Hadley, 1854-1922, cousin, dau of Thomas Marshall Hadley
**Aaron H. Mills, b.1860, John H. Mills, b.1843, sons of William Clarkson Mills

Monday, September 30, 1872

Tolerable pleasant. Will nor Irv either one worked. Guess they went to the

speaking at Monrovia. That's the way. Father gathering the pears. Aaron

and I went to school. Four more new scholars in our room. I guess school

went off all right. Ruth stayed at home, she was not well enough to go.

Emma Hadley* fetched the spinning wheel home. She stayed 2 or 3 hours.

Aaron went to Uncle Perry's** to see about getting a book but did not get it.

*Emma Hadley, 21, dau of Elias Hadley
**Perry T. Macy, 45, brother of WMM

Tuesday, October 1, 1872

A heavy frost in the morning. Will and Irv took six horses and hauled a log from Scottens*. About the time they got to the road gate Will*** took sick and told Irv to go on to the barn with the team. He kept getting worse and could not get to the house. He layed on the ground an hour or so. He finally got here and almost died. He cramped all over and vomited. He is some better just now. Aaron and Ruth and I went to school. Father gathered some apples. We had one more scholar in our room.

Mary Neese, wife of John Neese** died today of Typhoid Fever. She was 26 years.

Apple cutting at Aunt Patsy Mills' but I wasn't there.

*John Scotten, 59, b. NC, farmer, $2000/600

**John R. Neese, 36, b. NC, planing mill operator, $1000/350

***Will Carlisle, farm laborer

Wednesday, October 2, 1872

A little warmer than usual. Will was much better this morning. He was very sore. He went home. Father and Irv hauled a log from Scottens. Took six horses. Mother went to town and got $5.21 worth of goods at Woodard's. I gathered about 2 bushels of apples. Lydia stayed at Terrel's while mother was gone to town. Aaron dug about 2 bushels of potatoes. Physiology is nice, Latin is hard, Algebra is a vexation. We had two visitors and one new scholar.

Thursday, October 3, 1872

A nice day. Tolerable warm. Father and Irv hauled a log from Scottens and then come home and took 4 horses and hauled some lumber about the mill. We all went to school. Wayne* and Ella** and Lottie** come home with us. We killed two chickens for breakfast. Aaron gathered about a bushel of apples. The school was adjourned to get to the Quaker wedding at the meeting house. The fair at Indianapolis is now going on.

Henry Millhouse married Eliza Harvey in Meeting.

Cousin Noah Hadley married to Susannah Cook – he didn't invite anybody.

*Wayne Hadley, 8, cousin, son of Levi Hadley
**Ida Ellen Macy, 10, Charlotte L. Macy, 15, cousins, dautrs of Perry Macy

Friday, October 4, 1872

A nice day. Tolerable warm. We all went to school. Irv hauled a log from Scottens with six horses. Will come over but did not work. I heard that Alva Hadley was married yesterday but do not know sure. Father gathered some apples. Fogleman* killed a beef. Terrel cut some corn. Aaron and I pulled a few apples after we come home. Aaron got his watch of the silversmith but it does not run regular. Fogleman* has got one more steer in the pasture.

*John Fogleman, b. NC1827, M/C1848, butcher, Dem, Methodist, $1000/500

Saturday, October 5, 1872

Looks like Indian summer. Very warm and pleasant. Irv hauled a log from Scottens. Father and Aaron and I gathered about 30 or 35 bushels of apples. John D. Carter* and (Goam) and Ellis Conduitt (Frecky) speak at Mooresville tonight. Aaron and I killed two kittens, about 5 old cats and kittens ought to be killed. Terrel has bargained for a house with Samuel Moore**. He went over and cleaned it up today. Is to pay six hundred for it.

*John D. Carter, b. NC1811, M/C1822, farmer, Republican, Quaker, 1 ½ mi SE of
    Mooresville, $27300/3000
**Samuel Moore, retired merchant, b. NC1799, Founder of Mooresville,

Sunday, October 6, 1872

Warm in the morning and cool in the evening. We all went to Albert

Mendenhall's*. We had a very nice visit. Rila Moon and part of his family

were there. Elias and his girl have stayed there since they were married.

Martha** and Albert have been sick. It rained about noon and drizzled a

good deal of the afternoon but very slow and fine. I went with Elias and

some young folks to West Newton. I got a good bait of black hands. They

have a walnut tree by their milk house.

*Albert Mendenhall, 40, farmer, $8950/2600
**Martha Mendenhall, 29, b. OH, wife of Albert

Monday, October 7, 1872

Some cooler. Rained some during the night. Terrell moved to his house in town, Will Sumner* hauled them over. Had 3 loads. Aaron and I hauled them a load of wood and took some of their chickens. Joe Edwards come and brought Jim** and Kit**home. Father and Aaron and I gathered apples nearly all day. Ruth went to school. Terrell has a nice big lot but not such a good house. If he just had it paid for. Irv didn't come over.

*William P. Sumner, 33, teamster, ½ mi W of Mooresville, $/500
**Jim & Kit are work Horses

Tuesday, October 8, 1872

Voting day and quite warm. We all went to school. Lydia had a slight chill.

Father was about town all day. He settled up with Ben Perce*. Perce come

out 35 dollars behind. He paid father 10 dollars. Pa hired Al Clap** (20)

dollars per month. He will not come on for about a month. Four new

scholars this week so far. Fogleman killed another beef early in the

morning. Father got Cynthia a new double slate. Cost 40cts. Aaron got 10

cts worth of paper at Pool's*** & Hadley.

*Benjamin H. Perce, 34, b. MI, carriage painter, $3000/1000
**Alson Clapp, 23, b. NC, farm laborer,
***Joseph Pool, 36, druggist, $5500/5000

Wednesday, October 9, 1872

Nice day, warm and pleasant. Father worked with the apples part of the day. Terrell and 4 of his boys gathered apples. Father went to town to see Stephenson***. I changed seats with Ken Carter today. His seat was lower than mine. A man from Martinsville come to see father about some walnut logs but father was at town. Charity Mills and Ella Hadley and Huldah Hadley** come home with me. Robert H. Bishop* was married to Phenieyes ?????. Went to Minnesota.

*Robert H. Bishop, 26, RR clerk, $200/175
**Huldah Hadley, 1863-1889, cousin, dau of Thomas M. Hadley
***William L. Stephenson, 39, brick manufacturer, $300/500

Thursday, October 10, 1872

A nice day. Tolerable cool. We all went to school. Cynthia said she had a chill. Pa went to Martinsville. Lydia* had a light chill in the morning. Mother went to town and left Lydia at Huttons**. She got me a suit of clothes ($7.60) and some other things. 25cts worth of coloring notes and some garters (.15). Terrell picked up apples to make cider of. The mill was not in order so he did not get to make any. (Algebra) OK

* Lyddia Andrew, 3, adopted dau of WMM

**Joseph P.Hutton, b. NC 1839, M/C1869, toll keeper for
    Mooresville Monrovia Gravel Road Co., Dem, Protestant

Note: The toll gate for The Mooresville Monrovia Gravel Road Company was located on
    WMM's land between his home and White Lick Creek

Friday, October 11, 1872

Cold and frosty morning. The thermometer was 29F in the morning. Spoiled lot of late peaches. The water froze in the pan about one fourth inch thick. Father was at Martinsville nearly all day. We went to school. Aaron took the log wagon to Shrake's shop (Macy wagon) and one of the wheels of the other wagon. Took the big mules. Terrell made about a barrel and a half another of apple cider. One of the sows has pigs, all dead but 2, (9) at first. Bridge* has 5 missing children.

*Bridgeport the sow

Saturday, October 12, 1872

Nice day. Pretty cloudy and very big frost. Father and Aaron took 20 bushels of apples to Tom Taylor's*. Ed Dickenson** dug potatoes. I gathered apples and made some cider. (about ½ barrel) Ed got 20 bushel of potatoes for his work. Father and Aaron hauled about 65 bushel of potatoes and put in the cellar. Father got the wagon wheel fixed. I dug potatoes after dinner. Aaron Mills*** come down here in the evening.

*Thomas J. Taylor, b .OH1815, M/C1869, wagon maker, $2000/300
**Edward Dickenson, 37, b. KY, head sawyer @ Sawmill, $ /700
***Aaron Mills, 1821-1908, brother of Julia Ann Macy

Sunday, October 13, 1872

Pretty cool. Heavy frost. Aaron and mother and Lydia went to White Lick and to Uncle Perry's* after meeting. Father was about home all day. Aaron Mills and Ruth and I took a ride to Joe Edwards. We stayed till about four oclock and then come home. It snowed just a little. Uncle Henry Bray is in the settlement now. Guess he come to see about some of his father's business. Will Andrew** come over in the morning. He wanted to hire.

John Elliot married Miss Lucy Mcnak

*Perry T. Macy, 1825-1889, WMM's brother
**William Andrew, 28, teamster, previous employee of WMM

Monday, October 14, 1872

A pretty cool day. Some ice in standing water. We went to school. Two new

scholars. "Patia Breedlove and one of Joe Newby's girls". Will Andrew

helped father gather corn in the evening. We had a high time at noon

playing prison base. There was a beautiful aurora in the evening.

Deweese* come over in the evening to see if he could not buy some of our

mules. Did not come to any trade or make any offers.

*William Dewees, b. OH1837, M/C 1856, farmer, 1 mi W of Mooresville, $4500/1400

Tuesday, October 15, 1872

About the morning that fetched the leaves in a hurry. Father hauled a cord and fourth to John Mills*($3.15) and one load to William Bunnell**. He got 100 brick of A. Gregory ***(.15) to make a wall across the front of the sitting room fireplace. Lady**** has 6 pigs. Guess all of the other sows' pigs are dead, think the other hogs layed on them. The steers got the yard fence down somehow and got in the little orchard. I guess they had to get out again.

Charley Mills***** started for Texas today. He is going to peddle sewing machines---wish him good success.

*John H. Mills, 28, farmer/carriage maker, $4380/970

**William W. Bundle, b. KY1821, M/C1847, engineer, Rep, Methodist

***Abner B Gregory, 27, druggist/merchant, Rep, Methodist, $7700/3500

****Lady the sow

*****Charles H. Mills, 1848-1932, cousin of Alva Perry Macy, son of William Clarkson Mills

Wednesday, October 16, 1872

Cool and pleasant. Not quite so cold in the morning. Father hauled ¾ cord of wood to Mills' and 2/3 of a cord to Bunnell. He made a water gap for the hogs down to the bayou. We turned 5 more hogs with the fatlings. Bridgeport and Lady eat up all of Lady's pigs. Guess that is what has went with all of the pigs. We turned Aaron's sow in the little orchard. Dickenson's children* dug the rest of the potatoes, 20 bu. Father and Aaron hauled them up and we put them in the cellar.

*Edward Dickenson's children are 14, 12, 9, 7, & 4 yrs old

Thursday, October 17, 1872

Rained in the night some. Pretty warm in the morning. Did not rain much after daylight. We all went to school. Father went to Lewis Robbin's* to see Clapp. Guess he will not come till December. He bought two walnut trees of Moon and one of Will Deweese. Fogleman killed a beef and has 5 more in the pasture. I do not know when he turned them in. Aaron and I laid up the rails along the stubble (oats) fence. Anybody that can keep a Latin book clean must have clean hands.

*Lewis Robbins, b. OH1833, farmer, $14000/2500, 1 ½ mi S of
   Mooresville, current employer of Alson Clapp

Friday, October 18, 1872

A nice day. Tolerable cool. We all went to school. Father hauled ¼ cord of wood to Dorland* and Azar Johnson** ¾ of a cord. Wayne*** come home with us. We went up in the big woods and got some papaws. Ruth went to Levi's and got some lye to put in the blue dye. Fogleman killed a beef. Malinda Hadley****come and got Levi's chain. Emma Swamp lectures at the Methodist house (church). Subject: womans's rights etc.

*Edwin H. Dorland, 30, b. NY, hardware merchant, $3300/5700
**Elazar Johnson, 28, farm laborer
***Wayne C. Hadley, b.1854, cousin, son of Levi S Hadley
****Malinda J. Hadley, b. 1851, cousin, dau of Levi S Hadley

Saturday, October 19, 1872

Cool and pleasant. Aaron and I hauled three loads of pumpkins from the new ground and two loads of corn from the field below the barn. Father went to Moons to the sale. Did not get a cow. Got the promise of one of Tom Amick**. Several of the pumpkins were frozen and soft so they would not do to put away. A few very large ones. Achsah* and Ira* and Ora* come over about dark. Ira and Ona and Ruth*** are having a big time playing in the house. Killed a couple of chickens.

**Thomas O. Amick, 43, b. NC, farm laborer, $ /900
* Achshah, 16, Ira W., 9, Ora R. Hadley, 12, cousins, children of Levi S. Hadley
***Cynthia Ruth Macy, 11, sister of Alva Perry Macy

Sunday, October 20, 1872

Warm and pleasant. Some wind stirring. All went to meeting but Cynthia and Father. She had a chill and fever the rest of the day. Elwood White* said Frank Herman** was mending fast. His leg was healing up all right. Aaron and I went to Uncle Levi's after dinner. I went with Richard Mitchell*** to Uncle Perry's. Aunt Mary and Dickey Hadley's folks were at Perry's. Nobody was at home but Wayne and Richard. Melinda and Ella were at Perry's. Our visitors went home early in the morning.

*Elwood White, 38, farmer, ½ mi N of Mooresville, $19000/1200

**Frank Herman, 17, lives with Elwood White family

***Richardson Mitchell, 19, son of George W Mitchell

Monday, October 21, 1872

A nice day. We went to school, that is we boys. Ruth was not well enough to go. Father hauled 1 load of wood to Snoddy*, 5 loads to Dorland. Got 25cts worth of lime of Charley Wilson. I got a letter from Albert. Said he was doing well. He likes to stay there very well now. They started a game of baseball today at school. I don't believe I will belong. Plenty of other players, yes scrub will do for us little boys. Fogleman killed a beef. I got the heart to take to school to explain physiology with.

*John M. Snoddy, 39, physician, $5200/1000

Tuesday, October 22, 1872

A nice day to be raining. Did not rain much after noon. Aaron and I went to school. Ruth stayed at home. Father hauled one load to Terrell, one to Snoddy, one plus one (2) to Fansler* and three fourths of a cord to Samuel Moore***, three fourths of a cord to Azor Johnson and one load home and one load to William Ferguson**. Father took the log wagon to the blacksmith's shop. Mother went to town in the evening. I got a cap for 75cts. and a pair of suspenders for 50cts. (1.25) Mother got 14cts worth of cheese.

*David Fansler, 48, b. NC, M/C1849, wagon maker, $2500/500, Rep, Methodist
**William Ferguson, 46, b. NC, farmer, $ 520
***Samuel Moore, founder of Mooresville

Wednesday, October 23, 1872

Cool and clear. Some frost. Father went to town in the morning to see Sam Harriman*. He built part of the wall across the fireplace in the front room. We took the bureau that was standing in front of the fireplace upstairs. Aaron and I fixed the fence that extends from the meadow to the corner of the little orchard. One of the steers got out. We went to school and Ruth staid at home. Latin is pretty hard about now. Algebra not very easy.

*Samuel Harryman, b. VA1795, M/C 1837, chair maker, veteran of the war of 1812. Rep, Christian, $500/150

Thursday, October 24, 1872

A nice day. Clear nearly all day. Father fixed up the fireplace and put the stove up. So we are sitting in here by a large stove with a "bully" fire in it. Father is laying on the floor by the stove and Aaron is reading the Tribune. I took a half a gallon of lard to Aunt Achsah****. I went back in the evening and got some stockins. Aaron got a dimes worth of paper. Billy Carlisle*** wanted to buy some corn. Did not sell any.

Nattie Williams* was married to Maria Shanafelt** (and a big shiveree)

*Nathaniel C. Williams, 24, son of Isaa Williams
**Maria A. Shanafelt, 19, dau of Mary Shanafelt the milliner
***William HH Carlisle, 27, domestic servant, $ /150
****Achsah, wife of Ira C. Macy

Friday, October 25, 1872

Some cloudy and very warm. Looks like it would rain. Father hauled wood.

Two loads of sugar wood to Sam Moore, two to Billy McCracken*, one sugar

the other round and rough, one to Terrell, one to John Shrake**, one to

Tom Taylor***, one to Fansler****, one to John Elliott*****. We all three

went to school. School passed off alright for anything I know. We had a

short lecture on cider in the morning by ------- and ---------.

Uncle William Mills returned home from Kansas Yearly Meeting.

Milow Moon's house caught fire and burned a good deal of his property up. I

guess it caught by a spark. He is living with his father—Stanfield.

*William McCracken, b. NC1800, M/C1833, retired grocer, $8000/1000
**John Shrake, 36, blacksmith, $600/150
***Thomas J. Taylor, b. OH1815, M/C1869, wagon maker,
****David Fansler, b. NC1823, M/C1849, wagon maker,
*****John Elliot, b. NC1821, M/C1858, laborer,

Saturday, October 26, 1872

A nice day of course. Cloudy most of the forenoon but shine after dinner.

About 3 of us gathered 7 loads of corn and pumpkins. Mother went to

monthly meeting. All went to Uncle William's but Aaron and I. Uncle

William* arrived home yesterday. He has been to Kansas yearly meeting.

There was some talk of a little excursion of the grammar department (one

part of it) taking a two horse wagon load anyhow to the hickory flats

northwest (do not know what it amounted to).

*William Clarkson Mills, 1816-1899, brother of Julia Ann Macy

Sunday, October 27, 1872

Tolerable warm. Looks smoky along the horizon. Must have rained a little in the night. The ground was some wet, worse than dew anyhow. Aaron and I stayed about home all day. We stirred off some wax after 12 oclock. Joe Edwards come down or up or over in the evening. They got home a while before dark. Went to Uncle Miles'* after meeting. Said Johnny Mills** cut his foot pretty badly a while back. Cut it nearly in the instep. Guess the hickory nut party got one or two bushels.

Hugh Nichols died and was buried at Bethesda He lived in Illinois – had palpitation of the heart.

*Miles S. Hadley, b. 1828, farmer, $9000/2200
**John H. Mills, 28, farmer, $4380/970

Monday, October 28, 1872

Clear and cloudless. Big frost in the morning which brought an abundance of leaves down. Will Johnson* come and hired in the morning. Do not know how long him and father hauled logs from Zimri Allens**, one to Rubottom's mill and two to the depot. He went home after work was over. We went to school. Aaron and I were tardy. Aunt Rebecca**** come down to see if she could not get some yarn colored but as mother was done coloring she did not get any colored.

*William Johnson, 37, b. OH, farm laborer
**Zimri Allen, 71, b. NC, farmer, $7000/4000
***William L. Rubottom, 44, steam powered sawmill, $2000/2000
****Rebecca H. Bowles Hadley Macy, 39, wife of Perry Macy

Tuesday, October 29, 1872

The night was cool and clear. The wind was gently blowing. There was not much frost. Will hauled a log from Allen's. We went to school. Jackson come over here to see about buying the house. Father was about Stephe's* brick kiln a good part of the day. He sold the house in town to Harra Jackson for (1800) eighteen hundred dollars. $625.00 down. $875.00 in notes. $150.00 in one year and $150.00 in two years. I don't much like the trade.

* William S. Stephenson, b. 1835, brick maker

Wednesday, October 30, 1872

Raining a good part of the day. Johnson did not come. Dave Keller* come and hired, 1.00 per day. Him and father gathered 2 loads of corn and hauled a load of things from town. A cupboard and some barrels and other things. Clinton went to Illinois with his mother. I do not know when he will come back. We had considerable rioting in the house and therefore we got a lecture. Such will be the case on rainy days. I went to Uncle Levi's after school.

Harvey Chandelor was riding a young horse, it reared up with him and fell back upon him. It hurt his back and stomach, perhaps serious.

*David W. Keller, 21, farm laborer, son of Michael Keller

Thursday, October 31, 1872

Cool and clear. We went to school, that is Wayne and me. Johnson did not work. Pa and Dave hauled a load of wood to Albert Rardin and one to Mr. Page** and a load (3/4 cord) in each load. They got some shoes put on Nance* and Charley* (by Shrake). They hauled 2 loads of corn and pumpkins. Fogleman or his "hired help" hauled new rails from the new ground to the mule lot. He is going to fence off a part of it to feed his cattle in. Makes it from the ash tree by the spring to the orchard fence.

*Nance & Charley the horses
**William Page, 27, farmer

Friday November 1, 1872

The ground was frozen considerably and a big frost with it. Father and Dave

hauled corn. They put it in the log crib by the upper barn. Will hauled a log

from Allen's. We went to school. Cynthia stayed at home to take quinine.

Said she had a chill yesterday. I did not have a good latin lesson at all. It

was in pronouns. I got Albert Tansey's* drawing book, think some of buying

it, expect not though.

*Albert W. Tansey, 16, son of Jesse Tansey

Saturday, November 2, 1872

A nice day, pretty cool. We killed a hog in the morning. Father and Aaron and I scalded it and Pa cut it up and salted it away. Will hauled a log from Allen's. He got home at noon. Joe (I call him) and Aaron and I hauled corn. Will helped in the evening. Ruth went to Joe Edwards*, she stayed nearly all day. Martha** come home with her. Stephenson was here to buy the land of ours north of town but did not make any deal.

Boston caught fire somehow and was not stopped till it had burned over two hundred millions worth of property. This almost equaled to Chicago. It burnt up the main part (70 acres of houses burned).

*Joseph H. Edwards, 39, b. VA, farmer, $17850/535
**Martha A. Edwards, 11, daughter of Joseph Edwards

Sunday, November 3, 1872

Cool and pleasant. Father and mother went to meeting. We stayed at home and Ruth* and Mattie** had a pretty big time. Cynthia* had a chill after they come home but very light. Aaron and I rode Jim and Kit and Cynthia and Mattie rode Doll nearly to Joe's. Father put part of the steers in the barn lot. He kept the biggest ones in the mule lot. He bought 2 steers of Frank Troglin***. (60.00). Fogleman has got 4 or 5 steers in here.

*Cynthia Ruth Macy, 11, sister of Alva Perry Macy, 15
**Martha A. Edwards, 11
***Benjamin F. Trogdon, 25, farmer, b. NC, $800/800

Monday, November 4, 1872

Tolerable cool   Aaron and I went to school. Cynthia stayed home but she might as well have went. She thought she might chill but did not. Will and Dave gathered corn. Father went to Jessie Hadley's* and traded or sold the land to George Stephenson who was at Jesse's. He was to get $1700.00. But he has to wait with Stephenson. After dinner Pa and mother went to town, got some grinding done and consequently we had mush for supper. Mother got some stuff for -------.

A company of women and 2 men poured about a half barrel of whiskey into the street for a man that had been selling the liquor to the boys in town the Saturday night before at the Grant** rally. Hurrah for the women. It made the scamp look a little pale.

*Jesse Hadley, 54, b. NC, farmer, $10200/2714, in Guilford Twp, Hendricks County
**Ulysses S. Grant, b.OH1822, President of USA, running for 2nd term

Tuesday, November 5, 1872

Rained through the night and drizzled through the day. It was a good election day. The farmers could not work. Father settled with Thornburgh*. Paid him $96.13. Aaron and I went to school. We had a visitor in the evening. I did not know him. Aaron went to Uncle Levi's. There is one more new scholar downstairs. Cynthia stayed home. Will and Dave went to Monrovia to vote. Of course they did not come here.

*J. H. Thornburgh, 51, Merchant and farmer

324

Wednesday, November 6, 1872

More slow rain in the night but did not rain in the day. Will and Dave worked.

Will hauled logs from Allen's and Dave hauled gravel on the gravel road***.

Fogleman tore down two of the corn pens to make the cross fence of.

Father bought 13 trees (walnut) of Newton Hadley*. Give ($200.00) for all

and 16 of Uncle Levi** ($260.00) and 2 of William Mitchs' not long since

and one of Uncle John sometime since.

A train was thrown off the track by a board being across the rails

somewhere below Vincennes. Killed the engineer and fireman and

completely demolished the engine. As it happened none of the passengers

were hurt. I guess the board was put there by a rascal who was mad about

the road.

*Newton Hadley, 40, farmer, $6000/1225
**Levi S. Hadley, 45, farmer, $18690/3000
***Mooresville Monrovia Gravel Road...forerunner to State Road 42

Thursday, November 7, 1872

Cool and pleasant. Very clear in the night. Will did not come. Dave*****

plowed and hauled on the road. Father hauled one load to Billy Carlisle***

and 2 to McVay*. We all went to school. Chawner gave a very good talk

about profane language. This is literary night. Huldah** come home with

Cynthia. Lee Chandler**** has quit school. I guess on account of his

father's unfortunate fall. I guess Clinton has quit too.

*John McVey, 58, b. NC, carpenter,

**Huldah Hadley, 1863-1889, cousin, dau of Thomas M Hadley

***William Carlisle, b.1805NC, M/C1833, blacksmith, $12800/300, Rep, Methodist

****Lee J. Chandle, 18, son of Harvey Chandle, 44, saw mill operator

*****David W. Keller, 21, laborer, son of Mark Keller

Friday, November 8, 1872

Cool and pleasant. Very clear. Considerable big frost. Will hauled one from Allen's to Rubottom's* and one load of lumber to the depot. Dave and father gathered corn out of the sandy bottom. Husked two loads and jerked one. Burris (Kale)** come and borrowed the stirrups and the new wagon. Meeting at the Friends meeting house. We had a visitor at school in the afternoon, Dr. Harvey. I guess he went to meeting and then come up to school. We had a nice game of ball at noon.

*William L. Rubottom, 44, runs steam powered saw mill, $2000/2000
**Caleb Burris, 49, farmer, b. OH, $1000/300

Saturday, November 9, 1872

A pretty cool morning and a big frost. Quarterly meeting day. Father and mother and Aaron went to meeting. Cynthia and Lydia stayed at home. Dave and I gathered 2 loads of corn out of the sandy bottom. Susan Jones and her daughter come home with them. They have come in from Iowa. Johnson come but did not work. I went to town after we quit work and got a couple of slates and some hinges which are too large and I will take them back I expect.

Sunday, November 10, 1872

More frost. Ground frozen some. Cloudy most of the afternoon. We all went to meeting. Mrs. Jones went to Mr. Wilson Rooker's after meeting. Several good sermons preached. Quite a number of people there. Lydia went home with her father after meeting, has not brought her back yet. We arranged things upstairs a little better in the evening. Moved both beds and put the bureaus in better places. A man with the name of Garner had a meeting appointed at the meeting house this evening.

Monday, November 11, 1872

Rain in the night and cloudy and drizzly till noon then cleared off and was nice in the evening. Dave hauled as follows—

One load to Joe Page, two loads to Terrel, two to Billy Carlisle, one to McVay, one to Johnson.

I swoped the hinges for some smaller ones and paid up. Father went to town. The fatling hogs got out last night. Aaron put them back. They are about out of corn and water. Will did not come. We quit writing today and read after this. They write downstairs.

Tuesday, November 12, 1872

About the same temperature. Father went to the lawsuit, has not come home yet. Dave and Will hauled 2 logs (6 horses), one to Rubottoms and one to the depot. I took my boots to Terrel. His boys gathered corn in the field below the barn. One more new scholar. The reading was conducted by Mary R. Hadley. They had a big rally in town last night. Fogleman killed a beef. John Spoon*cut his foot very badly with the ax. He was out in the country and hobbled home.

*John Spoon, 27, farm laborer, $450/100

Wednesday, November 13, 1872

Rainy from daylight till noon. Cloudy all this afternoon. Will hauled one log to Rubottom's and a load of lumber to the depot. Father and Dave hauled corn till dinner. Aaron and father drove the fatlings up to the oats stubble and turned them in. They hauled them a load of corn. They hauled one load to Linzie Poe*, one to Bill Ray** and one to ------. Just moved today to town, one to Joe Hutton***. I took my boots to Terrel to get them regenerated. Terrel's boys husked corn for Moon.

*Linzie H. Poe, 39, b. NC, butcher, $400/100

**William H. Ray, 53, harness maker, $ /500

***Joseph Hutton, b. NC1839, toll keeper Mooresville Monrovia Gravel Road Co, Dem, Protestant, $ /100

Thursday, November 14, 1872

Snow in the evening and the thermometer was at 24F in the morning.

Father and David hauled wood. One load to Ferguson*, 2 to Azor

Johnson** Mendenhall*** one. They hauled one load of corn. We put the

apples in cellar. Good many rotten. Cynthia went to Uncle Ira's in the

evening and stayed all night. Bill Bunnell***** come over here to get

father to haul him a load of wood. Harvey Chandler**** had a load of

wood hauled from the crick.

*William B. Ferguson, 46, b. NC, farmer,
**Eleazor Johnson, 28, farm laborer
***Asa Mendenhall. 36, farm laborer
****Harvey Chandle, 44, $300/150, runs sawmill
*****W. W. Bundle, b. Ky 1821, MC1839, Engineer, Rep, Protestant

Friday, November 15, 1872

More snow but light. Kept on by spells all day. The wind was very keen.

Dave hauled one load of wood to Dick Woods. He paid for it. One load to

Thomas Taylor*, two loads to Bunnell***, one to McVay, one to Bill Elliott.

Father was about town all day. We all went to school. Aaron and Cynthia

were tardy. Johnson did not come. Father put the cellar doors on in the

evening. I took the White Pippins** out of the dry house and put them in

the cellar, just a barrel.

*Thomas J. Taylor, b. OH1815, M/C1869, wagon maker,

**Pippins are 'the prince of apples'

***William Bundlel, 51, b. KY, $400/150, stationary engineer

Saturday, November 16, 1872

Snowed more in the night, it is about two inches deep. The thermometer was at 19F in the morning. Dave hauled four loads of wood to Bunnell, two to Albert Rardin and one to Raford Arnold*. Father got Aaron and I some overcoats and boots. Aaron's coat was $9.00 and boots $6.90. My coat was $16.00 and boots $6.90. This looks like an outrage ($38.80). He got $1.20 worth of window glass. Joe Edwards come up and got his hames***. Mike Wilson**wanted father to furnish a team on the road next week (to work it).

*Raiford Arnold, 71, b. NC, carriage maker, $1500/200

**Michael M. Wilson, 33, b. NC, farmer, $3900/2450

***hames, a portion of horse harness

Sunday, November 17, 1872

Colder still. 13F in the morning. Some cloudy. We all went to school and meeting. Not so very many there. Preacher Hiet was there and spoke once or twice. We come home after meeting and kept the stove warm. Thawed a little in the evening. Our pumpkins are all frozen so that we will have to feed them out before they thaw. Riley Garner had an appointed meeting at the White Lick school house in the evening and has one at Bethel tomorrow.

Monday, November 18, 1872

Still pretty cold. 20F. Beautiful clouds in the morning and evening. Will and father hauled one log from Stanley's. David hauled gravel on the pike*. Aaron and father measured the "Big Field". Just 46 acres and 112 rods. We all went to school. We had a visitor. I do not know his name. He was there all day. We are reviewing Latin and Arithmetic. Lydia had another chill. I guess it is because she won't keep warm. She can't be still long enough to get good warmed.

*The 'Pike' is the MOORESVILLE MONROVIA GRAVEL ROAD, a toll road which has become Indiana State Road 42

Tuesday, November 19, 1872

Cloudy in the morning. Commenced snowing a while before noon and snowed slow and steady till dark and is still snowing. Dave hauled gravel from the creek from above the bridge to a hill yon side of William Harvey's*. Will hauled 2 logs from Elwood Stanley's**. Father got Jake shod at Carlisle's. Shod him on three feet. We went to school. Clinton has started again. His mother lives in town. We had a tolerable nice game of fox and goose at the last recess. Mush for supper. Good old mush.

*William Harvey, b. OH1830, M/C1830, farmer, $3150/1000, Rep, Quaker, 2 ½ mi SW of Mooresville

**Elwood Stanley, 36, farmer, $4450/900

Wednesday, November 20, 1872

Only 8 above OF this time. Pretty clear most of the day. Johnson did not come. Dave and father hauled a load of corn to the fatling hogs. They hauled 2 loads of corn out of the sandy bottom. Fogleman killed a beef. They shot it 5 times before they killed it. They had to get a lantern of us to see how to butcher it. They come and got our gun but it would not go off. They have not got done yet and it is 20 minutes after seven.

Thursday, November 21, 1872

Warmer again. Very cloudy most of the day. Father and Dave hauled Terrel a load of wood and gathered 2 loads of corn. Johnson did not come. We went to school. One visitor there, Miss Kellum. Aaron and I went to the addissonian*. I spoke a declamation. Had a pretty good time. I let a boy have my knife today and he let a couple of fools have it and they broke the little blade by playing with it on the floor. They have bought a few more books for the add library.

*addissonian....your guess is as good as mine! Can't find in dictionary.

Friday, November 22, 1872

Damp and chilly. Sleeted in the night. Very cloudy all day. David and father hauled one load of wood to Terrel and two loads to Raford and four to Tom Taylor*. Dave bought him a pair of gloves. (.15). Caldwell quit school today at noon. Do not know what he quit for. Two or three lamps were setting on the table or desk of the instructor when it was thrown over and the oil spilt and ink spilt and a general mess was made.

*Thomas Taylor, 56, b. OH, wagon maker, $2000/300

Saturday, November 23, 1872

Frosty and cool. Very cloudy and smoky most of the day. Dave and Aaron and I gathered 3 loads of corn. Father only helped one load, then he and mother went to monthly meeting. It thawed a good deal during the day. Jeptha Davidson* come over to get a load of wood but did not get it. We put the corn in the crib in the front of the house. Johnson did not come. Suppose he thought it was too muddy.

*Jeptha Davidson, 38, cooper, $ /150

Sunday, November 24, 1872

Cloudy still. Thought it would rain but it did not. We all went to school and meeting. Went to Uncle Tommy's* after meeting. The old folks went to the association in the evening. The younger set stayed there and took 3 or 4 games of author cards. Me and my partner got 2 games in. They have 3 boarders. Cynthia and Hulda** went to Uncle Ira's. This was Charlotte's last day as a ------.

*Thomas M. Hadley, b. NC1810, M/C1824, Rep, Quaker
**Huldah Hadley, 8, cousin, dau of Thomas Hadley

Monday, November 25, 1872

Warmer in the morning. Pretty cloudy. The wind a good part of the night. Dave and father gathered 2 loads of corn and hauled one load of wood to Hutton and one to Mr. Davidson. Aaron and I went to school. Cynthia stayed at home to take care of a bad cold. Mother and Cynthia made a tub full of cider out of some never fails that we did not gather. Maggie* come home with me. I am going to knit a comfort for her maybe.

*Maggie Hadley, 1854-1922, cousin, dau of Thomas M. Hadley

Tuesday, November 26, 1872

Clear and warm. Dave and father gathered corn. Two loads. We all went to school. Maggie went home as we went to school. Johnson did not make his appearance here. Fanny "mule" has hurt her foot pretty badly. Guess it is snagged. She can hardly walk. School was dismissed at half past 11 oclock to go to Charlotte Jones' wedding at the meeting house. The one room was full. Levi Jessup was there and a few other monthly preachers.

John Stout married to Charlotte Jones at the meeting house in meeting, of course. Several present besides all the high school.

Wednesday, November 27, 1872

Considerable colder. Mercury was at 19F. We all went to school. Father

and Dave and Aaron took 16 hogs to town in the morning. Sold them to

David Fogleman**. Fetched one hundred fifty one dollars and fifty five

cents. Pa and Dave gathered 2 loads of corn. Will Sumner* come over last

evening to see Fanny's*** foot. Did not find her as it was after dark. Think

it is a nail in her foot. She is extremely lame.

Charlotte Stout and her Sunday school class had their pictures taken

(except 2 or 3) at Calvert's Excelsiar Gallery. There were 13 of us.

*William P.Sumner, 33, teamster, $ /500
**David Fogleman, b. NC1828, M/C1864, farmer/stock trader, Rep, Methodist, $3250/5200
***Fanny, the horse

Thursday, November 28, 1872

Colder than has been lately. The branch was frozen over so that it would bear a person up almost anywhere. Father and Dave gathered two loads of corn. They cleared out the other pen and put the corn in it. I carried water while they were clearing the pen out in the morning. Fido* goes with the team that gathers corn every day. He caught a mouse, the first one by him. Will Johnson** did not come.

William Beeson's*** house caught fire from a broom which had been used about the fireplace. It burned the house to the ground with nearly all the furniture and the barn and all its implements. Very sad news.

Ella Thompson, daughter of Oswell Thompson died of croup. She was a loving little child only 4 or 5 years old. It almost broke the father's and grandmother's hearts.

*Fido the dog

**William G. Johnson, 37, b. OH, farm laborer, $ /500

***William F. Beeson, 47, b. OH, farmer, $12000/1200, trustee on the Mooresville High
    School board

Friday, November 29, 1872

Down to zero and one below. The creek was frozen over so that it would bear a horse and wagon. They did not work. Dave went home to stay till Monday. Elwood MacMellen, the family exhorter came around at about half past three oclock and talked or preached about 15 minutes. Cynthia did not go to school. Father bought 85cts of coffee and 15cts worth of oil of spike* for Fanny.

*Oil of Spike - made from lavender for skin medication

Saturday, November 30, 1872

Not quite so cold. Three degrees above zero. Johnson came but did not work. We did get cold cut up some wood and set in the house most of the time. Father and mother went to Aunt Mary's*** in the evening. I went to town and got two ounces of zepher. John Hadley* come home with me. Isaac Shelly** has some deer meat and flounder fish at his restaurant. Horace Greeley, a man of great genius died of exposure, anxiety, and loss of sleep. He was buried in New York City

*John J. Hadley, 1860-1937, cousin, son of Thomas M Hadley
**Isaac Shelly, b. 1844, confectioner/restaurateur
***Aunt Mary Ann Macy Hadley, 1831-1889, widow of Albert Hadley

Sunday, December 1, 1872

December day one was a snowy one and got dark early. We did not go anywhere. John* stayed till evening. Ed Williard come over about noon and went home about the same time as John. I plaited a whip for him. We went skating a little on the branch but the ice had so much snow on it, was not much fun. We put the horses in the stalk pasture below the barn. (Jim too)

*John Hadley, 11, cousin, son of Thomas Hadley

Monday, December 2, 1872

Rained in the night and thawed a good part of the snow off. I believe it turned a little colder in the evening. Father went to town and got 75cts worth of strychia to kill the rats which are getting too thick about the house and $6.00 worth of stuff for clothing. I guess Johnson did not come. Alson Clapp* come out in the evening. We took the mares and hack down to Robbin's** to get his trunk.

*Alson Clapp, 23, b. NC, farm laborer, live in, new hire of WMM
**Lewis Robbins, 39, b. OH, farmer, Clapp's previous employer, 1 ½ mi S of Mooresville, $14000/2500

343

Tuesday, December 3, 1872

The rising sun was very beautiful. Just above the trees was a bluish cloud, nearly horizontal. Above this the sky was red and above the red, blue. So it was very beautiful. It was nearly the same when it set, only alternate striped of red and bluish color. Dave and Al and Father gathered 3 loads of corn. We chose up yesterday and commenced passing and analyzing in earnest today (in grammar). One party jardes against the other.

Wednesday, December 4, 1872

Not quite as unpleasant. Some warmer of course. Guess our horses has got this horse disease which has been sent upon nearly all the middle and southern states. They cough and hack as though they had the distemper. It does not kill many unless they are worked while they have it. They gathered corn, I mean father and the hired men. We went to school. The game of "shinny" is winning.

Thursday, December 5, 1872

Very nice, not very cold. They finished the new-ground field and jerked one load out of the west field. Dave hauled a load of wood to Joseph Cummin's* yesterday. Fogleman has 2 steers in here now. We turned the milk cows and Fogleman's steers into the orchard. They were eating Dave Fogleman's corn. Nance** and Doll** cough considerable. I suppose they will all have it. It don't affect the mules as much as the horses.

*Joseph Cummins, b. NC1820, M/C1856, marshal/farmer, $12000/1000, Dem, Methodist
**Nance and Doll are horses

Friday, December 6, 1872

Pretty big frost in the morning. They pulled 4 loads of corn. Father built a corn pen north of the old orchard in the big woods. Joe Hutton* come and got the sausage grinder. He has killed his two hogs. Aaron went to North Branch to a series meeting which is going on. He went or was to go with Uncle Levi's. Cynthia went to Levi's or Perry's. I took my boots and Cynthia's shoes to Terrel in the morning.

*Joseph Hutton, 33, b. NC, farm laborer

Saturday, December 7, 1872

Just about right for gathering corn. We gathered six loads. Aaron come home in the morning. Cynthia come home in the evening. They both staid at Levi's. Father bought a scoop shovel ($2.00) of Dan Sheet's*. Dave went home after work was over. Al was not very well in the morning. Ausbury Thompson's** wife borrowed our sausage grinder. Nance*** has got the "epizoodic", the worst now. She runs at the nose a good deal.

*Daniel Sheets, 46, b. VA, dry goods merchant, $9750/10000
**Berry Thompson, 52, b. NC, farmer, $500/100
***Nance is a horse

Sunday, December 8, 1872

Pretty warm in the morning. Not even down to freezing but it got cloudy and turned cold and especially the wind whistled around through every crack in the house it could find. Father and mother went to meeting. Cynthia went to Sumner's in the afternoon. She got about a gallon of buttermilk of Ira. We turned all the horses into the orchard and then watered.

Monday, December 9, 1872

Pure cold. 10F above 0 with a piercing wind blowing. Dave did not come. Father and Al did not work. Father got some soda. Cara Monicle* has quit school on account of her health. Pa got 7cts worth of paper. Cynthia did not go to school. She thought it was too cold. Kit is running at the nose a good deal. The rats are getting our little chickens. Try to poison them.

*Cary Monical, 19, dau of James W. Monical, 44, farmer

Tuesday, December 10, 1872

A little colder. Wind did not blow much. Father and Al cut logs at Newton Hadley's* (walnut). We all went to school. Boss the dun cow had a calf in the morning. We were nearly out of milk. Black does not give only a pint or so. Lydia** is breaking out with the mettle rash or something else as bad. Did not commence hurting her till after she went to bed. She cries all the time. Large welts raise on her legs.

*Newton Hadley, 40, farmer, $6000/1225, 2 ½ mi SW of Mooresville
**Lyddia J. Andrew, 3, adopted dau of WMM, bio dau of William Andrew

Wednesday, December 11, 1872

Damp and chilly. Snowed a very little. Dave come and they gathered 5 loads of corn. Father's hands are cracked very badly so he cannot work very fast. The creek was frozen over very solid and smooth. Some of the boys went skating at noon. There was a large halo around the moon last. Perhaps it will rain or snow. Guess not much the matter of Lydia. She is laughing and just now wanted to hear Dave*** bray. She never heard the critter.

John Hutton* married Margaret Plunket**.

*John Hutton, 22, son of Elizabeth Hutton
**Margaret Plunket, 20, dau of Eli Plunket
***Dave, the mule

Thursday, December 12, 1872

Pretty cold. A very large frost in the morning. Before the frost melted the weeds and trees looked like they are adorned with diamonds and jewels. They finished gathering corn "U r e k a". Pa said he was very tired after they got done. Aaron come home after the last recess to finish writing his paper for the Society. I gave my contribution to Ella as she has one part of the OK. We intend to go as I am writing before I go.

Louisa Pool*, wife of Joseph Pool died. She has been weakly a long time. Will be buried December 14

*Louisa Pool, 35, wife of Joseph Pool, druggist

Friday, December 13, 1872

Pretty cool, cloudy most of the day and frost. Father and Dave stacked some lumber at Comer's* mill. Sold some culls (3409 ft.) to Mr. Likely. Al got the wood from the walnut tops at Newton Hadley's**. Hauled it to McVay. (three loads). We got through the physiology and commenced reviewing. Fogleman killed another beef. We got the feet to make oil of. Society done very well last night, not very many performances.

*Mathew Comer, b.1826, saw mill & lumber, Rep, Methodist
**Newton Hadley, 40, farmer, b. IN, $6000/1225

Saturday, December 14, 1872

Some warmer. Most warm enough to rain. Cloudy all day. Father, Dave and I worked with the lumber at town. Hauled some from Chandler's* Mill to where they stacked it up. Aaron fixed up the cow trough and made a barn door. I killed the old gobbler. Weighed 17lbs. extremely fat. Joseph and Sarah come about 10 oclock. Joe went into town and Sarah stayed till he come back.

*Harvey Chandle, 45, saw mill operator

Sunday, December 15 1872

Very nice day. Pretty cool. We all went to meeting. Father and mother went up to Mr. Pool's a little while before meeting. Said they were going to keep the corpse (Louisa Pool) till Wednesday next. We went to Uncle Perry's* after meeting. They were not home when we got there. Father and Ruth and I went to hear Alcana Beard lecture on the heathens of India. He exhibited 2 idols. God of love and God of wisdom.

*Perry Macy, 47, brother of WMM

Monday, December 16, 1872

Snowed some in the night. Seemed like the sun didn't get up till almost 8

oclock. Father and Al finished building the fence between sandy bottom

and the field Jones tended. After dinner they cut a sugar that was standing

by the G. R. (gravel road)* in sandy bottom and worked part of it into wood.

Cynthia** did not go the school. She was not very well.

*Mooresville Monrovia Gravel Road Co., toll road
**Cynthia Ruth Macy, 11, sister of Alva Perry Macy

Tuesday, December 17, 1872

Pretty cold. Some cloudy. Dave and Al cut another tree close to where they

cut one yesterday. It fell across the road. Father stayed at home and

helped about and fixed the hearth's which the rats have worked loose.

Lydia had a chill. Mother and Aunt Achsah* were at school part of the

evening. Father boiled the beef hoofs again today. Guess will not boil them

any more. Did not boil them yesterday.

*Achsah Macy, 38, wife of Ira C. Macy

Wednesday, December 18, 1872

Pretty heavy snow about 2 inches deep. Dave**** and Al**** cut wood.

Father helped them a while and then went with Mother to the burial of Mrs.

Pool. The high school was dismissed and went to the meeting house which

was very full. We were examined in physiology. Larken Macy*** from

Wayne County (my cousin) and Malinda Hadley* and Ellen** and Ida

Eurnet came here from meeting. The rhetoric and physical geography

classes were examined.

*Malinda A. Hadley, 9, cousin, dau of John F Hadley
**Ida Ellen Macy, 10, cousin, dau of Perry Macy
***Larkin Macy, 29, son of Mary Macy
****David W. Keller and Alson Clapp, laborers

Thursday, December 19, 1872

More snow! Pretty cloudy in the morning. A halo around the morning. There has been several halos lately. Cynthia and Ida* and Malinda** stayed at home. Larken*** went with us to school and stayed till recess then he come back here and stayed till evening. Him and Ida and Malinda went to Uncle Levi's. There is to be a social party at Uncle Perry's. Guess I will not go. Dave and Al cut wood. Father stayed about home. Snow is about 2 inches deep.

*Ida E. Macy, 10, cousin, dau of Perry T. Macy
**Malinda A. Hadley, 9, cousin, dau of John F. Hadley
***Larkin Macy, 29, cousin, son of Alva J. Macy

Friday, December 20, 1872

Very disagreeable. Sleeted enough in the night to make a tolerable thick crust on the snow. Dave and Al and father cut wood. They found an opossum in a hollow sycamore – killed it of course. School was out today. Good many there. Among the visitors were our Erlham Friends. Albert, Henry, Maria and some others I did not know. Evan Hadley from Iowa was there. I guess he aims to go to school next term. I did not know him when he came in.

Saturday, December 21, 1872

Down to 0 and the wind blowing. Keeps turning colder. None of us worked. I took the gun to Hill's* shop and took the breach-pin out. I got a dime's worth of powder of Scott**. We cleaned it out thoroughly. Aaron set the little clock to running. Dave went home. Lydia has a very bad cold. She coughs much of the time. Al went to town a while and to some other places to get his clothes mended and washed.

*J. M. Hill, b. OH1839, M/C1871, blacksmith, Rep, Christian
**Robert R. Scott, 37, merchant, $1000/2800

Sunday, December 22, 1872

Nineteen degrees below zero. We all stayed about the house and popped

corn and had chicken for dinner. We killed a rabbit too. Cynthia went to

Will Sumner's to take a bucket home. I went to Uncle Levi's in the evening.

Some of the older children and I went to Uncle Perry's and stayed till after

dark. Albert* was at home and Evan Hadley was there from Iowa. We held

a little meeting.

*Albert W. Macy, 19, cousin, son of Perry Macy

Monday, December 23, 1872

Warmer again but turned colder during the day. Father, Aaron and Al cut some wood and fed and kept fires. Jesse Hadley* come to settle some business with Pa and Stephenson**. Terrel come over and settled. Father owes him $78.87. More debts, no money, that's the way it goes. Enough to discourage a man all to pieces. One that is easy broken to pieces anyhow. Maybe better times will come. Indeed I hope so. (this is just my mind expanding).

*Jessee Hadley, 54, farmer, Guilford Twp, Hendricks Co.
**William L. Stephenson, 39, brick manufacturer, $300/500

Tuesday, December 24, 1872

Still below zero, kind of frosty wind which comes very close to the hide of a fellow, I tell you. Father went to town and got some coal oil. Joseph Edwards* come here and went with father to town. Al** and Aaron*** killed 2 rabbits while they were taking the cows to the stalk field. Wayne**** and Evan***** come down here and we went a little round and killed another rabbit. We had three. Wayne and Evan are going to stay all night with us.

Van Kinney married Mary Friddle

*Joseph H. Edwards, b.VA1833, M/C1856, farmer, $7850/535, 3 mi SW of Mooresville

**Alson Clapp, 23, employee of WMM

***Aaron Mills Macy, 17, son of WMM

****Wayne C Hadley, 8, cousin, son of Levi S Hadley

*****Evan Hadley, 26, cousin, son of Thomas Marshall Hadley

Wednesday, December 25, 1872

Pretty cold. Evan and Wayne and Aaron and I all went to Uncle Levi's before dinner. Then about a dozen of us young folk went to Uncle Aaron's to eat a Christmas dinner which was well gotten up. John Farmer* and his daughter was there. Will Swindler** and Maggie*** got there in the evening. Mother, father, Cynthia and Lydia went to Levi's but went home before night. Al**** went somewhere from here. Do not know where, has not come back yet. Dave come down to get some money but did not get any.

*John H. Farmer, 24, son of Peter Farmer
**William Swindler, 24, mill worker
***Maggie Hadley, 17, dau of Thomas M Hadley
****Alson Clapp, 23, WMM's live in laborer

Thursday, December 26, 1872

Damp and cloudy. Snowed some in the night. Aaron stayed at Uncle Perry's and I went to Levi's. We stayed till about 10 oclock in the night at Aaron Mills' and had a nice slow ride home or to our stopping places. Wayne drove the sled and the passengers were Malinda, Ella Hadley, Achsah, Emma, Elmira, Albert, Evan, Aaron, Julian Fulgom (Uncle Miles's hand) and I, of course. We had a very nice time. Father took some corn and wheat to mill. A crowd of cousins met at the gallerie and had their pictures in a group. Aaron and I were there. Joseph E. was here in the evening.

Friday, December 27, 1872

Some warmer. A kind of light snow or frost filled the air in the morning. Father and Aaron fixed up the sled in the forenoon. In the afternoon father fixed one of the mule stables. Aaron and I hauled 2 loads of fodder, one to the barn and one to the fence between the stubble (wheat) and new ground to feed the calves. Cynthia went to Uncle Ira's yesterday and come home in the morning. Al did not come. Lydia chilled again.

Saturday, December 28, 1872

Snowed about half the time. Very light so it did not amount to much. We all went to meeting but Cynthia and Lydia. Meeting held till near 4 oclock. Had a good amount of business to attend to and a good meeting for worship. I went home with Uncle William and then went with his children to Oak Ridge Society. They have a pretty full membership and a good society. Larken and some of Levi's folks were there.

Sunday, December 29, 1872

Damp and chilly. Cloudy most all day. I went with Uncle William's folks to White Lick meeting and school. Had a very good meeting. I went to Uncle Levi's and got dinner and stayed till time to go to meeting at town. Then Perry and Evan come there and went to meeting with us. Had a very good time. Father and the rest of us were there so I rode home with them. Al come in the evening.

Monday, December 30, 1872

A little rain but it was like mist, well not rain anyhow. We killed our hogs, 7 in all. Sold them to Terrel. Dave helped till noon and then he went to town. I went to town and got a box of caps. (10cts). I had the headache nearly all day. The meeting at town was continued last night and will be tomorrow night if nothing prevents. Albert* and Willy* were here a little while in the evening.

*Albert Macy, 19, William Macy, 12, cousins, sons of Perry Macy

Tuesday, December 31, 1872

A very nice day. Rain a little, snow a little, sleet a little. Seems like it can't be satisfied. There were some of the largest drops of snow I ever saw. Aaron and Al took Terrel's hogs to him. We salted our hogs away and rendered up the lard. Father went to town to get a barrel. Ben Butler come over to see about some business. I guess I have lost the knife. My good one, but it was just a knife.

William M Macy Sale of Toll Road Rejected - 1882

William Monroe Macy was the first and apparently only President of the MooresvilleMonrovia Gravel Road Co. It was a toll road owned and maintained by land owners whose land lay adjacent to the road. It appears that the MMGRC owners were willing to sell their interest in the road to the County in 1882. This 'evolution' involved the purchase of the stockholder's interest by the County commissioners who would then assume the maintenance and open it as a 'free to the public' gravel road.

The commissioners offered the Morgan County voters the choice via a ballot on the April 3, 1882 primary election. The voters rejected the idea by a margin of 2091 to 284.

Later, in 1889, David Fogleman presented the bankrupt MMGRC for disposition to the County. The Morgan County commissioners paid $950 for the road and thereby made it into a free public gravel road. A few iterations later, it became what is now known as Indiana State Road 42.

The documents which illustrate this story are recreated from Morgan County Library files.

Notice of Gravel Road Election

State of Indiana, Morgan County,

Notice is hereby given that the question of purchasing the Mooresville and Monrovia Toll Road for the purpose of making it a free gravel road will be submitted to the voters of Morgan County at the April election, 1882. At said election each voter who is in favor of such purchase shall assert on the ballot, "Purchase of Toll Road—Yes" and each voter opposed to the purchase "Purchase of Toll Road—No" And if in said election a majority of them voting on said question are in favor of said purchase, the Commissioners may make said purchase, but not otherwise

> Witness my hand and the
> seal of the Board of
> Commissioners of said
> county at Martinsville, this
> 26th day of March, 1882

(SEAL)   W.G. BAIN, auditor, M.C.

3-26-1882 Martinsville Republican newspaper

Gravel Road Election Results

Referendum 4-3-1882 (per Martinsville Republican)

Question
Shall the Morgan County Commissioners purchase The MooresvilleMonrovia Gravel Toll Road and make it a FREE Gravel road?

Township	Yes	No
Ashland	0	172
Baker	0	96
Ray	5	188
Monroe	148	120
Clay	20	213
Jackson	---	----
Washington	50	622
Madison	0	139
Brown	33	76
Gregg	22	195
Harrison	5	66
Green	1	204
TOTALS	284	2091

Commissioners Action on Petitions to Purchase Toll Road

1882

Morgan County Commissioners' Record Book
15, Page 423, Item 178

Date: June 7, 1882

William M. Macy, Et al   )
To purchase Toll Road   )   Dismissed

On motion the petition of **W. M. Macy**, et al to purchase Toll Road (Mooresville Monrovia Gravel Road Company) was taken up and it appearing to the satisfaction of the court that at the April election 1882 a majority of the voters of Morgan County voted "NO" as to the purchase of the Toll Road. It is therefore ordered that the above entitled cause die and the same is hereby **dismissed.**

The April 1882 Morgan County voter referendum rejected WMM's offer to sell the Toll road. WMM was president of the Mooresville Monrovia Gravel Road Co.

Macy after Mooresville

In 1882, William Monroe Macy had buried his

Mother	2/1866
Daughter	12/1866
Father	1/1869
Son	9/1877

in the White Lick Cemetery near Mooresville, IN.

Although his real estate had been appraised at $13200 in 1860 and $28000 in 1870, an 1880 farm census valued the real estate at $10000. While the interurban railway was destined to cut through the farm in 1902, we have no evidence that WMM was aware of that in 1882. His attempt to sell the Mooresville Monrovia Gravel Road Company to Morgan County was rejected by the voters in 1882. Soon after, he sold the Farmstead to Martin Ruble for $18000 (and carried Ruble for $2500 of that). Ruble "flipped" the property for $24000 to Alonzo Johnson within a year.

WMM appears to have been motivated to sell!

He migrated west with Julia Ann, Alva Perry, Cynthia Ruth, and Lydia (adopted) and purchased a farm near Dayton, Yamhill Co, OR. He built a wood frame home which was still standing when we visited the site in 2004.

About 1905, Alva relocated to Butte Co, CA (near Chico) where he and Ida May (Moore) raised their children—

Norman Kerr	b 8-27-1890
Maude LaVerne	b 3-8-1892
Bruce Ward	b 11-20-1893
Ruth W	b 1894

In 1905 William (at age 85) and Julia Ann migrated again to Greenleaf, Idaho where they owned another farm. In 1911, we find WMM dies at Cynthia's home in Denair, CA. Julia Ann subsequently succumbed in Cynthia's home which was now in Greenleaf, ID. Julia Ann was buried next to WMM in the Denair, CA cemetery.

Cynthia Ruth married Owen Hatfield (22 yrs her senior) and they are found in Oregon, California and Idaho over the years and usually near her parents. Their children included

Arthur William	b 11-10-1887
Bernice Macy	b 3-20-1890
Macy L.	b 5-26-1892

A book entitled *"From Sagebrush to Green Fields'* by Dilla Tucker Winslow documents the Macys and Hatfields were significant members of the Greenleaf, ID settlement in the first decade of the 20th century.

Another book , *'Fifty Years of Friends in Idaho'* by Ronald Eugene Stansell credits the Macys and the Hatfields with establishing the first academy of Greenleaf.

Family members who have visited The Macy Farmstead during the Robinson era include Madell Lucille Williams, (granddaughter of Cynthia Ruth) and Marilee Frances March, (great granddaughter of Alva Perry). During a trip to Oregon, we visited the George Fox University and talked with Kenneth Morgan Williams and Donald Keith Williams who are grandsons of Cynthia Ruth. As a part of that tour, we also visited Marjorie Watkins on Vashon Isle, Seattle, WA who is a g, g, grand niece of William Monroe Macy. Marjorie is the g,g,grandaughter of WMM's sister, Lucinda.

Each of them were major contributors to the story we've compiled on the Macy family and the Macy Farmstead. We are forever grateful to them all.

At Grandpa William M. Macy home near Dayton Ore. Around 1900.

16. Macys in Dayton, OR about 1900
Cynthia, Owen, Macy, Bernice, & Arthur Hatfield
William Monroe & Julia Ann Mills Macy

17. Robinson's 2004 Photo of Macy's Dayton, OR Home

Mooresville Monrovia Gravel Road Co Bankrupts

Morgan County Commissioners' Record Book 17, Page 384

Date: March 3, 1889
In the Matter of the
Mooresville & Monrovia
Gravel Road

     Comes now the Mooresville and Monrovia Gravel Road Company by David Fogleman, Receiver of said road and proposes to sell to the county of Morgan, the bridges, culverts and all appurtenances thereto belonging to said company on the line of its road from the town of Mooresville to the town of Monrovia in said county for the sum of $950. And abandon and turn to said county and the public their said gravel road with all the rights, privileges and accruements held and exercised by said company in and over said road without any further consideration.

     Which said proposition is now accepted by the board.

     This indenture witnesseth – that David Fogleman as receiver in the cause of the Farmer's Bank of Mooresville, Indiana vs the Mooresville Monrovia Gravel Road Company by order of the Morgan Circuit Court of Morgan County, Indiana entered in Order Book #20 of the record of said court on Page 532 conveys to Morgan County, Indiana the following described Highway and gravel road to wit:

     The gravel road leading from the town of Mooresville, Morgan County, Indiana to the town of Monrovia in said county and state known and styled as the "Mooresville and Monrovia Gravel Road" as the same is now used, laid out, constructed and runs over the lands of William M. Macy, Simon Hadley, Jonothan Doan, Lot M. Hadley, Jesse B. Johnson, Henry Brewer, Samuel Hadley, Evan Hadley, and Thomas E. Hadley together with the road-bed, culverts and bridges, and all appurtenances thereto belonging .

     In Witness thereof: the said David Fogleman, as receiver aforesaid, has hereinto set his hand and seal this 14th day of March, 1889.

                                        _____
                                        David Fogleman

Approved by me this 14th day of March, 1889
George W. Grubbs, Judge of the Morgan Circuit Court

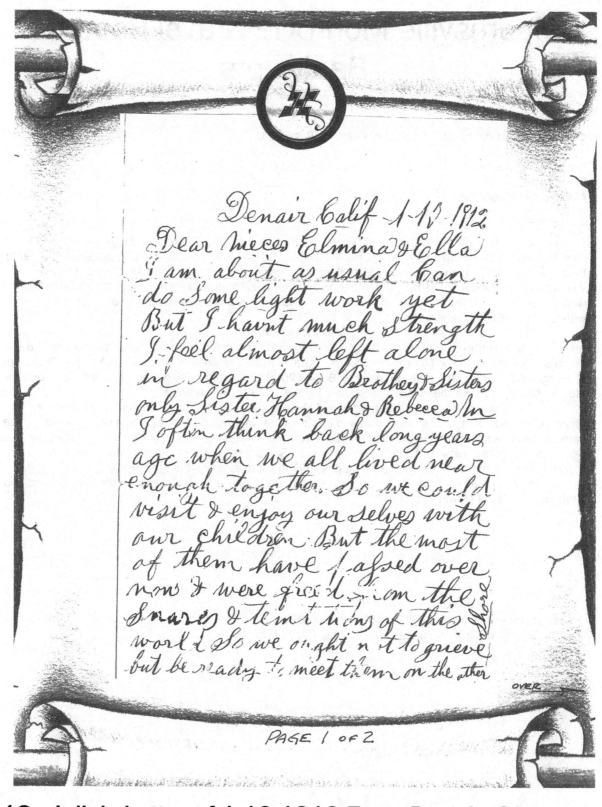

Denair Calif 1-13 1912
Dear Nieces Elmina & Ella
I am about as usual can
do Some light work yet
But I havnt much Strength
I feel almost left alone
in regard to Brothers & Sisters
only Sister Hannah & Rebecca In
I often think back long years
age when we all lived near
enough together So we could
visit & enjoy our selves with
our children But the most
of them have passed over
now & were freed from the
Snares & temtations of this
world So we ought n t to grieve
but be ready to meet them on the other

OVER

PAGE 1 OF 2

18. Julia's Letter of 1-13-1913 From Denair, CA to Nieces Elmina & Ella In Mooresville, IN

Rained last night we havent had
So much rain yet as last winter
Has been a great many frosty
mornings. Was about 16 above Zero
Evan Hadley & family & P.C Hadle
& Nathan & mollie Snodgrass &
Son where here at Xmas we
enjoyed there Co. I got Xmas cards
& collars & handkercheifs & a Small
painting of a lake & mts in Calif
from P.C Hadleys wife M.J Hadle
I dont think of much to write
would like to see you all I
get rather dull & lonesome Some
times Think this is a pretty nice
Settlement I go to meeting Some
times There is one lady goes
to church only 5 months older
than I am She is company
for me as we are the oldest there
To Elmina & Ella from aunt Julia

SIGNED: JULIA ANN MACY

OVER →

PAGE 2 OF 2

*Letter provided by Jo & Jim Hall

THE AFTERGLOW

Donovan Lee Robinson (b. 9-29-1934) and Joyce Ann Burke Robinson (b. 9-22-1935) purchased the William Monroe Macy Farmstead in Mooresville, IN, USA in October, 1981.

In the spring of 2004, we were alerted to an Indiana Department of Transportation (INDOT) project proposing to widen State Road 42 from 20 feet to 24 feet. The proposed design claimed a substantial portion of our front lawn, condemned 11 trees between our home and the highway, and would bless us with a 4 foot deep by 12 foot wide ditch covered with rip-rap. Within the following 48 months of wrangling with the tyranny of eminent domain we miraculously negotiated design modifications which substantially minimized the damage (proof again, that an engineer's first idea is not always his best idea!).

Our considerable efforts to deal with this calamity resulted in a mountain of documents which were compiled to highlight and defend the historical significance of the home. The information seemed too valuable to abandon but needed to be moved from manila folders to a comprehensible package which some local history 'students' might appreciate. That was the incentive for creating this book with history and genealogy focused on the William Monroe Macy Farmstead.

In the interim, Joyce had harbored thoughts of recording her own life story. (see <u>*I Was a Waif and Child Servant.... No Regrets*</u> published 2008 by Author House). Joyce's childhood was spent in a foster family home and she knew very little about her own family origins. While compiling her book and researching her own genealogy she became curious about whether her biological mother's maiden name, **Massie,** would possibly be connected to the **Macy** name of the Farmstead we now inhabit. We had observed that people spelled the name in a variety of ways. For example, we found Macxy, Massey, Massy, Massie, Macy, Mace, Macey, and Mascy were interchanged from generation to generation in the same family.

What a coincidence it would be if Joyce might be residing on the Farmstead where distant relatives once tread! Our curiosity thus energized, we began the very lengthy search to determine if Joyce might be connected to this Macy, Massie, Massey, etc. family. Anticipation accompanied our pursuit of the answers. It took both of us, our knowledge, and patient commitment to reach our conclusions.

During our 2007 visit to Plymouth and Nantucket where the Macy family ancestors settled upon arrival from England and the Mayflower, we found Macy to be a prominent and well documented name. All libraries and research centers were laden with Macy information. We were enthralled with the records we brought home for our story. After all, the Thomas Macy family was the first family to inhabit Nantucket Island; and was one of the nine initial owners of Nantucket Island. We found notable and pertinent evidence for our supposition.

Joyce's Massie ancestors were residing 150 miles south in Warrick County, Indiana at the same time the Macy family was residing in Mooresville, Morgan County, Indiana. We have accumulated files, marriage licenses, death certificates, tombstone photos (taken by us) too numerous to place in any book. Rewarding? Genealogy is like drilling for oil. The sweetness of developing a producing oil well trumps a series of drilled dry holes. We have enjoyed chasing this story of our Macy/Massie connection during our retirement years.

Our search led us to **Hugh de Coddington Massey** (1389-1456) of Cheshire, England and his **sons, William and John**. We found some contradictory dates which other genealogists have submitted, however, our analysis of a plethora of material from various sources concludes that the **William Monroe Macy** line are descendants of **William** de Coddington Massey. We also developed the tree branch which reveals that **Joyce Ann Burke Robinson's** ancestors are descendants of **John** de Coddington Massey. We concluded: Joyce Ann Burke Robinson is a 17th generation relative of Hugh de Coddington via son John; and William Monroe Macy is a 16th generation descendant of the same man via John's brother, William.

Direct Descendants of Hugh de Coddington Massey

```
1  Hugh de Coddington Massey   1389 - 1456
    +Ann Bold     1390 -
.. 2   William de Coddingham Massey 1440  <<<<<<<<<<<<<<<<<<<<<<<<<<<<<.
              +Alice Wooten
.... 3   John Massey
......    +Matilda
......  4   Robert Massey        -

.......   5   William of Coddington Massey
...........  +Alice Crew
..............  6   Robert Massey   1454 -
........................ +Dorothy Calveley    1460 -
................ 7   Roger Massey     1479 - 1532
..................         +Elizabeth Brereton
................. 8    John of Coddington Massey
..................          +Ellen Daniel
....................... 9   Thomas Macy    1585 -
...........................        + Mary Thomas 1594 -
........................... 10   Thomas Macy         1608 - 1682
..............................          +Sarah Hopcott    1612 - 1682
............................. 11   John Macy       1655 - 1691
....................................        +Deborah Gardner      1657/58 - 1712
..................................... 12   John Macy II 1675 - 1751
....................................          +Judith Worth      1689 - 1767
..................................... 13    John Macy III     1721 - 1795
.............................................          +Eunice Coleman       1724 - 1768
............................................. 14   Barachiah Macy     1760 - 1832
.................................................          +Lucinda Barnard       1767 - 1810
................................................. .15   William Macy     1786 - 1869
.................................................          +Hannah Hinshaw    1789 - 1866
.............................................................. 16 William Monroe Macy   1820 - 1911
```

Hugh de Coddington Massey>>>>>>> William Monroe Macy

Direct Descendants of Hugh De Coddington Massey

```
1   Hugh De Coddington Massey        1389 - 1456
..   +Anne/Agnes Bold   1390 -
.. 2   John of Broxton Massie  1429 - 1509    <<<<<<<<<<<<<<<<<<<<<<<<<
             +Margaret Larton
... 3   Edward Massey
             +Anne Snede
........ 4   Thomas of Broxton Massie  1540 - 1565
...........            +Elizabeth Middleton   1544 - 1623
...........  5   David Massey     1566 - 1623
...............            +Dorothy Leigh 1568 - 1623
...............   6   Hugh Massey          1580 - 1639
...................            +Anne Dod   1580 - 1610
...................   7   Thomas Massie          1610 - 1688
..........................        +Judith Brereton  1612 - 1688
........................8   Peter Massie 1639 - 1719
............................       +Penelope Ashley Cooper      1647 - 1711
............................  9   Thomas Massie        1675 - 1732
...............................          +Mary Walker     1677 - 1755
............................. 10   Peter Massie        1700 - 1762
.................................        +Ann Raymond 1710 -
.................................. 11   Sylvanus Massie          1738 - 1786
...................................+Hannah Ragland          1738 -
...................................12   John Massie          1760 - 1815
.......................................        +Polly Dial     1775 -
.........................................   13   Thomas B. Massie        1804 - 1878
...........................................        +Eliza Campbell 1813 - 1887
...........................................   14   James Burke Massie      1844 - 1898
.............................................        +Mary Jane Dancy    1854 - 1936
...............................................   15   Jesse Hall Massie     1887 - 1939
...................................................        +Blanche Oliver 1889 - 1922
.....................................................16   Helen  Mable Massie      1914 - 2002
......................................................        +Rollie Clarence Burke  1908 - 1994
```

.... **17   Joyce Ann Burke 1935 -**

Hugh de Coddington Massey >>>>>>>Joyce Ann Burke Robinson

Genealogists who read this book, may find it easy to identify with the fact the Robinsons found themselves immersed in the 1800's (mentally at least) much of our research time. Joyce, found herself reminiscing about how Julia Ann Mills Macy might have gathered her food from the garden, prepared it with "carried in" water and cooked it on a stove heated with wood chopped by the 'men folks'. Perhaps she even chopped her own wood sometimes. She had to feed the 'hired' hands meals every day, house many of them in her home for shelter while caring for her own family as well as her extended family as the need often arose.

The diary printed in this book speaks seldom of the mother's involvement in this household. However, after you have read the diary, you can easily surmise the amount of 'women's work' that was happening within the walls of this stately old home. Julia could not leisurely enjoy the home as we do ours today because the Macy Farmstead was a prominent 'gathering place' of the surrounding community of Mooresville, Indiana in the mid 1800's. It was busy! Julia utilized the help of neighbors, female relatives, as well as hired help in order to effectively run a household which served so many. She was busy making candles, butter, woolen yarns, clothing, and gathering eggs; all for sale from this farm. She bartered in town with her butter, maple sugar pralines, and dried peaches when in season. People needed their neighbors; and they worked and supported each other at many levels. She didn't have a car at her fingertip. The boys would take a break from working in the fields and bring her one of the work horses if she needed to go to town. How did they communicate their needs to each other? Well, they rode a horse or walked to deliver their messages.

Consider how many times the men got drenched with rain and brought all their wet clothing to Julia Ann to have them ready for the next day's work! The women were equally as industrious as the men in that day; the field work required the support of the household run by the women. Wouldn't Julia Ann Macy have loved an electric dishwasher or a hot, soft water shower?

We have loved our life on the Macy Farmstead. We remain mindful that what we share with others is the legacy of this Farmstead and the people who cleared, planted and reaped the products by hand and horse in the 1800's. Time passes, and people move on. The Macy family moved on west to Oregon. Everyone leaves their mark and the pioneers who tamed the wilderness of the 19th century were unique. We are all in their debt.

NOTE: Following are subsequent temporary owners of Macy Farmstead

1859 – 1882	William Monroe & Julia Ann Mills Macy
1882 – 1931	Alonzo Miller & Louisa Matilda Campbell Johnson
1931 - 1981	Willison (Willis) & Clara Sellars Richardson
1981 – ?	Donovan Lee & Joyce Ann Burke Robinson

AFTERGLOW:

Anything that lingers after something is finished, experienced or achieved; i.e. memory

ALSO:

The glow after the sunset,   (or)   the glow of an extinguished light bulb before it cools.

Appendix

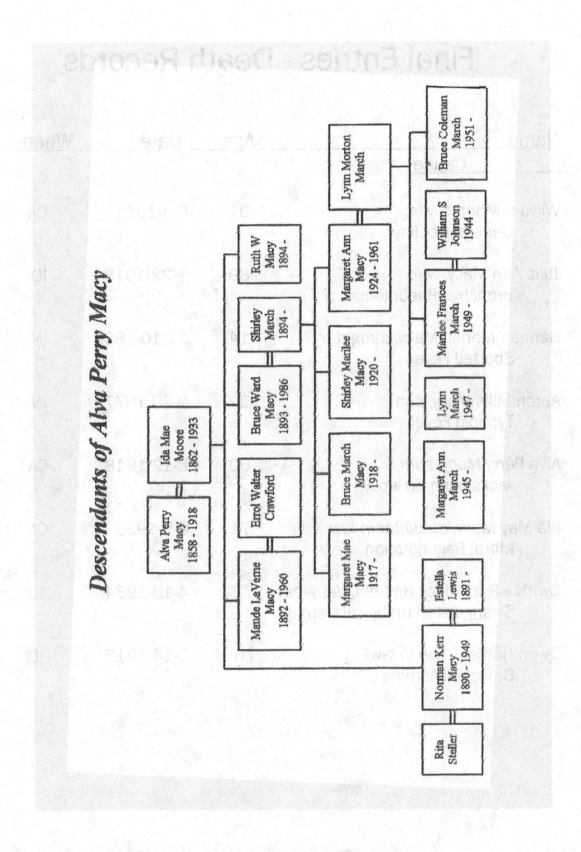

Descendants of Alva Perry Macy

19. Descendants of Alva Perry Macy

Final Entries - Death Records

Name	Age	Date	Where
Cause			
William Monroe Macy General Debility	91	6-4-1911	CA
Julia Ann Macy, *wife* Bronchial Pneumonia	89	7-22-1918	ID
Hannah Mariah Macy, *daughter* Spotted Fever	14	12-10-1866	IN
Aaron Mills Macy, *son* Typhoid Fever	22	9-25-1877	IN
Alva Perry Macy, *son* Jacksonian Epilepsy	60	8-12-1918	CA
Ida May Macy, *daughter in law* Mitral Regurgitation	71	8-9-1933	CA
Cynthia Ruth Macy Hatfield, *daughter* Strangulated Umbilical Hernia	72	4-18-1934	ID
Owen Hatfield, *son in law* Bronchial Asthma	76	2-14-1916	ID

COUNTY of STANISLAUS
MODESTO, CALIFORNIA

PLACE OF DEATH

COUNTY OF _Stanislaus_

TOWN OF _Near Denair_

CALIFORNIA STATE BOARD OF HEALTH
BUREAU OF VITAL STATISTICS

Original

~~DUPLICATE~~ CERTIFICATE OF DEATH   State Index No. _____

Local Registered No. _90_

CITY OF _____

(NO. _____ STREET _____ WARD)

[If death occurred in a Hospital or Institution, give its NAME instead of street and number.]

[If death occurs away from USUAL RESIDENCE, give facts called for under "Special Information."]

Full Name _William M. Macy_

PERSONAL AND STATISTICAL PARTICULARS

LENGTH OF RESIDENCE

At Place of Death _1_ years, _____ months.

In California _____ years, _____ months.

SEX _Male_   COLOR OR RACE _White_

DATE OF BIRTH _March 8, 1810_

AGE _91_ years _2_ months _26_ days.

SINGLE, MARRIED, WIDOWED OR DIVORCED _Married_

BIRTHPLACE _Tenn._ (State or Country)

OCCUPATION _Farmer_

NAME OF FATHER _William Macy_

BIRTHPLACE OF FATHER _N.C._ (State or Country)

MAIDEN NAME OF MOTHER _Anna Henshaw_

BIRTHPLACE OF MOTHER _Tenn._ (State or Country)

THE ABOVE STATED PERSONAL PARTICULARS ARE TRUE TO THE BEST OF MY KNOWLEDGE AND BELIEF

(INFORMANT) _Cynthia Hatfield_

(ADDRESS) _Denair, Cal_

MEDICAL CERTIFICATE OF DEATH _39 m._

DATE OF DEATH _June 4, 1901_ (Month) (Day) (Year)

I HEREBY CERTIFY that I attended deceased from _Feb 16_, 1901, to _May 31_, 1901; that I last saw him alive on _____, 1901; and that death occurred on the date stated above, at ___ M. The CAUSE OF DEATH was as follows: _This was a case of General Debility or Senile Decay. I saw him for three times some time ago, and then as I would do nothing for him. Had them report to me _____ (duration) ____ days Contributory He had been confined to his bed for several months, because of death would be general debility_

(Signed) _W. Lester Wilson_ M. D.

June 4, 1901 (Address) _Turlock, Cal_

SPECIAL INFORMATION only for Hospitals, Institutions, Transients, or Recent Residents

Former or Usual Residence _____

How long at Place of Death? _____ Days.

Where was disease contracted, if not at place of death? _____

PLACE OF BURIAL OR REMOVAL _Denair_   DATE OF BURIAL _June 5, 1901_

UNDERTAKER _G. S. Wright_   ADDRESS _Turlock_

FILED _June 6th 1901_ _E. L. Clough_ Subregistrar.

FILED _Sept. 15, 1901_ _H. C. Keeley_ Registrar or Deputy.

CERTIFIED COPY OF VITAL RECORDS

20. William Monroe Macy Death Certificate

21. Julia Ann Mills Macy Death Certificate

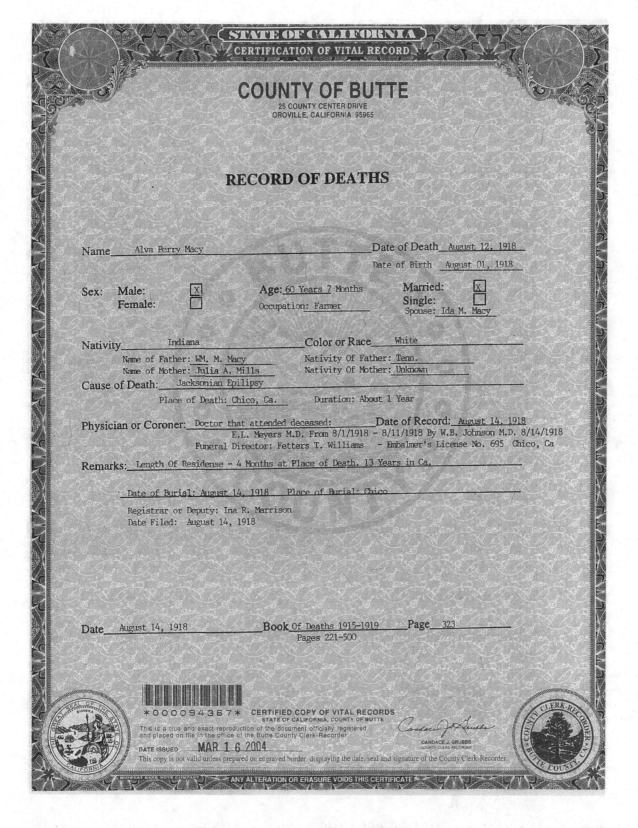

COUNTY OF BUTTE
25 COUNTY CENTER DRIVE
OROVILLE, CALIFORNIA 95965

RECORD OF DEATHS

Name___Alva Perry Macy_____   Date of Death __August 12, 1918_

Date of Birth __August 01, 1918_

Sex: Male: [X]   **Age:** _60 Years 7_ Months   **Married:** [X]
Female: [ ]   Occupation: _Farmer_____   **Single:** [ ]
Spouse: _Ida M. Macy_

Nativity_____Indiana_____Color or Race____White_____
Name of Father: _WM. M. Macy_____   Nativity Of Father: _Tenn._____
Name of Mother: _Julia A. Mills_____   Nativity Of Mother: _Unknown_____
Cause of Death:___Jacksonian Epilipsy_____
Place of Death: _Chico, Ca._   Duration: _About 1 Year_

Physician or Coroner:_Doctor that attended deceased:_____ Date of Record:_August 14, 1918_
E.L. Meyers M.D. From 8/1/1918 - 8/11/1918 By W.B. Johnson M.D. 8/14/1918
Funeral Director: Fetters T. Williams - Embalmer's License No. 695 Chico, Ca

Remarks:_Length Of Residense - 4 Months at Place of Death. 13 Years in Ca._____

Date of Burial: August 14, 1918   Place of Burial: Chico_____

Registrar or Deputy: Ina R. Marrison
Date Filed: August 14, 1918

Date ___August 14, 1918_____   Book_Of Deaths 1915-1919_____Page___323_____
Pages 221-500

22. Alva Perry Macy Death Certificate

23. Ida May Moore Macy Death Certificate

STATE OF IDAHO
IDAHO DEPARTMENT OF HEALTH AND WELFARE
BUREAU OF HEALTH POLICY AND VITAL STATISTICS

RECEIVED AT

STATE OF IDAHO
DEPARTMENT OF PUBLIC WELFARE
BUREAU OF VITAL STATISTICS

PLACE OF DEATH

County of *Canyon*

City of *Nampa*

CERTIFICATE OF DEATH

Registration District No. *1*

Primary Registration District No. *22-05*

DO NOT WRITE IN THIS SPACE

State File No. *88578*

Local Registrar's No. *37*

(No. _____) (If death occurred in a hospital or institution, give its name instead of street and number.)

2. FULL NAME *Cynthia Ruth Hatfield*

(a) Residence No. *New Plymouth Ida*

Length of residence in city or town where death occurred ___ yrs. ___ mos. ___ ds. How long in U.S., if of foreign birth? ___ yrs. ___ mos. ___ ds.

PERSONAL AND STATISTICAL PARTICULARS | MEDICAL CERTIFICATE OF DEATH

3. SEX *female* 4. COLOR OR RACE *white* 5. Single, Married, Widowed, or Divorced (write the word) *widow*

5a. If married, widowed, or divorced
HUSBAND of (or) WIFE of *Owen Hatfield*

6. DATE OF BIRTH (month, day, and year) *Sept 17 1861*

7. AGE Years *72* Months *7* Days *1* If LESS than 1 day, ___ hrs. or ___ min.

8. Trade, profession, or particular kind of work done, as spinner, sawyer, bookeeper, etc. *Housekeeping*

9. Industry or business in which work was done, as silk mill, saw mill, bank, etc.

10. Date deceased last worked at this occupation (month and year)

11. Total time (years) spent in this occupation

12. BIRTHPLACE (city or town) (State or country) *Mooresville Indiana*

13. NAME *William M. Macy*

14. BIRTHPLACE (city or town) (State or country) *not stated*

15. MAIDEN NAME *Julia A. Miller*

16. BIRTHPLACE (city or town) (State or country)

17. INFORMANT (Address) *M L Hatfield New Plymouth*

18. BURIAL, CREMATION, OR REMOVAL Place *McMinnville Ore* Date ___ 1934

19. UNDERTAKER (Address) *V. Peckham Caldwell Ida*

20. FILED *7/25* 193 *W M Montgomery* Registrar.

21. DATE OF DEATH (month, day, and year) *Apr 18 1934*

22. I HEREBY CERTIFY, That I attended deceased from *Mar 26* 1934 to *Apr 18* 1934

I last saw her alive on *April 18*, 1934; death is said to have occurred on the date stated above, at *5-8* m.

The principal cause of death and related causes of importance were as follows: | Date of onset

Strangulated Umbilical Hernia

Other contributory causes of importance:
operation
old age

Name of operation *Herniatomy* Date of *Apr 16 '34*

What test confirmed diagnosis? ___ Was there an autopsy? ___

23. If death was due to exter'l causes (violence) fill in also the following:

Accident, suicide, or homicide? ___ Date of injury ___, 193

Where did injury occur? ___ (Specify city or town, county, and State)

Specify whether injury occurred in industry, in home, or in public place.

Manner of injury ___

Nature of injury ___

24. Was disease or injury in any way related to occupation of deceased?

If so, specify ___

(Signed) *Thos G Mangum*, M.D.

(Address) *Nampa Idaho*

FAMILY RECORD ONLY

This is a true and correct reproduction of the document officially registered and placed on file with the IDAHO BUREAU OF HEALTH POLICY AND VITAL STATISTICS.

DATE ISSUED: **MAR 2 2 2004**

This copy is not valid unless prepared on engraved border displaying state seal and signature of the Registrar.

JANE S. SMITH
STATE REGISTRAR

GREAT SEAL OF THE STATE OF IDAHO

24. Cynthia Ruth Macy Hatfield Death Certificate

25. Owen Hatfield Death Certificate

Denair,
CA

McMinnville,
OR

26. William, Julia, Cynthia, & Owen Tombstones

Aaron Mills Macy Obituary

1855-1877

Obituary

The death of Aaron Mills Macy, son of Wm. M. and Julia Ann Macy which occurred on Tuesday morning, September 25, 1877 was a sudden and painful stroke to his numerous friends and acquaintances in this community. His disease was typhoid fever from which he suffered nineteen days previous to his death. He was born in Wayne County, IN May 24, 1855 so that he died when it seemed that his life gave greatest promise of usefulness and happiness. He was never robust in health, and was compelled to desist from study at Earlham College, Richmond, and returned to his father's farm, at which he was engaged when overtaken with this fatal disease. His death was peaceful. When he knew that he must die, he called the family and friends together, conducted a prayer meeting and gave sweet counsel and wholesome advice to all, not forgetting to send messages of love to some who were absent. He was a young man of good habits and affable bearing, and was making himself useful in the community. He was one of the superintendents of the Friends Sunday school in Mooresville. The funeral was attended by a large number of friends, especially young men and the teachers and scholars of the public schools. Persons present testified that he was a dutiful son, affectionate brother, devoted friend, docile scholar and diligent bible student. His death should prompt our surviving young men to a careful consideration of their duty to God.

Ida May Moore Macy Obituary

From the Chico Record, 8-10-1933

Death Takes Ida M. Macy

Mrs. Ida May Macy, who with her late husband, Alva P Macy, was prominent in the life of Chico 20 years ago, died at the home of her daughter, Mrs. Maude Crawford of 934 Chestnut Street last night.

Mrs. Macy, the next to the youngest of 13 children, was born in New Providence, IA. For 27 years she made her home in Chico and during that time a host of friends were acquired. Mr. Macy died in 1918 and is buried in the Chico Cemetery.

In addition to her daughter, Mrs. Crawford, at whose home she died, Mrs. Macy is survived by two sons, Norman Macy of Chico and Bruce Macy of Pomona; three brothers, Alfred E. Moore of Newberg, Ore., Rev. Frank L. Moore of Portland and J. B. Moore of Modesto, and eight grandchildren.

Mrs. Macy was a member of the First Methodist Church, where she was an active worker.

Westfall Funeral Home will announce funeral arrangements.

Genealogy

Descendants of John Howland

Generation No. 1

1. JOHN¹ HOWLAND *(HENRYᴬ, JOHNᴮ, JOHNᶜ, JOHNᴰ)* was born Abt. 1592 in Fenstanton, Huntingdonshire, England, and died 23 Feb 1671/72 in Jabez's home in Plymouth, MA. He married **ELIZABETH TILLEY** Abt. Mar 1622/23, daughter of JOHN TILLEY and JOAN HURST. She was born Abt. 1607 in Henlow, Bedfordshire, England, and died 21 Dec 1687 in Swansea, MA.

More about **JOHN HOWLAND**:
 1633, Admitted as a freeman in Plymouth, MA
Burial: 25 Feb 1671/72, Plymouth
Census: 1672, **Last survivor of Mayflower Passage**
Elected: Assistant Governor
Emigration: 1620, Indentured servant to John Carver
Family: 1621, Assumed head of the family when John Carver died
Immigration: 1620, **Passenger on the Mayflower**
Occupation: 1628, Managed trading station @ Augusta, MA
 1620, 13th signer of Mayflower Compact
Religion: Remained a faithful Separatist

More about **ELIZABETH TILLEY**:
Burial: Little Neck Cemetery, East Providence, RI
Family: 1621, mother, father, aunt & uncle died @ Plymouth, MA
Immigration: 1620, **Passenger on the Mayflower**

Children of **JOHN HOWLAND and ELIZABETH TILLEY** are:
2.   i.   **DESIRE² HOWLAND**, b. 13 Oct 1623, Plymouth; d. 23 Oct 1683, Barnstable, MA.
3.   ii.   JOHN HOWLAND II, b. 1627; d. Barnstable, MA.
4.   iii.   HOPE HOWLAND, b. 1629.
    iv.   ELIZABETH HOWLAND.
5.   v.   LYDIA HOWLAND, b. 1633.
    vi.   HANNAH HOWLAND.
    vii.   JOSEPH HOWLAND.
    viii.   JABEZ HOWLAND.
    ix.   RUTH HOWLAND, b. 1646.
    x.   ISAAC HOWLAND.

2. DESIRE² HOWLAND *(JOHN¹, HENRYᴬ, JOHNᴮ, JOHNᶜ, JOHNᴰ)* was born 13 Oct 1623 in Plymouth, and died 23 Oct 1683 in Barnstable, MA. She married JOHN GORHAM about. 1643, son of RALPH GORHAM and MARGARET STEPHENSON. He was born 28 Jan 1619/20 in England, and died 05 Feb 1674/75 in Barnstable, MA.

More about JOHN GORHAM:
Cause of death : 1676, Wounds of King Phillip's War (Indian War)
Military service: 1675, Captain of the Plymouth Company
Occupation: Owned a grist mill & tannery

Children of **DESIRE HOWLAND** and **JOHN GORHAM** are:
6.   i.   **SHUBAEL³ GORHAM**, b. 27 Oct 1664, Barnstable, MA; d. 07 Aug 1750, Hyannis, MA.
       ii.   JOHN GORHAM, b. 1650.
      iii. JABEZ GORHAM.
      iv. MERCY GORHAM.
       v.   LYDIA GORHAM.
      vi. HANNAH GORHAM.

3. JOHN² HOWLAND II *(JOHN¹, HENRYᴬ, JOHNᴮ, JOHNᶜ, JOHNᴰ)* was born 1627, and died in Barnstable, MA. He married MARY LEE 1651. She died in Barnstable, MA.

Children of JOHN HOWLAND and MARY LEE are:
       i.   ISAAC³ HOWLAND.
       ii.   HANNAH HOWLAND.
      iii. MERCY HOWLAND.
      iv. LYDIA HOWLAND.
       v.   EXPERIENCE HOWLAND.
      vi. ANNE HOWLAND.
     vii. SHUBAEL HOWLAND.
    viii. JOHN HOWLAND.

4. HOPE² HOWLAND *(JOHN¹, HENRYᴬ, JOHNᴮ, JOHNᶜ, JOHNᴰ)* was born 1629. She married JOHN CHIPMAN Abt. 1646.

Children of HOPE HOWLAND and JOHN CHIPMAN are:
       i.   ELIZABETH³ CHIPMAN.
       ii.   HOPE CHIPMAN.
      iii. LYDIA CHIPMAN.
      iv. JOHN CHIPMAN.
       v.   HANNAH CHIPMAN.
      vi. SAMUEL CHIPMAN.
     vii. RUTH CHIPMAN.
    viii. BETHIA CHIPMAN.
      ix. MERCY CHIPMAN.
       x.   JOHN II CHIPMAN.
      xi. DESIRE CHIPMAN.

5. LYDIA[2] HOWLAND *(JOHN[1],)* was born 1633. She married JAMES BROWN.

More about JAMES BROWN:
Military service: Served as Major in King Phillip War
Religion: One of original Swansea church members

Children of LYDIA HOWLAND and JAMES BROWN are:
- i.   JAMES[3] BROWN, b. 1655.
- ii. DOROTHY BROWN, b. 1666.
- iii. JABEZ BROWN, b. 1667.

Generation No. 3

6. SHUBAEL[3] GORHAM *(DESIRE[2] HOWLAND, JOHN[1])*, was born 27 Oct 1664 in Barnstable, MA, and died 07 Aug 1750 in Hyannis, MA. He married PUELLA HUSSEY May 1693 in Barnstable, MA, daughter of STEPHEN HUSSEY and MARTHA BUNKER. She was born 10 Oct 1677 in Nantucket, and died 23 Sep 1748 in Nantucket.

Children of **SHUBAEL GORHAM and PUELLA HUSSEY** are:
7.	i.	**DEBORAH[4] GORHAM**, b. Aft. 1713, Barnstable, MA; d. 21 Apr 1787, Nantucket.
	ii.	SALLY GORHAM.
	iii.	ABIGAIL GORHAM, b. 01 Mar 1698/99; d. 28 Jun 1778.
	iv.	LYDIA GORHAM, b. 14 May 1701; d. 01 Mar 1763.
	v.	HANNAH GORHAM, b. 28 Jul 1703; d. 16 Aug 1751.
8.	vi.	THEODORE GORHAM, b. 18 Jul 1705, Barnstable, Massachusetts, USA; d. 07 Apr 1787, Nantucket, Massachusetts, USA.
	vii.	DESIRE GORHAM, b. 26 Sep 1710; d. 05 Nov 1801.
	viii.	RUTH GORHAM, b. 07 May 1713.

Generation No. 4

7. DEBORAH[4] GORHAM *(SHUBAEL[3], DESIRE[2] HOWLAND, JOHN[1])* was born Aft. 1713 in Barnstable, MA, and died 21 Apr 1787 in Nantucket. She married BERIAH FITCH 11 Dec 1735, son of JEDEDIAH FITCH and ABIGAIL COFFIN. He was born 30 Aug 1713 in Nantucket, and died 04 May 1785 in Nantucket.

Children of **DEBORAH GORHAM and BERIAH FITCH** are:
9.	i.	**EUNICE[5] FITCH**, b. 12 Sep 1736, Nantucket; d. Nov 1792, Guilford Co, NC.
	ii.	LUCINDA FITCH, b. 1746.
	iii.	LYDIA FITCH, b. 13 Nov 1738.
	iv.	PUELLA FITCH.
	v.	JOHNATHAN GORHAM FITCH, b. 14 Sep 1740.
	vi.	PARNAL FITCH, b. 02 May 1742.
	vii.	PHEBE FITCH, b. 1744.
	viii.	BERIAH FITCH, b. 1748.
	ix.	RUEBEN FITCH, b. 1750.
	x.	DEBORAH FITCH, b. 1755.
	xi.	JEDEDIAH FITCH, b. 02 Oct 1762.

8. THEODORE[4] GORHAM *(SHUBAEL[3], DESIRE[2] HOWLAND, JOHN[1],)* was born 18 Jul 1705 in Barnstable, Massachusetts, USA[1], and died 07 Apr 1787 in Nantucket, Massachusetts, USA[1]. He married FRANCIS COFFIN[1] 02 Nov 1729 in Nantucket, MA, USA[1]. She was born 13 Sep 1706 in Nantucket, Massachusetts, USA[1], and died 04 Dec 1735 in Nantucket, Massachusetts, USA[1].

Child of THEODORE GORHAM and FRANCIS COFFIN is:
- i. PELEG[5] COFFIN, b. 08 Nov 1728, Sherburne, Nantucket, MA, USA[1].

9. EUNICE[5] FITCH *(DEBORAH[4] GORHAM, SHUBAEL[3], DESIRE[2] HOWLAND, JOHN[1])* was born 12 Sep 1736 in Nantucket, and died Nov 1792 in Guilford Co, NC. She married BENJAMIN BARNARD 09 Jan 1755, son of TIMOTHY BARNARD and MARY BUNKER. He was born 30 Jul 1735 in Barnstable, MA, and died 22 Dec 1792 in Guilford Co, NC.

Children of **EUNICE FITCH** and **BENJAMIN BARNARD** are:

10.   i.   **LUCINDA[6] BARNARD**, b. 17 Mar 1767, Nantucket Island, MA; d. 05 Apr 1810, Lost Creek, Jefferson Co. , TN.
     ii.   MARY BARNARD.
     iii.   LYDIA BARNARD.
     iv.   MATILDA BARNARD.
     v.   LIBNI BARNARD, b. 1764; m. ALMY MACY; b. 05 Nov 1766, Nantucket Island, MA; d. 1820.
     vi.   SHUBAEL BARNARD, b. 28 Jun 1774.
     vii.   FREDERICK BARNARD.
     viii.   ELISHA BARNARD.
     ix.   EUNICE BARNARD.
     x.   TIMOTHY BARNARD.

10. LUCINDA[6] BARNARD *(EUNICE[5] FITCH, DEBORAH[4] GORHAM, SHUBAEL[3], DESIRE[2] HOWLAND, JOHN[1],)* was born 17 Mar 1767 in Nantucket Island, MA, and died 05 Apr 1810 in Lost Creek, Jefferson Co. , TN. She married (2) **BARACHIAH MACY** 20 Mar 1783 in New Garden MM, NC, son of JOHN MACY and EUNICE COLEMAN. He was born 24 Feb 1760 on Nantucket Island, MA, and died 28 Aug 1832 in Economy, Wayne Co., Indiana.

More about **BARACHIAH MACY:**
Appointed: 21 May 1803, appointed clerk of Lost Creek MM
Migration 2: 18 Apr 1771, Moved Nantucket to North Carolina
Migration 3: 1801, Helped his Brother in law move to Jefferson Co. TN
Migration 4: 01 Jan 1802, Moved family to Jefferson Co TN
Migration 5: 27 Sep 1828, Cert. Springfield MM, Henry Co, IN

Children of **LUCINDA BARNARD** and **BARACHIAH MACY** are:

     i.   MARY[7] MACY, b. 08 Mar 1784, New Garden MM, Guilford Co.,NC; d. 1885, Guilford Co, NC.
11.   ii.   **WILLIAM MACY**, b. 04 Oct 1786, New Garden MM, Guilford Co, NC; d. 17 Jan 1869, Mooresville, IN.
     iii.   MARY MACY II, b. 17 Dec 1788, New Garden MM, Guilford Co., NC.
12.   iv.   JOHNATHAN MACY, b. 06 May 1791, New Garden MM, Guilford Co.,NC; d. 11 Oct 1865, Rogersville, Henry, Indiana, USA.
     v.   ANNA MACY, b. 15 Sep 1793, New Garden MM, Guilford Co.,NC.
     vi.   MATILDA MACY, b. 17 Feb 1796, New Garden MM, Guilford Co.,NC.
     vii.   EUNICE MACY, b. 07 Apr 1799, New Garden MM, Guilford Co.,NC; d. 15 May 1801, Guilford Co, NC.
     viii.   ELIHU MACY, b. 11 Jul 1801, New Garden MM, Guilford Co.,NC; d. 09 Mar 1802, Guilford Co, NC.
13.   ix.   ISAAC MACY, b. 02 Apr 1803, Lost Creek, Jefferson Co, TN; d. 16 Dec 1847, Wayne, Indiana, USA.
14.   x.   JOHN MACY, b. 03 Jun 1806, Lost Creek, Jefferson Co, TN; d. 1872, Oregon, USA.
     xi.   LYDIA MACY, b. 05 Nov 1808, Lost Creek, Jefferson, TN[1]; d. 05 Feb 1875, Dalton Township, Wayne, Indiana, USA; m. LEWIS THORNBURGH, 25 Mar 1829, Springfield Mm, Wayne, Indiana, USA; b. 20 Feb 1802, Lost Creek, Jefferson, Tennessee, USA; d. 12 Jul 1890, Dalton Township, Wayne, Indiana, USA.

11. WILLIAM[7] MACY (*LUCINDA[6] BARNARD, EUNICE[5] FITCH, DEBORAH[4] GORHAM, SHUBAEL[3], DESIRE[2] HOWLAND, JOHN[1],*) was born 04 Oct 1786 in New Garden MM, Guilford Co.,NC, and died 17 Jan 1869 in Mooresville, IN. He married **HANNAH HINSHAW** 01 Mar 1809 in Lost Creek MM, Jefferson Co, TN, daughter of WILLIAM HINSHAW and MARGARET HUNT. She was born 08 Feb 1789 in Lost Creek, Guilford Co., NC, and died 19 Feb 1866 in Mooresville, IN.

More about **WILLIAM MACY**:
Appointed: 1822, Clerk of Springfield Monthly Meeting
Burial: White Lick Cemetery, Mooresville, IN
Migration 1: 1801, Spent summer raising crop for family move
Migration 2: Jan 1802, Moved to Lost Creek, Jefferson Co, TN
Migration 3: Apr 1820, Moved to West River Twp. Randolph Co, IN
Migration 4: 27 Sep 1828, To Springfield MM, Wayne Co., IN
Migration5: 1856, Moved to Brown Twp. Morgan Co., IN
Military service: 1812, Refused to serve in Andrew Jackson's Army
Religion: Quaker
Retirement: Wrote his Autobiography

More about HANNAH HINSHAW:
Burial: White Lick Cemetery, Mooresville, IN

Children of **WILLIAM MACY** and **HANNAH HINSHAW** are:

15.	i.	JONATHON B.[8] MACY, b. 07 Mar 1810, Lost Creek MM, Jefferson Co, TN; d. 15 Sep 1850, Economy, Wayne Co., Indiana.
16.	ii.	NATHAN HINSHAW MACY, b. 16 Aug 1811, Lost Creek MM, Jefferson Co, TN; d. 23 Mar 1856, Raccoon River, Redfield, Dallas Co, IA.
17.	iii.	ALVAH J MACY, b. 26 Feb 1813, Lost Creek MM, Jefferson Co, TN; d. 09 Jul 1852, Economy, Wayne Co., Indiana.
	iv.	ELIHU C MACY, b. 25 Dec 1814, Lost Creek MM, Jefferson Co, TN; d. 23 May 1816, Jefferson Co, TN.
18.	v.	JOHN HINSHAW MACY, b. 28 Nov 1816, Lost Creek MM, Jefferson Co, TN; d. 01 Jun 1849, Economy, IN.
19.	vi.	LUCINDA MACY, b. 30 Aug 1818, Lost Creek MM, Jefferson, TN; d. 1893, Springbrook, Yamhill Co, OR.
20.	vii.	**WILLIAM MONROE MACY**, b. 08 Mar 1820, Lost Creek MM, Jefferson Co, TN; d. 04 Jun 1911, Denair, CA.
21.	viii.	MARGARET ANN MACY, b. 22 Mar 1822, Randolph Co, IN; d. 19 Aug 1899, Mooresville, IN.
22.	ix.	SARAH MACY, b. 23 Nov 1823, Randolph Co, IN; d. 10 Jun 1873.
23.	x.	PERRY T MACY, b. 17 Aug 1825, Randolph Co., IN; d. 07 May 1889, Mooresville, IN.
24.	xi.	IRA C MACY, b. 28 May 1828, Randolph Co, IN.
25.	xii.	RUTH ALMA MACY, b. 09 Jan 1830, Randolph Co, IN; d. 18 Dec 1909.
26.	xiii.	MARY ANN MACY, b. 01 Oct 1831, Randolph Co, IN; d. 03 Jan 1889, Newberg, Oregon, USA.
27.	xiv.	LYDIA ANN MACY, b. 16 Apr 1834, Randolph Co, IN; d. 24 Feb 1897.

12. JOHNATHAN[7] MACY *(LUCINDA[6] BARNARD, EUNICE[5] FITCH, DEBORAH[4] GORHAM, SHUBAEL[3], DESIRE[2] HOWLAND, JOHN[1],)* was born 06 May 1791 in New Garden MM, Guilford Co, NC, and died 11 Oct 1865 in Rogersville, Henry, Indiana, USA. He married HANNAH PIERCE 01 Sep 1809 in Lost Creek, Jefferson, Tennessee, USA. She was born 01 Jun 1792 in Guilford, North Carolina, USA, and died 14 Dec 1866 in Rogersville, Henry, Indiana, USA.

    Children of JOHNATHAN MACY and HANNAH PIERCE are:

      i.   DAVID[8] MACY, b. 22 Nov 1816, Lost Creek, Jefferson, Tennessee, USA; d. 30 Nov 1901, Kokomo, Howard, Indiana, USA.

      ii. ISAAC MACY, b. 20 Jun 1822, Lost Creek, Jefferson, Tennessee, USA; d. 1854, Springfield Mm, Indiana, USA.

     iii. EZRA MACY, b. 30 Aug 1812, Lost Creek, Jefferson, Tennessee, USA; d. Monroe, Randolph, Indiana, USA.

     iv. JETHRO MACY, b. 25 Jun 1825, Henry, Indiana, USA[1]; d. Monroe, Randolph, Indiana, USA.

      v. AARON MACY, b. 21 Sep 1829, Henry, Indiana, USA[1]; d. Farmland, Randolph, Indiana, USA.

     vi. WILLIAM MACY, b. 1825, Henry, Indiana, USA; d. 1828, Henry, Indiana, USA.

    vii. EUNICE MACY, b. 02 Sep 1809, Lost Creek, Jefferson, Tennessee, USA; d. Mount Harper, Kansas, USA.

   viii. MARY MACY, b. 14 Oct 1819, Lost Creek, Jefferson, Tennessee, USA; d. 18 Nov 1880, Springfield Mm, Indiana, USA.

13. ISAAC[7] MACY *(LUCINDA[6] BARNARD, EUNICE[5] FITCH, DEBORAH[4] GORHAM, SHUBAEL[3], DESIRE[2] HOWLAND, JOHN[1],)* was born 02 Apr 1803 in Lost Creek, Jefferson Co, TN, and died 16 Dec 1847 in Wayne, Indiana, USA[1]. He married (1) ELENOR[1] 05 Apr 1825 in New Garden, North Carolina, USA. She was born 28 Jul 1804 in Lost Creek Jefferson, Tennessee, USA, and died 10 Feb 1894 in West River Settlement , Wayne, Indiana, USA. He married (2) ELEANOR THORNBURG[1] 05 Apr 1825 in Jefferson, Tennessee, USA. She was born 28 Jul 1804 in Lost Creek, Jefferson, Tennessee, USA, and died 10 Feb 1894 in West River Settlement, Wayne, Indiana, USA.

    Child of ISAAC MACY and ELEANOR THORNBURG is:

      i.   ELVIRA[8] MACY[1], b. 06 May 1830, Wayne, Indiana, USA[1].

14. JOHN[7] MACY *(LUCINDA[6] BARNARD, EUNICE[5] FITCH, DEBORAH[4] GORHAM, SHUBAEL[3], DESIRE[2] HOWLAND, JOHN[1],)* was born 03 Jun 1806 in Lost Creek, Jefferson Co, TN, and died 1872 in Oregon, USA. He married (2) ALICE MILLS[1] 10 Jun 1827[1]. She was born 24 May 1811 in Lost Creek Mm, Jefferson, Tennessee, and died 1894

    Child of JOHN MACY and ALICE MILLS is:

      i.   DEWITT CLINTON[8] MACY[1], b. 1844[1]; d. 1924[1].

    Children of JOHN MACY and ALICE MILLS are:

      ii. JONATHAN[8] MACY, b. 1834, Wayne, Indiana, USA[1]; d. 1860, Oregon, USA.

     iii. JOHN MACY, b. 1832, Wayne, Indiana, USA[1]; d. 1860, Oregon, USA.

     iv. MARY MACY, b. 1836, Vermilion, Illinois, USA.

      v. EUNICE MACY, b. 1838, Vermilion, Illinois, USA.

     vi. ASA L MACY, b. 1828, Wayne, Indiana, USA.

    vii. DAVID MACY, b. 1842, Vermilion, Illinois, USA.

   viii. EZRA MACY, b. 1840, Vermilion, Illinois, USA.

     ix. JUDITH MACY b. 1844, Vermilion, Illinois, USA.

      x. ALVIN G MACY, b. 1830, Wayne, Indiana, USA.

15. JONATHON B.[8] MACY *(WILLIAM[7], LUCINDA[6] BARNARD, EUNICE[5] FITCH, DEBORAH[4] GORHAM, SHUBAEL[3], DESIRE[2] HOWLAND, JOHN[1],)* was born 07 Mar 1810 in Lost Creek MM, Jefferson Co, TN, and died 15 Sep 1850 in Economy, Wayne Co., Indiana. He married MATILDA PIERCE 14 Feb 1833 in Wayne Co, IN. She was born 1817 in OH and died 9-5-1877 in IN.

Children of JONATHON MACY and MATILDA PIERCE are:

    i.   CHARLOTTE[9] MACY, b. 1837, Indiana.
   ii.   LUCINDA MACY, b. 1839, Indiana.

16. NATHAN HINSHAW[8] MACY *(WILLIAM[7], LUCINDA[6] BARNARD, EUNICE[5] FITCH, DEBORAH[4] GORHAM, SHUBAEL[3], DESIRE[2] HOWLAND, JOHN[1],)* was born 16 Aug 1811 in Lost Creek MM, Jefferson Co, TN, and died 23 Mar 1856 in Raccoon River, Redfield, Dallas Co, IA. He married SUSANNAH LEWIS[1] 15 Mar 1834 in Wayne, Indiana, USA. She was born 1810 in TN, and died 1870 in Iowa, USA.

Children of NATHAN MACY and SUSANNAH LEWIS are:

    i.   WILLIAM LEWIS MACY, b. 21 Oct 1834, Mooresville, Morgan, Indiana, USA; d. 21 Sep 1921, Adel, Dallas, Iowa, USA.
   ii.   MARY ANN MACY, b. 26 Apr 1836, Wayne, Indiana, USA; d. 15 Dec 1873, Worth, Missouri, USA.
  iii.   OLIVER CLINTON MACY, b. 12 Nov 1837, Wayne, Indiana, USA; d. 15 Oct 1895.
  iv.   THOMAS COLEMAN MACY, b. 10 Aug 1839, Wayne, Indiana, USA; d. 1870.
   v.   HANNAH MACY, b. 04 May 1841, Wayne, Indiana, USA; d. 28 Sep 1850, Wayne, Indiana, USA.
  vi.   MARGARET MALINDA MACY b. 23 Mar 1844, Wayne, Indiana, USA; d. 21 Sep 1850, Wayne, Indiana, USA.

17. ALVAH J[8] MACY *(WILLIAM[7], LUCINDA[6] BARNARD, EUNICE[5] FITCH, DEBORAH[4] GORHAM, SHUBAEL[3], DESIRE[2] HOWLAND, JOHN[1],)* was born 26 Feb 1813 in Lost Creek MM, Jefferson Co, TN, and died 09 Jul 1852 in Economy, Wayne Co., Indiana. He married MARY LEWIS 06 Oct 1833 in Economy, IN. She was born 1812 and died 5-1-1893.

Children of ALVAH MACY and MARY LEWIS are:

    i.   HANNAH MACY, b. 1836, Indiana.
   ii.   MALINDA MACY, b. 1837, Indiana.
  iii.   MINERVA MACY, b. 1840, Indiana.
  iv.   MATILDA MACY, b. 1840, Indiana.
   v.   HULDAH MACY, b. 1842, Indiana.
  vi.   LARKIN MACY, b. 1843, Indiana.
  vii.   WILLIAM MACY, b. 1845, Indiana.
 viii.   WAYNE MACY, b. 1847, Indiana.

18. JOHN HINSHAW[8] MACY *(WILLIAM[7], LUCINDA[6] BARNARD, EUNICE[5] FITCH, DEBORAH[4] GORHAM, SHUBAEL[3], DESIRE[2] HOWLAND, JOHN[1],)* was born 28 Nov 1816 in Lost Creek MM, Jefferson Co, TN, and died 01 Jun 1849 in Economy, IN. He married ELMIRA MARSHALL 02 Dec 1838 in Chester MM Wayne Co, IN. She was born 13 Nov 1815 in Whitewater, IN.

Children of JOHN MACY and ELMIRA MARSHALL are:

    i.   MILES[9] MACY, b. 02 Jan 1840, Wayne Co, IN.
   ii.   EUSTATIA MACY, b. 15 Jan 1842, Wayne Co, IN; d. 19 Dec 1898.
  iii.   ELVIRA MACY, b. 1843, Randolph Co, IN.
  iv.   ELISA MACY, b. 1845.

19. LUCINDA[8] MACY *(WILLIAM[7], LUCINDA[6] BARNARD, EUNICE[5] FITCH, DEBORAH[4] GORHAM, SHUBAEL[3], DESIRE[2] HOWLAND, JOHN[1],)[1]* was born 30 Aug 1818 in Lost CreekMM, Jefferson, TN[1], and died 1893 in Springbrook,Yamhill Co, OR. She married THOMAS MARSHALL HADLEY[1] 25 Nov 1838 in Mooresville, Morgan, Indiana, USA[1], son of ISAAC HADLEY and RUTH MARSHILL. He was born 14 Dec 1810 in Rowan, North Carolina, USA[1], and died 23 Oct 1893 in Newberg, Yamhill, Oregon, USA[1].

Children of LUCINDA MACY and THOMAS HADLEY are:
   i.   ENOS[9] HADLEY, b. 1838, Indiana, USA.
   ii. HANNAH HADLEY, b. 25 Sep 1840, Mooresville, Morgan, Indiana, USA[1]; d. 1905[1].
   iii. MARIAH HADLEY, b. 1841.
   iv. MELISSA HADLEY, b. 1841, Indiana, USA.
   v.   LYDIA ELLEN HADLEY, b. 14 Jan 1842, Mooresville, Morgan, Indiana, USA[1]; d. 21 Aug 1842, Morgan, Indiana, USA.
   vi. MALINDA HADLEY, b. 1843.
   vii. MATILDA HADLEY, b. 20 May 1843, Mooresville, Morgan, Indiana, USA; d. Oregon, USA.
   viii. SIMON HADLEY, b. 1844, Indiana, USA.
   ix. WILLIAM MACY HADLEY, b. 21 Feb 1845, Mooresville, Morgan, Indiana, USA; d. 21 Nov 1882, Yamhill County, Oregon; m. HATTIE FUSON, 11 Sep 1872, Mooresville, IN.
   x.   EVAN HADLEY, b. 1846, Indiana, USA.
   xi. RUTH ALMA HADLEY, b. 04 Oct 1847, Mooresville, Morgan, Indiana, USA; d. 11 Apr 1931.
   xii. MARY LUCINDA HADLEY, b. 17 Mar 1850, Mooresville, Morgan, Indiana, USA[1]; d. Rush, Indiana, USA.
   xiii. IVA HADLEY, b. 1852; d. 1852.
   xiv. IRA C HADLEY, b. 03 Dec 1852, Mooresville, Morgan, Indiana, USA; d. 23 Dec 1853, Morgan, Indiana, USA.
   xv. ELIZABETH A HADLEY, b. 1853, Mooresville, Morgan, Indiana, USA.
   xvi. MARGARET ANN HADLEY, b. 16 Feb 1854, Mooresville, Morgan, Indiana, USA; d. 1922.
   xvii. CORNELIA HADLEY, b. 13 Feb 1858, Mooresville, Morgan, Indiana, USA; d. 25 Nov 1876, Morgan, Indiana, USA.
   xviii. JOHN J HADLEY, b. 17 May 1860, Mooresville, Morgan, Indiana, USA; d. 1937.
   xix. FRANK HADLEY, b. 1863, Indiana.
   xx. HULDA P HADLEY, b. 25 Jul 1863, Mooresville, Morgan, Indiana, USA; d. 16 Jan 1889.

20. WILLIAM MONROE[8] MACY *(WILLIAM[7], LUCINDA[6] BARNARD, EUNICE[5] FITCH, DEBORAH[4] GORHAM, SHUBAEL[3], DESIRE[2] HOWLAND, JOHN[1],)* was born 08 Mar 1820 in Lost Creek MM, Jefferson Co,TN, and died 04 Jun 1911 in Denair, CA. He married **JULIA ANN MILLS** 16 Oct 1849 in Morgan Co, IN by JP John S Hubbard, daughter of HENRY MILLS and HANNAH WOODWARD. She was born 03 Jul 1829 in Wayne Co, IN, and died 22 Jul 1918 in Caldwell, ID of Bronchial Pneumonia.

More about **WILLIAM MONROE MACY:**
Assets1: 1850, $1600 in Wayne Co., IN
Assets2: 1860, $13200 RE & $4065 PP
Assets3: 1870, $28000 & $6000 PP
Builder1: 1859, Built 11room Italianate home on 343 acres
Builder2: 1861, Built Quaker Academy Building
Builder3: 1864, Built White Lick Meeting House in Mooresville, IN
Burial: Denair, CA Grave #32-A-07
Contributions: 12 Sep 1860, 1 of 13 Original donors for Quaker Academy
Elected: 22 Dec 1865, 1st President of Mooresville Monrovia Gravel Road Co.
Migration 2: 1854, Moved to Brown Twp. Morgan Co., IN
Migration 3: 1882, Moved to Dayton, OR
Migration 4: 1907, Moved to Greenleaf, ID
Member: 1861, Mooresville HS Assoc. Board of Trustees
Occupation: Farmer, Timber buyer, Fruit Orchard, Maple Syrup camp,
Property: 18 Apr 1882, Macy Farmstead and #342 acres sold to Martin Ruble for $18000
Religion: Quaker

More about **JULIA ANN MILLS:**
Burial: 24 Jul 1918, Denair, CA Grave #32-A-08

Children of **WILLIAM MACY** and **JULIA MILLS** are:

28.   i.   **ALVA PERRY[9] MACY**, b. 30 Jan 1858, Brown Twp Morgan Co, IN; d. 12 Aug 1918, Chico, CA of Jacksonian Epilepsy.

       ii. **AARON MILLS MACY**, b. 24 May 1855, Wayne Co., IN; d. 25 Sep 1877, Mooresville, IN of typhoid fever.
           Burial: White Lick Cemetery, Mooresville, IN
           Occupation: 1876, Teacher @ Bethel School
           Religion: Quaker

29.   iii. **CYNTHIA RUTH MACY**, b. 17 Sep 1861, Mooresville, IN; d. 18 Apr 1934, Greenleaf, ID or New Plymouth, ID of strangulated umbilical hernia.

       iv. **HANNAH MARIAH MACY**, b. 26 Jan 1853, Wayne Co., IN; d. 10 Dec 1866, Mooresville, IN.
           died of spotted fever
           Burial: White Lick Cemetery, Mooresville, IN

       v. LYDDIA JANE ANDREW (ADOPTED), b. 1869.

21. MARGARET ANN[8] MACY *(WILLIAM[7], LUCINDA[6] BARNARD, EUNICE[5] FITCH, DEBORAH[4] GORHAM, SHUBAEL[3], DESIRE[2] HOWLAND, JOHN[1],)* was born 22 Mar 1822 in Randolph Co, IN, and died 19 Aug 1899 in Mooresville, IN. She married LEVI S HADLEY[1] 25 May 1850 in Morgan Co, IN, son of SIMON HADLEY and SARAH HADLEY. He was born 30 Oct 1826 in Morgan, Indiana, USA[1], and died 13 Mar 1891 in Morgan, Indiana, USA[1].

Children of MARGARET MACY and LEVI HADLEY are:

    i.   MALINDA JANE[9] HADLEY[1], b. 08 Apr 1851, Morgan, Indiana, USA[1]; d. 14 Mar 1925[1].
    ii.   LYDIA ELLEN HADLEY[1], b. 22 Jun 1852, Morgan, Indiana, USA[1]; d. 10 Aug 1934[1].
    iii. WAYNE COLEMAN HADLEY[1], b. 05 Dec 1853, Morgan, Indiana, USA[1]; d. 05 Sep 1913[1].
    iv. ACHSA ANN HADLEY[1], b. 28 Sep 1855, Indiana, USA[1]; d. 22 Aug 1920[1].
    v.   GULIA ELLEN HADLEY, b. 17 Nov 1858, Indiana, USA[1]; d. 14 Aug 1890[1].
    vi. ORA RUTH HADLEY[1], b. 15 Dec 1860, Morgan, Indiana, USA[1]; d. 21 Sep 1921[1].
    vii. IRA W HADLEY[1], b. 20 Feb 1863, Morgan, Indiana, USA[1]; d. 23 Feb 1948, Morgan, Indiana, USA[1].
   viii. LUCINDA M HADLEY[1], b. 20 Jul 1865, Morgan, Indiana, USA[1]; d. 08 Jan 1920[1].

22. SARAH[8] MACY *(WILLIAM[7], LUCINDA[6] BARNARD, EUNICE[5] FITCH, DEBORAH[4] GORHAM, SHUBAEL[3], DESIRE[2] HOWLAND, JOHN[1],)* was born 23 Nov 1823 in Randolph Co, IN, and died 10 Jun 1873. She married THOMAS LINDLEY HADLEY 17 Nov 1841 in Randolph Co, IN, son of JOSHUA HADLEY and SARAH LINDLEY. He was born 07 Jul 1821 in Chatham Co., NC, and died 23 Jul 1883 in Mooresville, IN.

Children of SARAH MACY and THOMAS HADLEY are:

    i.   MARY E[9] HADLEY, b. 15 Feb 1843.
    ii.   PERRY MACY HADLEY, b. 04 Dec 1845, Morgan Co, IN; d. 01 Apr 1925, Earlham, IA.
    iii. JOSHUA HADLEY, b. 02 May 1847, Morgan Co, IN.
    iv. ZIMRI HADLEY, b. 27 Mar 1849, Morgan Co, IN.
    v.   HANNAH E HADLEY, b. 16 Oct 1850, Morgan Co, IN.
    vi. WILLIAM L HADLEY, b. 13 Apr 1852, Morgan Co, IN.
    vii. AARON HADLEY, b. 21 Jun 1854, Morgan Co, IN.
   viii. IRWIN A HADLEY, b. 19 Jun 1857, Morgan Co, IN.
    ix. EDWIN J HADLEY, b. 19 Jun 1857, Morgan Co, IN.
    x.   RUANNA HADLEY, b. 09 Sep 1859, Morgan Co, IN; d. 02 Dec 1931, Greenleaf, ID.
    xi. SARAH RUTH HADLEY, b. 05 Oct 1861, Morgan Co, IN.
    xii. JOHN B HADLEY, b. 1864, Morgan Co, IN.

23. PERRY T[8] MACY *(WILLIAM[7], LUCINDA[6] BARNARD, EUNICE[5] FITCH, DEBORAH[4] GORHAM, SHUBAEL[3], DESIRE[2] HOWLAND, JOHN[1],)* was born 17 Aug 1825 in Randolph Co., IN, and died 07 May 1889 in Mooresville, IN. He married (1) REBECCA BOWLES, daughter of GEORGE BOWLES and ELIZABETH BAILEY. She was born 24 Oct 1833 in Randolph Co, Indiana, USA, and died 12 Apr 1912 in Mooresville, Indiana, USA. He married CHARITY MILLS 14 Sep 1848, daughter of HENRY MILLS and HANNAH WOODWARD. She was born 24 Oct 1833, and died 27 Dec 1863 in Mooresville, IN.

More about PERRY T MACY:
Burial: White Lick Cemetery,
   Mooresville, IN

More about CHARITY MILLS:
Burial: White Lick Cemetery
   Mooresville, IN

Children of PERRY MACY and CHARITY MILLS are:
30.   i.   ALBERT W[9] MACY, b. 18 Jan 1853, Hendricks Co., IN.
        ii.   CHARLES L MACY.
        iii.   IDA ELLEN MACY, b. 12 Apr 1862, Mooresville, IN.

Children of PERRY MACY and REBECCA BOWLES are:
        iv.   ALBERT[9] MACY, b. 1853, Indiana.
        v.   CHARLOTTE L MACY, b. 1857, Indiana.
        vi.   WILLIAM SEWARD HADLEY, b. 19 Mar 1860, Stuart Co, Iowa; d. 09 Apr 1897.
        vii.   IDA E MACY, b. 1862, Indiana.
        viii.   OLIVER MACY, b. 1870, Indiana.
        ix.   VERNON MACY, b. 26 Jul 1875, Morgan Co, Indiana.

24. IRA C[8] MACY *(WILLIAM[7], LUCINDA[6] BARNARD, EUNICE[5] FITCH, DEBORAH[4] GORHAM, SHUBAEL[3], DESIRE[2] HOWLAND, JOHN[1],)* was born 28 May 1828 in Randolph Co, IN. He married ACHSAH JOHNSON 31 Aug 1853 in Morgan Co, IN. She was born 16 Jun 1834.

Children of IRA MACY and ACHSAH JOHNSON are:
        i.   ZERNAH ELLEN[9] MACY, b. 30 Oct 1855, Randolph Co., IN; d. 19 Jan 1955, Morgan Co, IN.
        ii.   EMMA M MACY, b. 1862.
        iii.   JERAMIAH MACY.
        iv.   MILES H MACY.

25. RUTH ALMA[8] MACY *(WILLIAM[7], LUCINDA[6] BARNARD, EUNICE[5] FITCH, DEBORAH[4] GORHAM, SHUBAEL[3], DESIRE[2] HOWLAND, JOHN[1],)* was born 09 Jan 1830 in Randolph Co, IN, and died 18 Dec 1909. She married MILES S HADLEY[1] 29 Mar 1850 in Morgan Co, IN, son of SIMON HADLEY and SARAH HADLEY. He was born 18 Jun 1828 in Mooresville, Morgan, Indiana, USA, and died 29 Dec 1911 in Mooresville, Morgan, Indiana, USA.

Children of RUTH MACY and MILES HADLEY are:
        i.   ALVAH MACY[9] HADLEY[1], b. 15 Jan 1851, Mooresville, Morgan, Indiana, USA[1]; d. 03 Nov 1924.
        ii.   HANNAH ELMINA HADLEY[1], b. 1856, Indiana; d. 16 Dec 1939, Mooresville, Morgan, Indiana, USA.
        iii.   GULIA EFFIE HADLEY[1], b. 16 Jan 1868[1]; d. 26 Feb 1868.

26. MARY ANN⁸ MACY *(WILLIAM⁷, LUCINDA⁶ BARNARD, EUNICE⁵ FITCH, DEBORAH⁴ GORHAM, SHUBAEL³, DESIRE² HOWLAND, JOHN¹)* was born 01 Oct 1831 in Randolph Co, IN, and died 03 Jan 1889 in Newberg, Oregon, USA. She married ALBERT HADLEY 03 Apr 1852 in Mooresville, son of JOSHUA HADLEY and MARY T. He was born 14 Feb 1831 in Hendricks, Indiana, USA, and died 24 Mar 1866 in Hendricks Co., IN.

Children of MARY MACY and ALBERT HADLEY are:
- i. CALVIN R⁹ HADLEY, b. 1853, Indiana.
- ii. EDITH HADLEY, b. 1855, Indiana.
- iii. ALONZO HADLEY¹, b. 19 Feb 1857, Mooresville, Morgan, Indiana, USA; d. 30 Apr 1925, Newberg, Yamhill, Oregon, USA¹.
- iv. MACY B HADLEY, b. 1858, Indiana.
- v. ELI HADLEY, b. 1860, Indiana.
- vi. LAURA HADLEY, b. 1862, Indiana.
- vii. MIRANDA HADLEY, b. 1863, Indiana.
- viii. HANNAH E HADLEY, b. 1866, Indiana.

27. LYDIA ANN⁸ MACY *(WILLIAM⁷, LUCINDA⁶ BARNARD, EUNICE⁵ FITCH, DEBORAH⁴ GORHAM, SHUBAEL³, DESIRE² HOWLAND, JOHN¹)* was born 16 Apr 1834 in Randolph Co, IN, and died 24 Feb 1897. She married JOHN FRANKLIN HADLEY 13 Mar 1859 in Morgan Co, IN. He was born 14 Jan 1840 in Indiana, and died 04 Apr 1898 in Morgan Co, IN.

Children of LYDIA MACY and JOHN HADLEY are:
- i. WILLIAM AARON⁹ HADLEY, b. 1860, Indiana.
- ii. MALINDA ALMA HADLEY, b. 1863, Indiana.
- iii. MAHLON J HADLEY, b. 1867, Indiana.
- iv. CORA H HADLEY, b. Indiana.
- v. LINNIE HADLEY, b. Indiana.

28. ALVA PERRY⁹ MACY *(WILLIAM MONROE⁸, WILLIAM⁷, LUCINDA⁶ BARNARD, EUNICE⁵ FITCH, DEBORAH⁴ GORHAM, SHUBAEL³, DESIRE² HOWLAND, JOHN¹)* was born 30 Jan 1858 in Brown Twp Morgan Co, IN, and died 12 Aug 1918 in Chico, CA of Jacksonian Epilepsy. He married IDA MAY MOORE 29 Sep 1886, daughter of ALFRED MOORE and MARTHA KERR. She was born 14 Apr 1862 in New Providence, IOWA, and died 10 Aug 1933 in Chico, CA.

More about **ALVA PERRY MACY:**
Burial: Chico, CA
Contributions: 1872, Diary of life on Macy Farmstead
Emigration 2: 1905, Moves to California
Immigration 1: 1882, Moves to Dayton, OR with father, mother, & sister
Occupation: Farmer

More about **IDA MAY MOORE:**
Burial: Chico, CA
Family: She was the niece of Samuel Moore, founder of Mooresville

Children of **ALVA MACY** and IDA MOORE are:
  i. NORMAN KERR¹⁰ MACY, b. 27 Aug 1890, Oregon; d. 15 Nov 1949, Los Angeles; m. (1) RITA STELLER; m. (2) ESTELLA LEWIS, 02 Jun 1915; b. 1891, IL.
  ii. MAUDE LAVERNE MACY, b. 08 Mar 1892, Oregon; d. 07 Jul 1960, Chico, CA; m. ERROL WALTER CRAWFORD, 01 Jun 1916.
31. iii. BRUCE WARD MACY, b. 20 Nov 1893, Dayton, Oregon; d. 27 Jan 1986, Magalia, Butte Co., CA.
  iv. RUTH W MACY, b. 1894, Oregon.

29. CYNTHIA RUTH⁹ MACY *(WILLIAM MONROE⁸, WILLIAM⁷, LUCINDA⁶ BARNARD, EUNICE⁵ FITCH, DEBORAH⁴ GORHAM, SHUBAEL³, DESIRE² HOWLAND, JOHN¹,)* was born 17 Sep 1861 in Mooresville, IN, and died 18 Apr 1934 in Greenleaf, ID or New Plymouth, ID of Strangulated umbilical hernia. She married OWEN HATFIELD 17 Sep 1886 in Dayton, OR. He was born 17 May 1839 in Dayton, OR, and died 14 Feb 1916 in Greenleaf, ID of Mephutis Bronchial Asthma.

More about CYNTHIA RUTH MACY: More about OWEN HATFIELD:
Burial: McMinnville, OR   Burial: McMinnville, OR
Cause of death: Herniotomy, (operation for strangulated hernia)
Children of **CYNTHIA MACY** and OWEN HATFIELD are:
32. i. ARTHUR WILLIAM¹⁰ HATFIELD, b. 10 Nov 1887, Dayton, OR.
33. ii. BERNICE MACY HATFIELD, b. 20 Mar 1890, Dayton, OR; d. 1976.
34. iii. MACY L HATFIELD, b. 26 May 1892, Dayton, Oregon; d. 10 Dec 1945, Payette, ID.

30. ALBERT W⁹ MACY *(PERRY T⁸, WILLIAM⁷, LUCINDA⁶ BARNARD, EUNICE⁵ FITCH, DEBORAH⁴ GORHAM, SHUBAEL³, DESIRE² HOWLAND, JOHN¹,)* was born 18 Jan 1853 in Hendricks Co., IN. He married EMMA K MILLS, daughter of JEHU MILLS and SARAH C. She was born 11 Sep 1857.

Children of **ALBERT MACY** and EMMA MILLS are:
  i. ROY W¹⁰ MACY, b. 06 Dec 1879.
  ii. FLORENCE M MACY, b. 04 Nov 1886.
  iii. LUCILLE B MACY, b. 16 Dec 1893.

31. BRUCE WARD[10] MACY *(ALVA PERRY[9], WILLIAM MONROE[8], WILLIAM[7], LUCINDA[6] BARNARD, EUNICE[5] FITCH, DEBORAH[4] GORHAM, SHUBAEL[3], DESIRE[2] HOWLAND, JOHN[1],) was* born 20 Nov 1893 in Dayton, Oregon, and died 27 Jan 1986 in Magalia, Butte Co., CA. He married SHIRLEY MARCH 27 Sep 1916, daughter of O. W. MARCH. She was born 23 Jun 1894.

Children of BRUCE MACY and SHIRLEY MARCH are:
- i. MARGARET MAE[11] MACY, b. 15 Nov 1917.
- ii. BRUCE MARCH MACY, b. 11 Nov 1918.
- iii. SHIRLEY MARILEE MACY, b. 18 Jul 1920.
- 35.   iv. MARGARET ANN MACY, b. 13 Dec 1924; d. 16 Jun 1961.

32. ARTHUR WILLIAM[10] HATFIELD *(CYNTHIA RUTH[9] MACY, WILLIAM MONROE[8], WILLIAM[7], LUCINDA[6] BARNARD, EUNICE[5] FITCH, DEBORAH[4] GORHAM, SHUBAEL[3], DESIRE[2] HOWLAND, JOHN[1],)* was born 10 Nov 1887 in Dayton, OR. He married STELLA WATSON.
Children of ARTHUR HATFIELD and STELLA WATSON are:
- i. CHESEL[11] HATFIELD.
- ii. ARLIE LAWRENCE HATFIELD.

33. BERNICE MACY[10] HATFIELD *(CYNTHIA RUTH[9] MACY, WILLIAM MONROE[8], WILLIAM[7], LUCINDA[6] BARNARD, EUNICE[5] FITCH, DEBORAH[4] GORHAM, SHUBAEL[3], DESIRE[2] HOWLAND, John)* was born 20 Mar 1890 in Dayton, OR, and died 1976. She married (1) FLOYD WENDELL WILLIAMS 16 Feb 1910 in Greenleaf, ID. He was born 13 Apr 1887 in Lynnville, IA, and died 16 Nov 1925 in Greenleaf, ID. She married (2) SEBURN DORLAND WILLIAMS 09 Jun 1932.
Children of BERNICE HATFIELD and FLOYD WILLIAMS are:
- i. RONALD RICHMOND[11] WILLIAMS, b. 29 Dec 1910.
- ii. **MADELL LUCILLE WILLIAMS**, b. 17 Jun 1913; m. FRANCIS WONDERLY.
- iii. RUTH QUIMBY WILLIAMS, b. 05 Jun 1915.
- iv. FLOYD WENDELL WILLIAMS, b. 09 Feb 1918.
- v. **KENNETH MORGAN WILLIAMS**, b. 09 Feb 1920.
- vi. **DONALD KEITH WILLIAMS**, b. 13 Apr 1921.
- vii. LEWIS HAROLD WILLIAMS, b. 04 Aug 1922.
- viii. MACY LEDRU WILLIAMS, b. 1911.

34. MACY L[10] HATFIELD *(CYNTHIA RUTH[9] MACY, WILLIAM MONROE[8], WILLIAM[7], LUCINDA[6] BARNARD, EUNICE[5] FITCH, DEBORAH[4] GORHAM, SHUBAEL[3], DESIRE[2] HOWLAND, JOHN[1],)* was born 26 May 1892 in Dayton, Oregon, and died 10 Dec 1945 in Payette, ID. He married EMMA BOREN 26 May 1935.
Child of MACY HATFIELD and EMMA BOREN is:
- i. NORA MAE[11] HATFIELD, b. 1942.

35. MARGARET ANN[11] MACY *(BRUCE WARD[10], ALVA PERRY[9], WILLIAM MONROE[8], WILLIAM[7], LUCINDA[6] BARNARD, EUNICE[5] FITCH, DEBORAH[4] GORHAM, SHUBAEL[3], DESIRE[2] HOWLAND, JOHN[1],)* was born 13 Dec 1924, and died 16 Jun 1961. She married LYNN MORTON MARCH 03 Mar 1945.

Children of MARGARET MACY and LYNN MARCH are:

    i.   MARGARET ANN[12] MARCH, b. 26 Dec 1945.

    ii. LYNN MARCH, b. 29 Dec 1947.

    iii. **MARILEE FRANCES MARCH**, b. 07 Sep 1949; m. WILLIAM S JOHNSON; b. 1944.

         More About MARILEE FRANCES MARCH:

         Assets: 2006, Charitable descendent of John Howland

         Contributions: 2004, Donated family history items to Earlham College

               Sep 2006, Visited WMMacy Farmstead

    iv. BRUCE COLEMAN MARCH, b. 10 Jan 1951.

Endnotes

1. Ancestry.com, One World Tree (sm), Provo, UT, USA: The Generations Network, Inc., n.d., Online publication - Ancestry.com. OneWorldTree [database on-line]. Provo, UT, USA: The Generations Network, Inc.

Descendants of Thomas Macy

Generation No. 1

1. THOMAS MACY was born 1608 in Chilmark, Co Witshire, England, and died 19 Apr 1682 in Nantucket. He married SARAH HOPCOTT Abt. 1643 in England. She was born 1612 in Chilmark, England, and died 1682 in Nantucket.

More about **THOMAS MACY**:
Appointed: 1654, Deputy to the General Court
Confirmation: 06 Sep 1639, Made a freeman
Elected: 04 Mar 1642/43, 1 of 7 selectmen of Salisbury
migration: 1659, Among 1st settlers of Nantucket
Religion: Baptist
Residence: Lived on mainland Mass. for 20 years

Children of **THOMAS MACY and SARAH HOPCOTT** are:

	i.	SARAH² MACY, b. 09 Jul 1644; d. 1645.
	ii.	SARAH MACY II, b. 01 Aug 1646, Salisbury; d. 1701, Nantucket; m. WILLIAM WORTH, 01 Apr 1665, Nantucket; b. 1640, England; d. 1723, Nantucket.
	iii.	MARY MACY, b. 04 Dec 1648; d. 06 Jun 1712, Nantucket; m. WILLIAM BUNKER; b. 1640; d. 1712.
	iv.	BETHIA MACY, b. 1650; d. 1732, Nantucket; m. JOSEPH GARDNER, 30 Mar 1670.
	v.	THOMAS MACY, b. 22 Sep 1653; d. 03 Dec 1675, Nantucket; m. UNMARRIED.
2.	vi.	JOHN MACY, b. 14 Jul 1655, Salisbury, Mass; d. 14 Oct 1691, Nantucket.
	vii.	FRANCIS MACY, b. 1657; d. 1658.

Generation No. 2

2. JOHN MACY I was born 14 Jul 1655 in Salisbury, Mass, and died 14 Oct 1691 in Nantucket. He married **DEBORAH GARDNER** 1676 on Nantucket, daughter of RICHARD GARDNER and SARAH SHATTUCK. She was born 12 Feb 1657/58, and died 02 Apr 1712 on Nantucket.

Children of **JOHN MACY and DEBORAH GARDNER** are:

3.	i.	JOHN³ MACY II, b. Abt. 1675, Nantucket; d. 28 Nov 1751, Nantucket.
	ii.	SARAH MACY, b. 03 Apr 1677, Nantucket; d. 18 Mar 1747/48; m. JOHN BARNARD.
4.	iii.	DEBORAH MACY, b. 03 Mar 1678/79, Nantucket; d. 16 Aug 1742.
	iv.	BETHIAH MACY, b. 08 Apr 1683, Nantucket; d. 26 Jun 1738.
5.	v.	JABEZ MACY, b. 1684, Nantucket; d. 07 Aug 1776.
	vi.	MARY MACY, b. 1685, Nantucket; d. 27 Jun 1716.
	vii.	THOMAS MACY, b. 1687, Nantucket; d. 16 Mar 1759.
	viii.	RICHARD MACY, b. 22 Sep 1689, Nantucket; d. 25 Dec 1779.

3. **JOHN MACY II** *(John2, Thomas1)* was born Abt. 1675 in Nantucket, and died 28 Nov 1751 in Nantucket. He married **JUDITH WORTH** 25 Apr 1707 in Nantucket, daughter of JOHN WORTH and MIRIAM GARDNER. She was born 22 Dec 1689 in Nantucket, and died 08 Nov 1767 in Nantucket.

Children of **JOHN MACY II and JUDITH WORTH** are:

	i.	CALEB[4] MACY.
	ii.	MIRIAM MACY, b. 16 Feb 1707/08; d. 01 Aug 1736.
	iii.	SILVANUS MACY, b. 16 Aug 1709; d. 06 Sep 1719.
	iv.	SETH MACY, b. 22 Aug 1710; d. 06 Jul 1790.
	v.	ELIAB MACY, b. 20 Dec 1712; d. Apr 1723.
	vi.	DAVID MACY, b. 12 Sep 1714; d. New Garden MM, Guilford Co.,NC.
	vii.	ANNA MACY, b. 17 Dec 1717; d. 13 Dec 1756.
	viii.	BETHIAH MACY, b. 16 Jan 1718/19; d. 1729.
6.	ix.	**JOHN MACY III**, b. 23 Dec 1721, Nantucket; d. 18 Jul 1795, New Garden, NC @ home of son **Barachiah**.
	x.	JUDITH MACY, b. 20 Mar 1722/23; d. 25 Jun 1795.
	xi.	JOHNATHAN MACY, b. 20 Apr 1725; d. 17 Jun 1798.
	xii.	WILLIAM MACY, b. 23 Jan 1725/26; d. 06 Feb 1753.
	xiii.	SARAH MACY, b. 25 Jun 1729.
	xiv.	ABIGAIL MACY, b. 26 May 1731; d. 25 Nov 1763.

4. **DEBORAH MACY** *(JOHN[2], THOMAS[1],)* was born 03 Mar 1678/79 in Nantucket, and died 16 Aug 1742. She married DANIEL RUSSELL.

Child of DEBORAH MACY and DANIEL RUSSELL is:

7.	i.	WILLIAM RUSSELL.

5. **JABEZ MACY** *(JOHN2, THOMAS1)* was born 1684 in Nantucket, and died 07 Aug 1776. He married SARAH STARBUCK.

Children of JABEZ MACY and SARAH STARBUCK are:

	i.	GEORGE[4] MACY, b. 11 Mar 1719/20, Nantucket.
	ii.	EUNICE MACY, b. 14 Nov 1721, Nantucket.
	iii.	DORCAS MACY, b. 16 Jun 1724, Nantucket.
	iv.	DANIEL MACY, b. 21 May 1731, Nantucket; d. 28 Mar 1785, Nantucket.
	v.	MATTHEW MACY, b. 19 Oct 1732, Nantucket.
	vi.	LYDIA MACY, b. 18 Sep 1734, Nantucket; d. 04 Sep 1822.
	vii.	SARAH MACY, b. 26 Sep 1737, Nantucket; d. 17 Nov 1800.
	viii.	JABEZ MACY, b. 30 Oct 1739, Nantucket; d. 18 Sep 1767.

6. **JOHN MACY III** *(JOHN³, JOHN², THOMAS¹,)* was born 23 Dec 1721 in Nantucket, and died 18 Jul 1795 in New Garden, NC @ home of son Barachiah. He married **EUNICE COLEMAN** 13 Aug 1743 in Nantucket, daughter of ELIHU COLEMAN and JEMIMA BARNARD. She was born 17 Oct 1724 in Nantucket, and died 28 Dec 1768 in Nantucket.

More about **JOHN MACY III**:
Emigration: 18 Apr 1771, From Nantucket to New Garden,NC
John Macy III died at the home of **Barachiah Macy** in Guilford Co, NC

Children of **JOHN MACY III and EUNICE COLEMAN** are:
- i. BETHIAH⁵ MACY, b. 03 Aug 1744, Nantucket Island, MA; d. 29 Sep 1810.
- ii. JUDITH MACY, b. 20 May 1746, Nantucket Island, MA.
- iii. ELIAB MACY, b. 09 Jun 1748, Nantucket Island, MA; d. 15 Aug 1749, Nantucket.
- iv. JEMIMA MACY, b. 15 May 1750, Nantucket Island, MA.
- v. EUNICE MACY, b. 12 May 1752, Nantucket Island, MA; d. Nantucket.
- vi. JOHN IV MACY, b. 09 Feb 1754, Nantucket Island, MA; d. 30 Nov 1785.
- vii. ELIHU MACY, b. 20 Nov 1755, Nantucket Island, MA.
- viii. EUNICE MACY, b. 27 Dec 1757, Nantucket Island, MA; d. 04 Jul 1759, Nantucket.
- 8. ix. **BARACHIAH MACY**, b. 24 Feb 1760, Nantucket Island, MA; d. 28 Aug 1832, Economy, Wayne Co., Indiana.
- 9. x. MERAB MACY, b. 30 Nov 1761, Nantucket, Nantucket, Massachusetts, USA; d. 22 Jan 1844, New Garden MM, Guilford Co.,NC.
- xi. ABIGAIL MACY, b. 06 Dec 1763, Nantucket Island, MA; d. 05 Jan 1764, Nantucket.
- xii. MICAJAH MACY, b. 25 Nov 1764, Nantucket Island, MA.
- xiii. ALMY MACY, b. 05 Nov 1766, Nantucket Island, MA; d. 1820; m. LIBNI BARNARD; b. 1764.
- xiv. CLEMENT MACY, b. 24 Dec 1768, Nantucket Island, MA.
- xv. DINAH MACY, b. Nantucket Island, MA.

7. **WILLIAM RUSSELL** *(DEBORAH MACY, JOHN², THOMAS¹,)* He married RUTH SWAIN 1737.

Child of **WILLIAM RUSSELL** and **RUTH SWAIN** is:
- i. TIMOTHY RUSSELL.

8. BARACHIAH¹⁵ MACY *(JOHN⁴, JOHN³, JOHN², THOMAS¹,)* was born 24 Feb 1760 in Nantucket Island, MA, and died 28 Aug 1832 in Economy, Wayne Co., Indiana. He married (1) **LUCINDA BARNARD** 20 Mar 1783 in New Garden MM, NC, daughter of BENJAMIN BARNARD and EUNICE FITCH. She was born 17 Mar 1767 in Nantucket Island, MA, and died 05 Apr 1810 in Lost Creek, Jefferson Co., TN. He married (2) ELIZABETH WOODWARD 01 Nov 1815 in Lost Creek MM, Jefferson Co., TN. She was born 08 Apr 1769.

More about **BARACHIAH MACY:**
Appointed: 21 May 1803, appointed clerk of Lost Creek MM
Migration 1: 1771, Quakers settled S&W of Guilford Co. NC
Migration 2: 18 Apr 1771, Moved to North Carolina
Migration 3: 1801, Helped his Brother in law move to Jefferson Co. TN
Migration 4: 01 Jan 1802, Moved family to Jefferson Co TN
Migration 5: 27 Sep 1828, Cert. Springfield MM, Henry Co.,IN

Children of **BARACHIAH MACY and LUCINDA BARNARD** are:

	i.	MARY⁶ MACY, b. 08 Mar 1784, New Garden MM, Guilford Co.,NC; d. 1885, Guilford Co, NC.
10.	ii.	**WILLIAM MACY**, b. 04 Oct 1786, New Garden MM, Guilford Co.,NC; d. 17 Jan 1869, Mooresville, IN.
	iii.	MARY MACY II, b. 17 Dec 1788, New Garden MM, Guilford Co.,NC.
11.	iv.	JOHNATHAN MACY, b. 06 May 1791, New Garden MM, Guilford Co.,NC; d. 11 Oct 1865, Rogersville, Henry, Indiana, USA.
	v.	ANNA MACY, b. 15 Sep 1793, New Garden MM, Guilford Co.,NC.
	vi.	MATILDA MACY, b. 17 Feb 1796, New Garden MM, Guilford Co.,NC.
	vii.	EUNICE MACY, b. 07 Apr 1799, New Garden MM, Guilford Co.,NC; d. 15 May 1801, Guilford Co, NC.
	viii.	ELIHU MACY, b. 11 Jul 1801, New Garden MM, Guilford Co.,NC; d. 09 Mar 1802, Guilford Co, NC.
12.	ix.	ISAAC MACY, b. 02 Apr 1803, Lost Creek, Jefferson Co, TN; d. 16 Dec 1847, Wayne, Indiana, USA.
13.	x.	JOHN MACY, b. 03 Jun 1806, Lost Creek, Jefferson Co, TN; d. 1872, Oregon, USA.
	xi.	LYDIA MACY¹, b. 05 Nov 1808, Lost Creek, Jefferson, TN¹; d. 05 Feb 1875, Dalton Township, Wayne, Indiana, USA¹; m. LEWIS THORNBURGH¹, 25 Mar 1829, Springfield Mm, Wayne, Indiana, USA¹; b. 20 Feb 1802, Lost Creek, Jefferson, Tennessee, USA¹; d. 12 Jul 1890, Dalton Township, Wayne, Indiana, USA¹.

9. MERAB¹⁵ MACY *(JOHN⁴, JOHN³, JOHN², THOMAS¹,)* was born 30 Nov 1761 in Nantucket, Nantucket, Massachusetts, USA¹, and died 22 Jan 1844 in New Garden MM, Guilford Co, NC.

Children of MERAB MACY are:

	i.	ANNA⁶ MACY¹, b. 03 Oct 1803, New Garden MM, Guilford, North Carolina, USA¹; d. 19 Jul 1806, New Garden Mm, Guilford, North Carolina, USA¹.
	ii.	JETHRO MACY¹, b. 11 Mar 1792, New Garden MM, Guilford, North Carolina, USA¹; d. 13 Jul 1796, New Garden Mm, Guilford, North Carolina, USA¹.
	iii.	DAVID MACY¹, b. 26 Sep 1798, New Garden MM, Guilford, North Carolina, USA¹; d. 24 Apr 1808, New Garden Mm, Guilford, North Carolina, USA¹.
	iv.	EUNICE MACY¹, b. 18 Jun 1786, New Garden MM, Guilford, North Carolina, USA¹; d. 05 Nov 1847, Indiana, USA¹.
	v.	JETHRO MACY¹, b. 25 Feb 1805, New Garden MM, Guilford, North Carolina, USA¹; d. 01 Jan 1831, Indiana, USA¹.
	vi.	ELIZABETH MACY¹, b. 19 Apr 1784, New Garden MM, Guilford, North Carolina, USA¹; d. 05 Nov 1847, Indiana¹.

10. WILLIAM MACY *(BARACHIAH[5], JOHN[4], JOHN[3], JOHN[2], THOMAS[1],)* was born 04 Oct 1786 in New Garden MM, Guilford Co., NC, and died 17 Jan 1869 in Mooresville, IN. He married HANNAH HINSHAW 01 Mar 1809 in Lost Creek MM, Jefferson Co, TN, daughter of WILLIAM HINSHAW and MARGARET HUNT. She was born 08 Feb 1789 in Lost Creek, Guilford Co, NC, and died 19 Feb 1866 in Mooresville, IN.

More about **WILLIAM MACY:**
Appointed: 1822, Clerk of Springfield Monthly Meeting
Burial: White Lick Cemetery, Mooresville, IN
Migration 1: 1801, Spent summer in TN raising crop for family move
Migration 2: Jan 1802, Moved to Lost Creek, Jefferson Co, TN
Migration 3: Apr 1820, Moved to West River Twp. Randolph Co, IN
Migration 4: 27 Sep 1828, To Springfield MM, Wayne Co., IN
Migration 5: 1856, Moved to Brown Twp. Morgan Co., IN
Military service: 1812, Refused to serve in Andrew Jackson's Army (War of 1812)
Religion: Quaker
Retirement: Wrote his Autobiography

More about HANNAH HINSHAW:
Burial: White Lick Cemetery, Mooresville, IN

Children of **WILLIAM MACY** and **HANNAH HINSHAW** are:

14.	i.	JONATHON B.[7] MACY, b. 07 Mar 1810, Lost Creek MM,Jefferson Co, TN; d. 15 Sep 1850, Economy, Wayne Co., Indiana.
15.	ii.	NATHAN HINSHAW MACY, b. 16 Aug 1811, Lost Creek MM,Jefferson Co, TN; d. 23 Mar 1856, Raccoon River, Redfield, Dallas Co, IA.
16.	iii.	ALVAH J MACY, b. 26 Feb 1813, Lost Creek MM, Jefferson Co, TN; d. 09 Jul 1852, Economy, Wayne Co., Indiana.
	iv.	ELIHU C MACY, b. 25 Dec 1814, Lost Creek MM, Jefferson Co, TN; d. 23 May 1816, Jefferson Co, TN.
17.	v.	JOHN HINSHAW MACY, b. 28 Nov 1816, Lost Creek MM, Jefferson Co, TN; d. 01 Jun 1849, Economy, IN.
18.	vi.	LUCINDA MACY, b. 30 Aug 1818, Lost Creek MM, Jefferson, TN; d. 1893, Springbrook, Yamhill Co, OR.
19.	vii.	**WILLIAM MONROE MACY**, b. 08 Mar 1820, Lost Creek MM, Jefferson Co, TN; d. 04 Jun 1911, Denair, CA.
20.	viii.	MARGARET ANN MACY, b. 22 Mar 1822, Randolph Co, IN; d. 19 Aug 1899, Mooresville, IN.
21.	ix.	SARAH MACY, b. 23 Nov 1823, Randolph Co, IN; d. 10 Jun 1873.
22.	x.	PERRY T MACY, b. 17 Aug 1825, Randolph Co., IN; d. 07 May 1889, Mooresville, IN.
23.	xi.	IRA C MACY, b. 28 May 1828, Randolph Co, IN.
24.	xii.	RUTH ALMA MACY, b. 09 Jan 1830, Randolph Co, IN; d. 18 Dec 1909.
25.	xiii.	MARY ANN MACY, b. 01 Oct 1831, Randolph Co, IN; d. 03 Jan 1889, Newberg, Oregon, USA.
26.	xiv.	LYDIA ANN MACY, b. 16 Apr 1834, Randolph Co, IN; d. 24 Feb 1897.

11. JOHNATHAN MACY (*BARACHIAH*[5], *JOHN*[4], *JOHN*[3], *JOHN*[2], *THOMAS*[1]) was born 06 May 1791 in New Garden MM, Guilford Co, NC, and died 11 Oct 1865 in Rogersville, Henry, Indiana, USA. He married HANNAH PIERCE[1] 01 Sep 1809 in Lost Creek, Jefferson, Tennessee, USA. She was born 01 Jun 1792 in Guilford, North Carolina, USA, and died 14 Dec 1866 in Rogersville, Henry, Indiana, USA.

Children of JOHNATHAN MACY and HANNAH PIERCE are:
i. DAVID[7] MACY[1], b. 22 Nov 1816, Lost Creek, Jefferson, Tennessee, USA[1]; d. 30 Nov 1901, Kokomo, Howard, Indiana, USA[1].
ii. ISAAC MACY[1], b. 20 Jun 1822, Lost Creek, Jefferson, Tennessee, USA[1]; d. 1854, Springfield Mm, Indiana, USA[1].
iii. EZRA MACY[1], b. 30 Aug 1812, Lost Creek, Jefferson, Tennessee, USA[1]; d. Monroe, Randolph, Indiana, USA[1].
iv. JETHRO MACY[1], b. 25 Jun 1825, Henry, Indiana, USA[1]; d. Monroe, Randolph, Indiana, USA[1].
v. AARON MACY[1], b. 21 Sep 1829, Henry, Indiana, USA[1]; d. Farmland, Randolph, Indiana, USA[1].
vi. WILLIAM MACY[1], b. 1825, Henry, Indiana, USA[1]; d. 1828, Henry, Indiana, USA[1].
vii. EUNICE MACY[1], b. 02 Sep 1809, Lost Creek, Jefferson, Tennessee, USA[1]; d. Mount Harper, Kansas, USA.
viii. MARY MACY[1], b. 14 Oct 1819, Lost Creek, Jefferson, Tennessee, USA[1]; d. 18 Nov 1880, Springfield Mm, Indiana, USA[1].

12. ISAAC MACY (*BARACHIAH*[5], *JOHN*[4], *JOHN*[3], *JOHN*[2], *THOMAS*[1],) was born 02 Apr 1803 in Lost Creek, Jefferson Co, TN, and died 16 Dec 1847 in Wayne, Indiana, USA. He married (2) ELEANOR THORNBURG[1] 05 Apr 1825 in Jefferson, Tennessee, USA. She was born 28 Jul 1804 in Lost Creek, Jefferson, Tennessee, USA, and died 10 Feb 1894 in West River Settlement, Wayne, Indiana, USA.

Child of ISAAC MACY and ELEANOR THORNBURG is:
i. ELVIRA[17] MACY[1], b. 06 May 1830, Wayne, Indiana, USA[1].

13. JOHN MACY (*BARACHIAH*[5], *JOHN*[4], *JOHN*[3], *JOHN*[2], *THOMAS*[1],) was born 03 Jun 1806 in Lost Creek, Jefferson Co, TN, and died 1872 in Oregon, USA[1]. He married (2) ALICE MILLS[1] 10 Jun 1827 in Wayne Co, Indiana, USA. She was born 24 May 1811 in Lost Creek MM, Jefferson, Tennessee, USA.
Children of JOHN MACY and ALICE MILLS are:
i. DEWITT CLINTON[7] MACY[1], b. 1844[1]; d. 1924[1].
ii. JONATHAN[7] MACY[1], b. 1834, Wayne, Indiana, USA[1]; d. 1860, Oregon, USA[1].
iii. JOHN MACY[1], b. 1832, Wayne, Indiana, USA; d. 1860, Oregon, USA[1].
iv. MARY MACY[1], b. 1836, Vermilion, Illinois, USA.
v. EUNICE MACY[1], b. 1838, Vermilion, Illinois, USA.
vi. ASA L MACY[1], b. 1828, Wayne, Indiana, USA.
vii. DAVID MACY[1], b. 1842, Vermilion, Illinois, USA.
viii. EZRA MACY[1], b. 1840, Vermilion, Illinois, USA.
ix. JUDITH MACY[1], b. 1844, Vermilion, Illinois, USA.
x. ALVIN G MACY[1], b. 1830, Wayne, Indiana, USA.

Generation No. 7

14. JONATHON B. MACY (*WILLIAM*[6], *BARACHIAH*[5], *JOHN*[4], *JOHN*[3], *JOHN*[2], *THOMAS*[1]) was born 07 Mar 1810 in Lost Creek MM, Jefferson Co, TN, and died 15 Sep 1850 in Economy, Wayne Co., Indiana. He married MATILDA PIERCE 14 Feb 1833 in Wayne Co, IN. She was born 1817 in OH.
Children of JONATHON MACY and MATILDA PIERCE are:
i. CHARLOTTE[18] MACY, b. 1837, Indiana.
ii. LUCINDA MACY, b. 1839, Indiana.

15. NATHAN HINSHAW[7] MACY *(WILLIAM[6], BARACHIAH[5], JOHN[4], JOHN[3], JOHN[2], THOMAS[1],)* was born 16 Aug 1811 in Lost Creek MM, Jefferson Co, TN, and died 23 Mar 1856 in Raccoon River, Redfield, Dallas Co, IA. He married SUSANNAH LEWIS[1] 15 Mar 1834 in Wayne, Indiana, USA. She was born 1810 in TN, and died 1870 in Iowa, USA.

Children of NATHAN MACY and SUSANNAH LEWIS are:

    i.   WILLIAM LEWIS[8] MACY[1], b. 21 Oct 1834, Mooresville, Morgan, Indiana, USA[1]; d. 21 Sep 1921, Adel, Dallas, Iowa, USA[1].

    ii.   MARY ANN MACY[1], b. 26 Apr 1836, Wayne, Indiana, USA[1]; d. 15 Dec 1873, Worth, Missouri, USA[1].

    iii.   OLIVER CLINTON MACY[1], b. 12 Nov 1837, Wayne, Indiana, USA[1]; d. 15 Oct 1895[1].

    iv.   THOMAS COLEMAN MACY[1], b. 10 Aug 1839, Wayne, Indiana, USA[1]; d. 1870[1].

    v.   HANNAH MACY[1], b. 04 May 1841, Wayne, Indiana, USA[1]; d. 28 Sep 1850, Wayne, Indiana, USA[1].

    vi.   MARGARET MALINDA MACY[1], b. 23 Mar 1844, Wayne, Indiana, USA[1]; d. 21 Sep 1850, Wayne, Indiana, USA[1].

16. ALVAH J[7] MACY *(WILLIAM[6], BARACHIAH[5], JOHN[4], JOHN[3], JOHN[2], THOMAS[1],)* was born 26 Feb 1813 in Lost Creek MM, Jefferson Co, TN, and died 09 Jul 1852 in Economy, Wayne Co., Indiana. He married MARY LEWIS 06 Oct 1833 in Economy, IN. She was born 1812.

Children of ALVAH MACY and MARY LEWIS are:

    i.   HANNAH[8] MACY, b. 1836, Indiana.

    ii.   MALINDA MACY, b. 1837, Indiana.

    iii.   MINERVA MACY, b. 1840, Indiana.

    iv.   MATILDA MACY, b. 1840, Indiana.

    v.   HULDAH MACY, b. 1842, Indiana.

    vi.   LARKIN MACY, b. 1843, Indiana.

    vii.   WILLIAM MACY, b. 1845, Indiana.

    viii.   WAYNE MACY, b. 1847, Indiana.

17. JOHN HINSHAW[7] MACY *(WILLIAM[6], BARACHIAH[5], JOHN[4], JOHN[3], JOHN[2], THOMAS[1],)* was born 28 Nov 1816 in Lost CreekMM, Jefferson Co, TN, and died 01 Jun 1849 in Economy, IN. He married ELMIRA MARSHALL 02 Dec 1838 in Chester MM Wayne Co, IN. She was born 13 Nov 1815 in Whitewater, IN.

Children of JOHN MACY and ELMIRA MARSHALL are:

    i.   MILES[8] MACY, b. 02 Jan 1840, Wayne Co, IN.

    ii.   EUSTATIA MACY, b. 15 Jan 1842, Wayne Co, IN; d. 19 Dec 1898.

    iii.   ELVIRA MACY, b. 1843, Randolph Co, IN.

    iv.   ELISA MACY, b. 1845.

18. LUCINDA[7] MACY *(WILLIAM[6], BARACHIAH[5], JOHN[4], JOHN[3], JOHN[2], THOMAS[1])* was born 30 Aug 1818 in Lost CreekMM, Jefferson, TN[1], and died 1893 in Springbrook, Yamhill Co, OR. She married THOMAS MARSHALL HADLEY[1] 25 Nov 1838 in Mooresville, Morgan, Indiana, USA, son of ISAAC HADLEY and RUTH MARSHILL. He was born 14 Dec 1810 in Rowan, North Carolina, USA[1], and died 23 Oct 1893 in Newberg, Yamhill Co, Oregon, USA.

Children of LUCINDA MACY and THOMAS HADLEY are:

    i.   ENOS[8] HADLEY[1], b. 1838, Indiana, USA[1].
    ii.   HANNAH HADLEY[1], b. 25 Sep 1840, Mooresville, Morgan, Indiana, USA[1]; d. 1905[1].
    iii.   MARIAH HADLEY, b. 1841.
    iv.   MELISSA HADLEY[1], b. 1841, Indiana, USA[1].
    v.   LYDIA ELLEN HADLEY[1], b. 14 Jan 1842, Mooresville, Morgan, Indiana, USA[1]; d. 21 Aug 1842, Morgan, Indiana, USA[1].
    vi.   MALINDA HADLEY, b. 1843.
    vii.   MATILDA HADLEY[1], b. 20 May 1843, Mooresville, Morgan, Indiana, USA[1]; d. Oregon, USA[1].
    viii.   SIMON HADLEY[1], b. 1844, Indiana, USA[1].
    ix.   WILLIAM MACY HADLEY[1], b. 21 Feb 1845, Mooresville, Morgan, Indiana, USA[1]; d. 21 Nov 1882, Yamhill County, Oregon; m. HATTIE FUSON, 11 Sep 1872, Mooresville, IN.
    x.   EVAN HADLEY[1], b. 1846, Indiana, USA[1].
    xi.   RUTH ALMA HADLEY[1], b. 04 Oct 1847, Mooresville, Morgan, Indiana, USA[1]; d. 11 Apr 1931[1].
    xii.   MARY LUCINDA HADLEY[1], b. 17 Mar 1850, Mooresville, Morgan, Indiana, USA[1]; d. Rush, Indiana, USA[1].
    xiii.   IVA HADLEY[1], b. 1852[1]; d. 1852[1].
    xiv.   IRA C HADLEY[1], b. 03 Dec 1852, Mooresville, Morgan, Indiana, USA[1]; d. 23 Dec 1853, Morgan, Indiana, USA[1].
    xv.   ELIZABETH A HADLEY[1], b. 1853, Mooresville, Morgan, Indiana, USA[1].
    xvi.   MARGARET ANN HADLEY[1], b. 16 Feb 1854, Mooresville, Morgan, Indiana, USA[1]; d. 1922[1].
    xvii.   CORNELIA HADLEY[1], b. 13 Feb 1858, Mooresville, Morgan, Indiana, USA[1]; d. 25 Nov 1876, Morgan, Indiana, USA[1].
    xviii.   JOHN J HADLEY[1], b. 17 May 1860, Mooresville, Morgan, Indiana, USA[1]; d. 1937[1].
    xix.   FRANK HADLEY, b. 1863, Indiana.
    xx.   HULDA P HADLEY[1], b. 25 Jul 1863, Mooresville, Morgan, Indiana, USA[1]; d. 16 Jan 1889[1].

19. WILLIAM MONROE[7] MACY (*WILLIAM[6], BARACHIAH[5], JOHN[4], JOHN[3], JOHN[2], THOMAS[1]*) was born 08 Mar 1820 in Lost CreekMM, Jefferson Co,TN, and died 04 Jun 1911 in Denair, CA. He married **JULIA ANN MILLS** 16 Oct 1849 in Morgan Co, IN (by JP John S Hubbard), daughter of HENRY MILLS and HANNAH WOODWARD. She was born 03 Jul 1829 in Wayne Co., IN, and died 22 Jul 1918 in Caldwell, ID of Bronchial Pneumonia.

More about **WILLIAM MONROE MACY**:
Assets1: 1850, $1600 in Wayne Co., IN
Assets2: 1860, $13200 RE & $4065 PP
Assets3: 1870, $28000 & $6000 PP
Builder1: 1859, Built 11room Italianate home on 343 acres
Builder2: 1861, Built Quaker Academy Building
Builder3: 1864, Built White Lick Meeting House in Mooresville, IN
Burial: Denair, CA Grave #32-A-07
Contributions: 12 Sep 1860, 1 of 13 Original donors for Quaker Academy
Elected: 22 Dec 1865, 1st President of Mooresville Monrovia Gravel Road Co.
Migration 2: 1854, Moved to Brown Twp. Morgan Co., IN
Migration 3: 1882, Moved to Dayton, OR
Migration 4: 1907, Moved to Greenleaf, ID
Member: 1861, Mooresville HS Assoc. Bd of Trustees
Occupation: Farmer, Timber buyer, Fruit Orchard, Maple Syrup camp,
Property: 18 Apr 1882, Macy Farmstead and #343 acres sold to Martin Ruble for $18000
Religion: Quaker

More about **JULIA ANN MILLS**:
Burial: 24 Jul 1918, Denair, CA Grave #32-A-08

Children of **WILLIAM MACY** and **JULIA MILLS** are:
27.   i.   **ALVA PERRY[8] MACY**, b. 30 Jan 1858, Brown Twp Morgan Co, IN; d. 12 Aug 1918, Chico, CA of Jacksonian Epilepsy.
       ii.   AARON MILLS MACY, b. 24 May 1855, Wayne Co., IN; d. 25 Sep 1877, Mooresville, IN of typhoid fever.

             More About AARON MILLS MACY:
             Burial: White Lick Cemetery, Mooresville, IN
             Occupation: 1876, Teacher @ Bethel School
             Religion: Quaker

28.   iii. CYNTHIA RUTH MACY, b. 17 Sep 1861, Mooresville, IN; d. 18 Apr 1934, Greenleaf, ID or New Plymouth, ID of Strangulated umbilical hernia.
       iv.   HANNAH MARIAH MACY, b. 26 Jan 1853, Wayne Co., IN; d. 10 Dec 1866, Mooresville, IN.

             More About HANNAH MARIAH MACY:
             Died of spotted fever
             Burial: White Lick Cemetery, Mooresville, IN

       v.   LYDDIA JANE ANDREW (ADOPTED), b. 1869.

20. MARGARET ANN[7] MACY *(WILLIAM[6], BARACHIAH[5], JOHN[4], JOHN[3], JOHN[2], THOMAS[1],)* was born 22 Mar 1822 in Randolph Co, IN, and died 19 Aug 1899 in Mooresville, IN. She married LEVI S HADLEY[1] 25 May 1850 in Morgan Co, IN, son of SIMON HADLEY and SARAH HADLEY. He was born 30 Oct 1826 in Morgan, Indiana, USA, and died 13 Mar 1891 in Morgan, Indiana, USA.

Children of MARGARET MACY and LEVI HADLEY are:

- i. MALINDA JANE HADLEY[1], b. 08 Apr 1851, Morgan, Indiana, USA[1]; d. 14 Mar 1925[1].
- ii. LYDIA ELLEN HADLEY[1], b. 22 Jun 1852, Morgan, Indiana, USA[1]; d. 10 Aug 1934[1].
- iii. WAYNE COLEMAN HADLEY[1], b. 05 Dec 1853, Morgan, Indiana, USA[1]; d. 05 Sep 1913[1].
- iv. ACHSA ANN HADLEY[1], b. 28 Sep 1855, Indiana, USA[1]; d. 22 Aug 1920[1].
- v. GULIA ELLEN HADLEY, b. 17 Nov 1858, Indiana, USA[1]; d. 14 Aug 1890[1].
- vi. ORA RUTH HADLEY[1], b. 15 Dec 1860, Morgan, Indiana, USA[1]; d. 21 Sep 1921[1].
- vii. IRA W HADLEY[1], b. 20 Feb 1863, Morgan, Indiana, USA[1]; d. 23 Feb 1948, Morgan, Indiana, USA[1].
- viii. LUCINDA M HADLEY[1], b. 20 Jul 1865, Morgan, Indiana, USA[1]; d. 08 Jan 1920[1].

21. SARAH[7] MACY *(WILLIAM[6], BARACHIAH[5], JOHN[4], JOHN[3], JOHN[2], THOMAS[1])* was born 23 Nov 1823 in Randolph Co, IN, and died 10 Jun 1873. She married THOMAS LINDLEY HADLEY 17 Nov 1841 in Randolph Co, IN, son of JOSHUA HADLEY and SARAH LINDLEY. He was born 07 Jul 1821 in Chatham Co., NC, and died 23 Jul 1883 in Mooresville, IN.

Children of SARAH MACY and THOMAS HADLEY are:

- i. MARY E[8] HADLEY, b. 15 Feb 1843.
- ii. PERRY MACY HADLEY, b. 04 Dec 1845, Morgan Co, IN; d. 01 Apr 1925, Earlham, IA.
- iii. JOSHUA HADLEY, b. 02 May 1847, Morgan Co, IN.
- iv. ZIMRI HADLEY, b. 27 Mar 1849, Morgan Co, IN.
- v. HANNAH E HADLEY, b. 16 Oct 1850, Morgan Co, IN.
- vi. WILLIAM L HADLEY, b. 13 Apr 1852, Morgan Co, IN.
- vii. AARON HADLEY, b. 21 Jun 1854, Morgan Co, IN.
- viii. IRWIN A HADLEY, b. 19 Jun 1857, Morgan Co, IN.
- ix. EDWIN J HADLEY, b. 19 Jun 1857, Morgan Co, IN.
- x. RUANNA HADLEY, b. 09 Sep 1859, Morgan Co, IN; d. 02 Dec 1931, Greenleaf, ID.
- xi. SARAH RUTH HADLEY, b. 05 Oct 1861, Morgan Co, IN.
- xii. JOHN B HADLEY, b. 1864, Morgan Co, IN.

22. PERRY T[7] MACY *(WILLIAM[6], BARACHIAH[5], JOHN[4], JOHN[3], JOHN[2], THOMAS[1])* was born 17 Aug 1825 in Randolph Co., IN, and died 07 May 1889 in Mooresville, IN. He married (1) REBECCA BOWLES 1869, daughter of GEORGE BOWLES and ELIZABETH BAILEY. She was born 24 Oct 1833 in Randolph, Indiana, USA, and died 12 Apr 1912 in Morgan, Indiana, USA. He married (2) CHARITY MILLS 14 Sep 1848, daughter of HENRY MILLS and HANNAH WOODWARD. She was born 24 Oct 1833 in Randolph Co, Indiana, and died 27 DEC 1863 in Mooresville, IN.
More about PERRY T MACY: and Charity Mills
Burial: both in White Lick Cemetery, Mooresville, IN

Children of PERRY MACY and CHARITY MILLS are:

- 29.　i. ALBERT W[8] MACY, b. 18 Jan 1853, Hendricks Co., IN.
- ii. CHARLOTTE L MACY, b 1857, Mooresville, Indiana
- iii. IDA ELLEN MACY, b. 12 Apr 1862, Mooresville, IN.

Children of PERRY MACY and REBECCA BOWLES are:

- iv. WILLIAM SEWARD HADLEY, b. 19 Mar 1860, Stuart Co, Iowa; d. 09 Apr 1897.
- v. OLIVER MACY, b. 1870, Indiana.
- vi. VERNON MACY, b. 26 Jul 1875, Morgan Co, Indiana.

23. IRA C[7] MACY *(WILLIAM[6], BARACHIAH[5], JOHN[4], JOHN[3], JOHN[2], THOMAS[1],)* was born 28 May 1828 in Randolph Co, IN. He married ACHSAH JOHNSON 31 Aug 1853 in Morgan Co, IN. She was born 16 Jun 1834.

Children of IRA MACY and ACHSAH JOHNSON are:

    i.   ZERNAH ELLEN[8] MACY, b. 30 Oct 1855, Randolph Co., IN; d. 19 Jan 1955, Morgan Co, IN.
    ii. EMMA M MACY, b. 1862.
    iii. JERAMIAH MACY.
    iv. MILES H MACY.

24. RUTH ALMA[7] MACY *(WILLIAM[6], BARACHIAH[5], JOHN[4], JOHN[3], JOHN[2], THOMAS[1],)* was born 09 Jan 1830 in Randolph Co, IN, and died 18 Dec 1909. She married MILES S HADLEY 29 Mar 1850 in Morgan Co, IN, son of SIMON HADLEY and SARAH HADLEY. He was born 18 Jun 1828 in Mooresville, Morgan, Indiana, USA, and died 29 Dec 1911 in Mooresville, Morgan, Indiana, USA.

Children of RUTH MACY and MILES HADLEY are:

    i.   ALVAH MACY[8] HADLEY[1], b. 15 Jan 1851, Mooresville, Morgan, Indiana, USA[1]; d. 03 Nov 1924[1].
    ii. HANNAH ELMINA HADLEY[1], b. 1856, Indiana; d. 16 Dec 1939, Mooresville, Morgan, Indiana, USA[1].
    iii. GULIA EFFIE HADLEY[1], b. 16 Jan 1868[1]; d. 26 Feb 1868[1].

25. MARY ANN[7] MACY *(WILLIAM[6], BARACHIAH[5], JOHN[4], JOHN[3], JOHN[2], THOMAS[1],)* was born 01 Oct 1831 in Randolph Co, IN, and died 03 Jan 1889 in Newberg, Oregon, USA. She married ALBERT HADLEY 03 Apr 1852 in Mooresville, son of JOSHUA HADLEY and MARY T. He was born 14 Feb 1831 in Hendricks, Indiana, USA, and died 24 Mar 1866 in Hendricks Co., IN.

Children of MARY MACY and ALBERT HADLEY are:

    i.   CALVIN R[8] HADLEY, b. 1853, Indiana.
    ii.   EDITH HADLEY, b. 1855, Indiana.
    iii. ALONZO HADLEY[1], b. 19 Feb 1857, Mooresville, Morgan, Indiana, USA[1]; d. 30 Apr 1925, Newberg, Yamhill, Oregon, USA[1].
    iv. MACY B HADLEY, b. 1858, Indiana.
    v.   ELI HADLEY, b. 1860, Indiana.
    vi. LAURA HADLEY, b. 1862, Indiana.
    vii. MIRANDA HADLEY, b. 1863, Indiana.
   viii. HANNAH E HADLEY, b. 1866, Indiana.

26. LYDIA ANN[7] MACY *(WILLIAM[6], BARACHIAH[5], JOHN[4], JOHN[3], JOHN[2], THOMAS[1]* was born 16 Apr 1834 in Randolph Co, IN, and died 24 Feb 1897. She married JOHN FRANKLIN HADLEY 13 Mar 1859 in Morgan Co, IN. He was born 14 Jan 1840 in Indiana, and died 04 Apr 1898 in Morgan Co, IN.

Children of LYDIA MACY and JOHN HADLEY are:

    i.   WILLIAM AARON[8] HADLEY, b. 1860, Indiana.
    ii. MALINDA ALMA HADLEY, b. 1863, Indiana.
    iii. MAHLON J HADLEY, b. 1867, Indiana.
    iv. CORA H HADLEY, b. Indiana.
    v. LINNIE HADLEY, b. Indiana.

27. ALVA PERRY[8] MACY *(WILLIAM MONROE[7], WILLIAM[6], BARACHIAH[5], JOHN[4], JOHN[3], JOHN[2], THOMAS[1])* was born 30 Jan 1858 in Brown Twp Morgan Co, IN, and died 12 Aug 1918 in Chico, CA of Jacksonian Epilepsy. He married IDA MAY MOORE 29 Sep 1886, She was the daughter of ALFRED MOORE and MARTHA KERR. She was born 14 Apr 1862 in New Providence, IOWA, and died 10 Aug 1933 in Chico, CA.

More about **ALVA PERRY MACY:**
Burial: Chico, CA
Contributions: 1872, Diary of life on Macy Homestead
Emigration: 1905, Moves to California
Immigration 1: 1882, Moves to Dayton, OR with father, mother, & sister
Occupation: Farmer

More about **IDA MAY MOORE:**
Burial: Chico, CA
Family: She was the niece of Samuel Moore, founder of Mooresville

Children of **ALVA MACY and IDA MAY MOORE** are:
- i. NORMAN KERR[9] MACY, b. 27 Aug 1890, Oregon; d. 15 Nov 1949, Los Angeles; m. (1) RITA STELLER; m. (2) ESTELLA LEWIS, 02 Jun 1915; b. 1891, IL.
- ii. MAUDE LAVERNE MACY, b. 08 Mar 1892, Oregon; d. 07 Jul 1960, Chico, CA; m. ERROL WALTER CRAWFORD, 01 Jun 1916.
- 30. iii. BRUCE WARD MACY, b. 20 Nov 1893, Dayton, Oregon; d. 27 Jan 1986, Magalia, Butte Co., CA.
- iv. RUTH W MACY, b. 1894, Oregon.

28. CYNTHIA RUTH[8] MACY *(WILLIAM MONROE[7], WILLIAM[6], BARACHIAH[5], JOHN[4], JOHN[3],John2 Thomas1)* was born 9-17- 1861 at Mooresville, IN, and died 4-8- 1934 in Greenleaf, ID or New Plymouth, ID of Strangulated umbilical hernia. She married OWEN HATFIELD 17 Sep 1886 in Dayton, OR. He was born 17 May 1839 in Illinois, and died 14 Feb 1916 in Greenleaf, ID of Mephutis Bronichial Asthma.

More about CYNTHIA RUTH MACY: Cause of Death
Burial: McMinnville, OR   Herniotomy, operation for stangulated hernia

More about OWEN HATFIELD:
Burial: 14 Feb 1916, McMinnville, OR
Military service: Vet. Jun 1861 - Jul 1862, Civil War–Corporal, Co. H, 7th Illinois Infantry

Children of **CYNTHIA MACY and OWEN HATFIELD** are:
- 31. i. ARTHUR WILLIAM[9] HATFIELD, b. 10 Nov 1887, Dayton, OR.
- 32. ii. BERNICE MACY HATFIELD, b. 20 Mar 1890, Dayton, OR; d. 1976.
- 33. iii. MACY L HATFIELD, b. 26 May 1892, Dayton, Oregon; d. 10 Dec 1945, Payette, ID.

29. ALBERT W[8] MACY *(PERRY T[7], WILLIAM[6], BARACHIAH[5], JOHN[4], JOHN[3], JOHN[2], THOMAS[1],)* was born 18 Jan 1853 in Hendricks Co., IN. He married EMMA K MILLS, daughter of JEHU MILLS and SARAH C. She was born 11 Sep 1857.

Children of ALBERT MACY and EMMA MILLS are:
- i.   ROY W[9] MACY, b. 06 Dec 1879.
- ii. FLORENCE M MACY, b. 04 Nov 1886.
- iii. LUCILLE B MACY, b. 16 Dec 1893.

Generation No. 9

30. BRUCE WARD[9] MACY *(ALVA PERRY[8], WILLIAM MONROE[7], WILLIAM[6], BARACHIAH[5], JOHN[4], JOHN[3], JOHN[2], THOMAS[1],)* was born 20 Nov 1893 in Dayton, Oregon, and died 27 Jan 1986 in Magalia, Butte Co., CA. He married SHIRLEY MARCH 27 Sep 1916, daughter of O. W. MARCH. She was born 23 Jun 1894.

Children of BRUCE MACY and SHIRLEY MARCH are:
- i.   MARGARET MAE MACY, b. 15 Nov 1917.
- ii. BRUCE MARCH MACY, b. 11 Nov 1918.
- iii. SHIRLEY MARILEE MACY, b. 18 Jul 1920.
- 34. iv. MARGARET ANN MACY, b. 13 Dec 1924; d. 16 Jun 1961.

31. ARTHUR WILLIAM[9] HATFIELD *(CYNTHIA RUTH[8] MACY, WILLIAM MONROE[7], WILLIAM[6], BARACHIAH[5], JOHN[4], JOHN[3], JOHN[2], THOMAS[1])* was born 10 Nov 1887 in Dayton, OR. He married STELLA WATSON.

Children of ARTHUR HATFIELD and STELLA WATSON are:
- i.   CHESEL HATFIELD.
- ii. ARLIE LAWRENCE HATFIELD.

32. BERNICE MACY[9] HATFIELD *(CYNTHIA RUTH[8] MACY, WILLIAM MONROE[7], WILLIAM[6], BARACHIAH[5], JOHN[4], JOHN[3], JOHN[2], THOMAS[1])* was born 20 Mar 1890 in Dayton, OR, and died 1976. She married (1) FLOYD WENDELL WILLIAMS 16 Feb 1910 in Greenleaf, ID. He was born 13 Apr 1887 in Lynnville, IA, and died 16 Nov 1925 in Greenleaf, ID. She married (2) SEBURN DORLAND WILLIAMS 09 Jun 1932.

Children of BERNICE HATFIELD and FLOYD WILLIAMS are:
- i.   RONALD RICHMOND WILLIAMS, b. 29 Dec 1910.
- ii.   **MADELL LUCILLE WILLIAMS**, b. 17 Jun 1913; m. FRANCIS WONDERLY.
- iii. RUTH QUIMBY WILLIAMS, b. 05 Jun 1915.
- iv.   FLOYD WENDELL WILLIAMS, b. 09 Feb 1918.
- v.   **KENNETH MORGAN WILLIAMS**, b. 09 Feb 1920.
- vi.   **DONALD KEITH WILLIAMS**, b. 13 Apr 1921.
- vii. LEWIS HAROLD WILLIAMS, b. 04 Aug 1922.
- viii. MACY LEDRU WILLIAMS, b. 1911.

33. MACY L[9] HATFIELD *(CYNTHIA RUTH[8] MACY, WILLIAM MONROE[7], WILLIAM[6], BARACHIAH[5], JOHN[4], JOHN[3], JOHN[2], THOMAS[1])* was born 26 May 1892 in Dayton, Oregon, and died 10 Dec 1945 in Payette, ID. He married EMMA BOREN 26 May 1935.

Child of MACY HATFIELD and EMMA BOREN is:
- i.   NORA MAE[20] HATFIELD, b. 1942.

34. MARGARET ANN MACY *(BRUCE WARD[9], ALVA PERRY[8], WILLIAM MONROE[7], WILLIAM[6], BARACHIAH[5], JOHN[4], JOHN[3], JOHN[2], THOMAS[1])* was born 13 Dec 1924, and died 16 Jun 1961. She married LYNN MORTON MARCH 03 Mar 1945.

Children of MARGARET MACY and LYNN MARCH are:
    i.   MARGARET ANN MARCH, b. 26 Dec 1945.
    ii. LYNN MARCH, b. 29 Dec 1947.
    iii. **MARILEE FRANCES MARCH**, b. 07 Sep 1949; m. WILLIAM S JOHNSON; b. 1944.

        More About MARILEE FRANCES MARCH:
        Assets: 2006, Charitable descendent of John Howland
        Contributions: 2004, Donated family history items to Earlham College
        migration: Sep 2006, **Visited WMMacy Farmstead**

    iv. BRUCE COLEMAN MARCH, b. 10 Jan 1951.

Endnotes

1. Ancestry.com, One World Tree (sm), Provo, UT, USA: The Generations Network, Inc., n.d., Online publication - Ancestry.com. OneWorldTree [database on-line]. Provo, UT, USA: The Generations Network, Inc.

About the Authors

Donovan and Joyce Robinson feel too little has been written of the generation which created a comfortable world for our 21st century life. Politicians and warriors have dominated the history taught in school, however, our culture was equally developed by people who converted the American wilderness into cities and production centers. The Macy story began with the Robinsons' effort to thwart an 'eminent domain powered condemnation' of the front lawn of the Farmstead. A basis for declaring the Farmstead an Historical Landmark was needed. The Macys (who built the home in 1859) lived long, left a trail of Quaker records, descended from Mayflower passengers, and were major players at each settlement they joined, while 8 generations of Macy genes proceeded from Plymouth Rock to California. As retirees, Donovan and Joyce had a reasonable excuse for going to California, Oregon, Washington, Massachusetts, Nantucket, North Carolina, and Tennessee. Long afternoons in historical libraries passed easily as they gathered bits and pieces of the Macy record. A lifetime of team effort was normal for the Robinsons. In pursuit of Macy ancestors, the evolution of Macy/Massie/Massey sparked a further study which concluded Joyce shared a Massie ancestor with the man who built the Farmstead where she lives. This is discussed in THE AFTERGLOW. Donovan's career was in product development which included 6 patents, 2 technical papers published by the Society of Automotive Engineers and other industrial reports. Compiling the Macy story and organizing the data was not far from engineering methodology. The shared authorship included severe editing by both parties. Joyce's book "I Was a Waif and Child Servant" was published in 2008. "THE 1872 DIARY of the MOORESVILLE MACY FARMSTEAD" is the culmination of nearly 5 years of effort by 'Team Robinson'.